New Structures in Jazz and Improvised Music since 1960

ROGER T. DEAN

Open University Press
Milton Keynes • Philadelphia

Open University Press
Celtic Court
22 Ballmoor
Buckingham
MK18 1XW

and

1900 Frost Road, Suite 101
Bristol, PA 19007, USA

First Published 1992

British Library Cataloguing-in-Publication Data

Dean, Roger T.
  New structures in jazz and improvised music since 1960.
  I. Title
  781.65

  ISBN 0–335–09898–3
  ISBN 0–335–09897–5 (pbk)

Library of Congress Cataloging-in-Publication Data

Dean, R.T.
  New structures in jazz and improvised music since 1960/Roger T. Dean.
      p.   cm.
  Includes bibliographical references and index.
  ISBN 0–335–09898–3 (hardback) – ISBN 0–335–09897–5 (pbk.)
  1. Jazz – History and criticism.   2. Improvisation (Music)
  I. Title.
  ML3506.D4   1991
  781.65′5–dc20   91–10511   CIP MN

Typeset by Graphicraft Typesetters Ltd, Hong Kong
Printed in Great Britain by Redwood Press Ltd, Melksham, Wilts

Contents

New structures in jazz and improvised music since 1960

Preface

In this book I present a systematic analysis (perhaps the first) of changes
in the nature and structure of improvised music between 1960 and around
1985. Inevitably the choice of dates is arbitrary and they form loose
boundaries which I penetrate freely. I am concerned primarily with
improvisation in western music, though I make some comparisons with
other musics. This concentration on western music is a consequence
partly of my particular involvement in it, and partly of my impression that
while changes in the period in western improvisation have been substantial, those in most other types of improvisation have been slighter.

I shall refer to some research materials which begin such musical
analyses of improvising. Written materials (books and articles) are refer-
enced in the text as A1, A2, etc., and are detailed in Appendix 2. Musical
scores, and volumes of transcriptions are given in the text as M1, M2,
etc., and are detailed in Appendix 3; but it should be noted that many
transcriptions are within the texts of the references in Appendix 2. Musical recordings and films are indicated by R1, R2, etc. (see Appendix 4)
and are a selection sufficient to demonstrate the point under discussion.
The date given for a recording is generally that of the earliest recording
on the LP. Section 3 discusses recordings which are listed separately at
the end of each chapter.

The references are supplemented by a list of 'core recordings' (Appendix 5) of improvisation whose availability would be desirable. Jazz
records in particular are covered in A21c, A53, A69 and A82; no comparable catalogue of recordings of other kinds of western improvisation
is available. The availability of recorded material is a real problem
which will not be rapidly overcome. That on compact disc is a very
limited selection compared with earlier vinyl recordings, and many of the
latter are no longer readily accessible. The music is sufficiently important
that these difficulties have to be accepted (and some possible solutions

are mentioned in Appendix 5); and the objective of the transcriptions is to provide a sufficient basis for my analyses even when the recorded material is unavailable. Inevitably the transcriptions are only a limited selection of the recorded material, and they have their own biases (see Appendix 1).

The improvised music I am discussing is not only jazz but also free improvisation, which may or may not retain connections with jazz; and improvisation within composed contexts, which again are not limited to any congruence with jazz. The numerous books and articles on modern jazz mostly have an extremely biographical approach, emphasising 'key' individuals in the music, with little consideration of musical structures. There is relatively little of substance published on other types of western improvisation. The extremes in styles of discussion of jazz can be seen in A57, where the only detailed and documented musical essay is that of Gunther Schuller. While Schuller's own *Early Jazz* (A130) is a classic musical analysis which goes far beyond any conventional limitations, Jost's excellent *Free Jazz* (A65) is probably the only significant book which attempts musical analysis of modern jazz and early free jazz: it was written nearly two decades ago and so only covers the period up to the mid-1960s. It, too, is largely arranged around individual musicians. Budds (A19) presents only a simple description of some of the events in 1960s jazz, with a few musical comments, and makes virtually no reference to jazz outside America. Litweiler (A78) offers no precise musical comments, and seems somewhat unfamiliar with European avant-garde improvising, which nevertheless falls clearly within his assumed brief.

In contrast to most of the previous works on jazz improvisation, I shall concentrate on the musical components of improvisation (such as rhythm, pitch, etc.), illustrating the changes in their usage and range which have occurred in the period under discussion, and not on biographical elements. I shall bring forward specific examples of the changes from the recorded literature, but drawn from many musicians rather than necessarily from those figuring in previous books. I will deal with the music first as object (the final sound heard by someone listening to a recording), and second as process (the means and approaches adopted by the improviser in producing that sound, and the relationship with the audience present at the time of performance). These two aspects are, of course, utterly continuous with each other, and are separated arbitrarily for the purposes of clarity of analysis. I shall make no great effort to attribute priority in a particular musical process to particular improvising musicians, though to a limited degree I shall attempt to counterbalance the American bias in the jazz literature, which largely springs from the fact that most jazz recordings and reviewers originate in the USA.

I will reveal continuous developments in all the musical parameters themselves; in the individual musical traditions and localities; in the behaviour of performing groups of improvisers; and in the work of the individual musicians active in the areas. Of course, history is not linear: every development is followed by diffusive waves in space and time. Thus developments are not always synchronous in the work of different individuals or countries. In addition, there are always individuals who fly before the wind, though not joined by a flock.

I shall largely resist the temptation to offer sociopolitical 'explanations' for the developments I identify. This is because I presently find the previous attempts at such explanations of musical developments unsatisfying. For example, the proposed explications of musical development in sociological terms lead to empirical questions which could test the validity of the proposals. Such tests have not been completed rigorously, and it is not my object to undertake such a test for the music under study here. I analyse these problems in the Introduction, and further in Appendix 1, and I present some ideas and analyses which could be tested in these terms, granted sufficient person-power to undertake the immense data gathering which would be necessary.

So many complex issues are hidden behind the analysis of music, and particularly within the literature on jazz, largely neglected, that I shall devote much of Appendix 1 to a discussion of musical entities, their interpretation and significance. From the wealth of possible approaches I will justify my choices of analysis of music as object and process, and of the comparative study of musical objects extracted from larger contexts. As there is far more published material on composed than on improvised music, I will make comparisons between developments in improvisation and in composition, but do so relatively briefly, in the hope of eliciting further response from analysts accustomed to concern themselves with composition.

My interpretation of the developments I identify is that they are largely a result of autonomous change within music, in which musical activities and the diffusion of their recorded products are the articulating forces which cause musical response in further practitioners, and which hence lead to further musical developments. This view can explain the simultaneous or successive exploitation in different countries, societies and musical spheres, of the musical parameters which I will discuss: for example, the virtually simultaneous development of free improvising in closely allied forms in American jazz, among American composers, in the UK (again with participants from both jazz and composed music backgrounds), and equally in eastern Europe. These ideas are open to future investigation, but I will also offer in the Introduction an interpretation of the developments in terms of the modern–postmodern divide, and the sociological implications proposed to relate to this in the work of Jameson (see A6). Again this proposal is accessible to further analysis granted relevant data, and I present it with not entirely frivolous motives.

This book is a companion to my *Creative Improvisation: Jazz, Contemporary Music and Beyond*, a practical work, with a musical tape, also published by Open University Press (A31). That book offers a brief background history of improvisation and accompanying references, which will not be reiterated here. Both books result largely from my own experience as improviser and composer within the contexts of western music they address; in some small sections of this book I will present that experience directly.

This book is intended for all those using the companion volume, *Creative Improvisation*; for advanced school students, and music students at universities; for the serious listener to contemporary music; for practitioners and academics in music; and, in an ambivalent sense, for sociologists of music. It owes a debt to the other improvising members of my ensembles, Lysis and austraLysis, whose improvisations are illustrated in the tape accompanying *Creative Improvisation*, as well as on commercial recordings. I thank Ashley Brown, Tony Buck, Hazel Smith and Torbjorn Hultmark for their extensive contributions.

I have also received helpful comments, advice and assistance from several people during the preparation of this book, and I thank in particular Georgina Born, Chris Clark, Graham Collier, the late Charles Fox, Shankar Ghosh, Bruce Johnson, Alan Marett, Richard Middleton, Jeff Pressing, Eddie Prevost and John Sloboda. They bear none of the responsibility for what is presented here, of course. It is a pleasure to acknowledge also, with the utmost gratitude, the unflagging support of the librarians at Brunel University, and of my editor, Peter Wright.

Roger Dean

Introduction

Improvised music and its elements

Musical improvisation can be taken for simplicity as the simultaneous conception and performance of music (A31). The further analysis of the concept in A31 will not be repeated here. Another relevant discussion of the concept is A51 (pp. 223–51). However, it is worth exploring one issue here. Some authors quite unnecessarily confuse composition with improvisation. Composition can be taken as an activity which precedes any sounding of the completed work, while improvisation is simultaneous with the sounding of a work and becomes complete when the sound finishes. This is not to imply that the activities of composition and improvisation are distinct in ways which are of fundamental importance to music: for example, a comparative analysis of improvisation in many cultures indicates that this is not so and that they are 'part of the same idea' (A97). Composition and improvisation often coexist to some degree, for instance in improvising based on formulaic 'referents' (see Pressing in A27) such as harmonies or rhythms. And the importance of limited improvised ornamentation of pre-existent musical elements varies very considerably from culture to culture, having perhaps the greatest significance in Arabian cultures (A60).

One major feature of improvisation, elaborated in A31, is that it permits interaction between individual musical creators at the time of conception of music; in this it is unlike composition. For instance, Derek Bailey (A23) states: 'there's so much of improvisation that's missing, that's not possible in solo performance'. Several authors have given detailed discussions of the concept of improvisation, and yet failed to take account of this feature of it (see, for example, A2, p. 24); often they also perpetuate the confusion between composition and improvisation (A2).

I have quoted some more sympathetic, if less rigorously philosophical definitions, than those of A2, in A31. Here I will only offer some suggestions from Evan Parker (sleeve notes to R110):

> We operate without rules (pre-composed material) or well-defined codes of behaviour (fixed tempi, tonalities, serial structures etc.) and yet are able to distinguish success from failure.
>
> If there are in any sense 'rules of play' in our music, they seem to me to accord well with ... [those] ... which according to Desmond Morris [*The Naked Ape*] govern all play activities ...
>
> 1 You shall investigate the unfamiliar until it has become familiar.
> 2 You shall impose rhythmic repetition on the familiar.
> 3 You shall vary this repetition in as many ways as possible.
> 4 You shall select the most satisfying of these variations and develop these at the expense of the others.
> 5 You shall combine and recombine these variations one with another.
> 6 You shall do all this for its own sake for an end in itself.

In proceeding next to discuss the apparent contradiction of rule 6 by recording and distributing the music Parker was well aware of the limitations of these rules. In particular, they again neglect the interactive elements of much improvisation, which encourages some performers to subordinate all these rules at times to the pursuits of the other musicians with whom they are playing.

The historical and sociopolitical process in improvised music

For the sake of clarity I would like here to summarise the key arguments of this book. I will reveal continuities in the development of all the major elements of music; and I will do so with reference to individual musicians, but also to areas of musical activity taken integrally (for example, compositions for improvisers, or use of rhythmic devices). I will illustrate that the developments have taken place in many countries concurrently, if in slightly different forms. I will argue that those differences are really differences between individuals interpreting the largely autonomous musical environment rather than between societies; and discuss the difficulties in sociopolitical interpretation of improvised music. However, I will illustrate in the final section of this Introduction how one aspect of the development of the arts in general since the 1960s (the modernist–postmodernist transition) may be reflected also in improvised music, and mention the possible sociological interpretations of this. In general I will later avoid such sociological interpretation for reasons I discuss here and further in Appendix 1.

What, then, is my general thesis concerning musical developments in the period? It is primarily that an evolution can be discerned as a gradual increase over time in the complexity of usage of most musical elements, and that this can be detected in the work of individuals and countries as much as in the field at large. 'Greater complexity' is used mainly in the sense of increased numbers of distinct musical events per unit time. These events are not simply increasing frequencies of exchangeable, equivalent events (such as having more quavers sounded within an 8/8 bar), but rather increasing numbers of distinctive events per unit time (for example, having in an 8/8 bar not only crotchets and quavers, but also triplets, dotted crotchets, etc.). The complexity may extend to simultaneity of elements usually present only separately or successively (multiple keys, multiple time signatures, multiple pitch centres within the sound of an individual musician, etc.).

The development and successful utilisation among a group of musicians of a range of such complex techniques is nearly always followed by a reaction, or consolidation, in which previous (less complex in the sense outlined) approaches are reasserted. So in response to modernism, there was subsequently a postmodern phase (see the next section of this Introduction) in which both complex and 'simpler' techniques coevolved. This may be a general feature, beyond modernism and postmodernism, in which reactive tendencies follow progressive phases.

Several times during the period, besides new structural tendencies, new musical sound sources and technologies have been brought to bear: for example, multiphonic and other 'extended' techniques of performing on acoustic instruments have been developed; digital control devices for activating electronic sound sources, and for controlling algorithms which activate them, have been introduced; and computerised sound synthesis has become accessible. Such developments are often anticipated by an analytical or imaginative few, such as Don Ellis in 1960, who exploited an array of compositional techniques which only in the next fifteen years came to be much exploited by other improvisers. In relation to each of these developments the cycle of increasing complexity and subsequent reaction can be observed. When one considers these changes in relation to the field at large it becomes more difficult (if, indeed, it is necessary) to decide whether to relate the developing phase in one area to the reactive or to the proactive elements of the whole field. The advantage of the analysis of individual musical entities, or small groups of musicians, is therefore obvious, and will underpin most of this book. The integration of reactive (proactive) elements in music at large and in its interpretation is the territory of a larger sociopolitical analysis, but I will offer only a preliminary foray at the end of this section. For more detailed coverage of some of the theoretical framework, see Appendix 1.

Before we can consider the validity of sociopolitical interpretations of the recent development of improvised music we need to discuss the nature of musical elements and their possible affects and references. Whereas language is a referential system (in which words have specific reference to objects outside themselves), music is largely not; it may be described as self-referential. Can music be referential at all? (See A35 for a useful introductory discussion.) It is interesting that whereas sounds can be characterised as loud or soft (a gradation which has no obvious bearing on other physical events besides sound), pitches are usually described as high or low (see Deutsch in A27). 'High' pitches have 'high' frequencies, and usually high energy content, so that a large number is associated with the energy level or frequency; and vice versa for low pitches. But why should 'high' and 'low' be associated with pitch (or energy), when really they are attributes of physical position? Does this indicate a referentiality in which pitches are associated with spatial positions? This might well be culturally entrained, for instance being only appreciated in societies which analyse music verbally, but might none the less be effective.

It is difficult to see what impact such referentiality might have. A more subtle example of referentiality is mentioned in Appendix 1, that of some Javanese musical sounds which have clear connotations in daily non-musical life. But one can reasonably conclude that such kinds of referentiality are of small importance. Thus music is a self-referential system for our purposes.

While all human activities are inevitably influenced by social and political events, in the crudest sense simply by definition of the terms, it is likely that the impact varies substantially between the different arts. Thus a referential system such as language has more points of contact with (and hence of influence by) society and politics than does abstract painting, which in turn has more than music, and particularly contemporary music. Abstract painting is to be seen commonly in daily situations such as magazines (in advertising elements) *and* objects similar to abstract paintings exist outside the art products themselves; while the same dual exposure does not occur with avant-garde music or environmental music or sound-sculpture. At the more referential extreme, on the other hand, representational art can clearly be highly political (take for example, Picasso's *Guernica*). This implies that the influence on the development of an art of the complementary (non-sociopolitical) factor, its internal, autonomous but changing system of reference, may be of complementary magnitude to the sociopolitical influence: so that the autonomous factors in the development of verbal arts are lesser than those in the development of visual art; and so that music is the most autonomously developing of the arts.

I will argue, therefore, that a broad social interpretation of the development of improvised music is unlikely to be valuable or very convincing. I will summarise some of the kinds of social interpretation which have been offered, and illustrate some of their interests and weaknesses. Nevertheless, it is clear that the ethnography of improvisation has much to tell us yet, and one cannot exclude that longer-term, more extensive sociological information on the impact and origins of improvisation will become available and reliably interpretable.

But I do not wish to be solely destructive of such sociological interpretations: and so I offer at the end of this section a new interpretation of
the development of jazz in terms of the modernist–postmodernist divide
which has been taken, at least by Jameson (see A6; A60) to be an
important reflection in the arts of social forces in the last thirty years.

Improvisation as social interaction

> This free kind of ensemble music is made in the spirit of mutual
> tolerance, whereby the musical intuition of each individual is entirely
> responsible for the form the work takes (W. Goldschmidt, sleeve of
> R105a).

> What makes [free music] relevant is that it's a group activity. You
> have to look for this other organism which is the group mind. You
> block access to that group mind if [your own] personality is too
> strong (Evan Parker, quoted in A77).

Before proceeding to a discussion of the sociological interpretations of
improvisation, it is necessary to divert briefly again to the social psychology of the improvising process. For improvisation, unlike most western
musical production in the last 200 years, can involve the simultaneous
participation of several cocreators. Composition rarely involves more
than one musician; and the various performers who contribute to the final
process act later, and thus usually do not interact directly with the
composer, and virtually never change the written form of the work. This
interaction is one of the key attractions of improvisation, and one of the
features which may make it at least as valuable as composition. Indeed,
composition by individuals working alone is not a widesprread activity in
most societies; improvisation by groups is more widespread and is also
used in the production of musical entities learned by rote, and which
remain firmly fixed (and hence 'composed') for several performances.

Thus the question arises as to what are the social interactions within
the improvised performance. Improvisers' views on this are very varied,
ranging from expressions of personal fulfilment through improvising
(which would imply autonomy of musical action by the individual) to the
idea that group improvising is a kind of problem-solving. A selection of
individual statements and some of my own views have been illustrated
previously (A31). Here I will only mention some further contrasts. A77
illustrates the stances of several improvisers in the UK. John Stevens,
founder of the Spontaneous Music Ensemble and pioneer of free improvisation, describes group workshop procedures for improvisers which
induce a 'spiritual' or 'meditative' attitude towards improvising. Paul
Burwell (who reappears in Chapter 11 as a member of the Bow Gamelan)
and David Toop talk of the playing process as 'a circular figure whose
motion describes a path through spontaneous improvisation, crystalliz-
ation, decomposition toward the potential for reintegration on an intuitive

level'. In the same article, AMM, as represented by Lou Gare and Eddie Prevost, refer to creating a 'state of awareness', and of the importance of audience and of silence during improvisations.

Perhaps all social interactions are problem-solving events in some sense; but what problems are tackled within a group of free improvisers? Are they problems deriving from the autonomous self-referentiality of music? For instance, they might concern how to make a sound on an individual instrument, perhaps a string instrument, converge with two other simultaneous sounds from other instruments. This might be achieved empirically by changing the mode of attack of the string instrument until an appropriate combination of multiphonic tones (seeming to have several pitch centres) is produced on each of several strings, so that the various components of the sound have sufficient overlap (or metonymy) with the other sounds. (In literary theory, objects or word-objects are metonymic with each other when they display part–whole relationships; this often depends on physical characteristics (for example fingers–hand).)

Or might the problems be larèer, üuch ás hoÑ to persuade the whole of a group to move to playing in a single pitch register and in a sustained manner, compressing violently the range of pitches in use? How would an individual musician lead to this? Perhaps by a process of playing pitches related to successively chosen other members of the ensemble, and then migrating from those pitches to the desired pitch range and sustaining a new sound therein?

Conversely, could these same problems be seen rather as the solving of sociopolitical problems, or as referring to such a process? Certainly a dialogic analogy can be made (A1; A116; discussed in A31). And it would not be so readily made with much referent-based jazz improvising, where the roles of the soloist and rhythm section do not converge: that is, any attempted dialogue has limited output. Here is Griffiths' (A49a) description, quoting Rzewski, of Musica Elettronica Viva (MEV):

> 'MEV's [aims] suggest . . . music as social therapy. "Spacecraft", an improvised [piece] was intended to lead each player from his "occupied space" of personal inclination to "a new space which was neither his nor another's, but everybody's." For "Sound Pool" (1969) musicians were asked "to act as naturally and free as possible without the odious role-playing ceremony of traditional concerts."'

So free improvisation as a process can be seen as a socially egalitarian, dialogic activity. However, a comparably dialogic element is present in some of the sections, particularly the fast concluding rhythmic sections, of some classical Indian music, where the sitar or veena might duet with a percussion instrument (tabla or mridangam). Indian musical structures contain as much 'inequality' and inflexibility of roles (the drone instrument versus the harmonium playing the raga pitches repetitively versus the improvising string or wind instrument) as does conventional modern jazz. One therefore cannot argue that the emergence of a dialogic mode of improvisation was a feature unique to the development of free improvisation in the 1960s. Thus a clear-cut correlation with social change outside music cannot be made: the dialogic Indian music was present within a highly stratified society, showing relatively little change, while free improvisation in the 1960s arose in many different western societies, from communist to capitalist.

Sociopolitical interpretations of developments in contemporary improvisation

> The term 'jazz' has come to mean the abuse and exploitation of black musicians; it has come to mean cultural prejudice and condescension ... and that is why I am presently writing a book, *I Hate Jazz*. It's not my name and it means my oppression as a man and musician.
>
> ... I am often asked. 'Can whites play your kind of music?' My answer is, 'Yes, anybody can play something that's already been set out there. If a painter paints a certain thing, I can imitate it. But no whites have ever contributed to the creative or innovative aspects of black music' (Max Roach, jazz drummer, A119).

This statement is at first sight appallingly prejudiced (what of Bill Evans, Scott LaFaro, Jimmy Giuffre, Lee Konitz, etc.) and in some aspects possibly totally ignorant (of Breuker, Schlippenbach, etc.). The difficulty in interpreting it is the lack of a satisfactory definition of 'black music' in this or other writings (nor is it my aim to provide one in this book: I doubt the possibility and utility of so doing). But the statement probably reflects a considerable experience of racism directed against black musicians; while viewing this with sympathy one has nevertheless to question whether the statement has not itself become racist (reverse racism in this case). It forms a fitting challenge with which to open this section; and clearly indicates that for some there are overt sociopolitical influences on improised music.

What might be the reasons for the changes in the rhythmic structures used in improvisation between 1950 and 1965, as illustrated by Figs A1.5–A1.7 in Appendix 1? What might be behind the development of increased metrical complexity, the dissolution of regular 4/4 playing, and the emancipation of the drums to a position of total equality with other instruments in a free jazz group, contributing on the levels of rhythm, pitch and timbre (see Chapters 1–3)? Can one relate these changes to alterations in the fabric of the societies in which they occurred?

Can they be related to an increasing interest of US blacks in African and oriental music? Yusef Lateef, Sahib Shihab and Archie Shepp visited Africa, studied African music and were influenced by Islam to some degree in the early 1960s, and there were parallel changes in their own music (A19). But there are major difficulties in showing that the African influence in early and in 1960s jazz was direct or significant rather than superficial (A85). If such a real connection were established, one would then have to seek the origins of the increased interest in matters of African music.

A common sociological description of the development of free jazz, its consequences, and of the coincident movements (A70; A76) uses the concept of revolt of a new order against an old and repressive (A132) order, and the idea that such a revolt occurred in music at least partly because there was a comparable revolt within society. Reinforcing this revolt was the occurrence of discrimination against the black musicians in work, and the lack of credit for their music; and an assertion of ethnic roots (A132). Hear LeRoi Jones's poem on his recording (R82) with the New York Arts Quartet (two white and two black musicians) for a more intuitive impression of some of the issues. A bibliography of relevant writings is available (A30). Perhaps the main limitation of these ideas is a lack of explicit realisation that there are always, besides dominant forces, contrary forces within society, as emphasised in the writings of Raymond Williams.

Nevertheless, might these ideas have explicative power in relation to developments in the USA? Was the black musician, the exploited and oppressed under revolt, responsible for the musical revolution? And the white, largely the thieving bystander? Attali (A6, p. 109) expresses (unusually for him) some stereotypic views when he says:

> A music of the body, played and composed by all, jazz expressed the alienation of blacks. Whites would steal from them this creativity born of labour ... and then turn around and sell it back ...

And again (p. 140):

> Free jazz, a meeting of black popular music and the more abstract theoretical explorations of European music, eliminated the distinction between popular and learned music, broke down the repetitive hierarchy. It also shows how the refusal to go along with the crisis of proliferation created locally the conditions for ... a new music.

But one can question the idea of a 'local' creation: rather one should ask how a comparable revolution occurred in other countries with very different social formulations at the time, and with relatively little sign or chance of social change, for example, in West Germany (Mangelsdorff, Dauner, Brotzmann, Schlippenbach), England (where a black influence might be suggested in the work of West Indian Joe Harriott, but a white was also evident in AMM, Spontaneous Music Ensemble, Parker, and Bailey), and in eastern Europe, particularly East Germany and Poland. I do not mean to imply by this discussion a lack of regard for the innovations of some of my musical heroes such as Parker, Davis, Coltrane, Coleman, Taylor and Ra; merely to question the forces at work, and to point to European, Russian, Japanese, and non-jazz American contributions to free jazz and freely improvised music not bound by jazz conventions, as well as to point to changes in jazz itself. The arguments have by now moved a long way from those of 1970, only three years after Coltrane's death, mentioned above (A70). For example:

the People who work in free music often find themselves venturing afterwards into extra-musical areas, with a social concern – John Stevens' concern for children in deprived environments, the evolution of a radical Marxist policy in the Scratch Orchestra, possibilities of free music workshops for mental hospital patients and so on (A77).

On the other hand, although 'protesters saw bop as protest music [the musicians'] cause was fundamentally musical' (A94).

Thus there is considerable difficulty in making a causal sociopolitical theory of the origins of free jazz (A70; A76) go beyond a crude level of description, little more than given above (see also Lewis in A153, for a critique of the ideas of black revolt in jazz development). And there is also difficulty in making it applicable to societies other than the USA: indeed Nanry (A94, p. 180) states that free jazz is not black nationalist and thus directly undermines some of the arguments of A70.

The reverse relationship, an influence of musical freedom on social action, is also plausible, as illustrated particularly in the Europeans (A6). As Jameson (A6, p. xi) mentions, Attali points to

the possibility of a superstructure to anticipate historical developments, to foreshadow new social formations in a prophetic and annunciatory way. The argument of *Noise* [the book in question] is that music, unique amongst the arts ... has precisely this annunciatory vocation; and that the music of today stands as a promise of a new, liberating mode of production ...

And yet the so-called black revolution is the main example in improvised music since 1960 in which a sociological interpretation has taken any hold.

The sociologist might object that developments in countries besides the USA were secondary, derivative of the socially driven change in the USA. This argument is difficult to sustain in terms of the precise nature of the musical developments introduced: they differ significantly in the different countries, as already indicated. For example in the mid-1960s composition for free improvisers was far more important in Europe than in the USA, while later it was in Europe that totally free improvising (without predetermined referents) remained active (in the work of Parker, Bailey, Breuker, Brotzmann, etc.) while in the USA it was often submerged again within more conventional compositions. Finally, if it were accepted that the precise nature of the musical change need not be similar in the different cases for the sociological argument still to hold similarly, then the sociologist would have reached a position of admitting the immense power of the autonomous forces of change within music.

It is worth noting the utterly contrasting view of Murray Schafer (A126, p. 7; p. 99): 'the general acoustic environment of a society' (by which he refers to noises more than to music) 'can be read as an indicator of social conditions which produce it and may tell us something about the trending and evolution of that society'.

Most of the sociological and historical literature on jazz is by Americans. It is unfortunately necessary here to illustrate the general insularity and bias of their approaches, which becomes particularly important after the origins of free jazz. As noted earlier, I am unapologetically redressing the balance somewhat in the book, but at this point in the arguments on sociological interpretation it is important to be clear that there is such a limitation in the American literature. I will illustrate this primarily by reference to a single detailed and scholarly introductory book, Nanry's *The Jazz Text* (A94), which makes claim to be objective and analytical, and which certainly has many such virtues. By way of preamble it should be pointed out that the likelihood that there are more jazz musicians in the USA than in any other country has no particular bearing on sociological interpretations, for the developments in other countries require explanations, too; in addition, it is not obvious that the proportion of the US population professional within jazz is higher than in some other countries (it would be very interesting to obtain the necessary data to decide this).

Nanry starts with some very dubious and unquestioned assumptions. For example, on p. 11 he states that 'There must be enough common understanding [in jazz performances] for the music to make sense to participants', and uses this idea to assert that rules are needed. If this statement is anything other than tautologous it is difficult to support. On the same page he continues: 'Jazz tends to be more successful the closer it adheres to conventional and recognizable melodic lines'. This is again an assertion which he makes no attempt to justify, and which seems unlikely to be a necessary feature of any music. The assertion is denied even by studies on the 'silent theme' tradition in bebop, which emphasise quite the opposite: that the bebop revolution exploited harmonic patterns without their originally attendant melodies, and without necessarily installing any substitute melody in their place (A149).

These dubious assumptions tend in the same direction: to support and publicise the insular maintenance of a jazz tradition with limited potential for technical enlargement, rather than the alternative of opening improvising musicians to the fullest possible range of opportunities. They might still maintain swing and related rhythmic accentuation (discussed later); Nanry (p. 16) asserts that swing can exist in relation to monorhythm (by which he means pulse) and seems unconvinced that in 'advanced modern groups' swing can still be present when desired. For 1979 this seems a remarkably reactionary statement. He also (p. 14) fails to appreciate that African rhythms are often not based on shared bar lines. Rather, each part (other than the time line) may have loose repeating rhythmic cycles, but they do not necessarily coincide with each other (A64; see also developments in subsequent studies such as A112, discussed in Chapter 2 of the present book). Thus Nanry's discussion of jazz rhythms, which he assumes derive significantly from African rhythms, is dangerously under-mined. On p. 245, Nanry admits that he cannot produce a satisfactory definition of jazz, and therefore admits that, little as he might like it, drastic changes in the music have occurred and so will continue to.

These misleading assumptions are supported by a lack of overt aware-ness of European jazz and free improvising. Thus, on p. 25 he says: 'Although jazz is played in communities throughout the US, New York is still the *mecca* of jazz' (emphasis added). One wonders, of what kind of jazz? And a mecca for the listener or the musician? This is clearly a debatable statement which would be difficult to substantiate; and, more importantly, are there no other countries? The statement is especially disturbing because Nanry seems only to be aware of European musicians who work in America: the only reference to Europeans occurs on pp. 190–1 and all six musicians he names have worked in jazz-rock groups in the USA.

Similarly, though less extremely, Litweiler (A78) in a sympathetic biographical survey of European free jazz makes major omissions and several errors of fact (for example, in relation to Joe Harriott, whose recordings are described incorrectly). These examples of US insularity, and perhaps misinterpretation, could be multiplied readily.

Thus the somewhat chauvinist bias of most writers on jazz has an impact on their interpretation of jazz development, whether sociological or otherwise (this will inevitably be true to some extent also of the present book) and it would be unwise to neglect this impact (see also supporting views of Lewis in A153).

Perhaps the most important criterion of the value of one of these sociological theories would be whether it leads to testable predictions and, if so, whether these are sustainable. This would require independent definition of the degree of musical and of social change sufficient to qualify for consideration. Such quantisations, let alone their application, are lacking from the sociological literature describing US black jazz of the 1960s, or, for that matter, in relation to the other musical changes mentioned above.

Here is Eddie Prevost (A23) on mid- and late 1960s free improvisa-tions:

The high rise block for instance – a very structured way of organising people. Even the Welfare State [in the UK] which was a marvellous thing when it began, began from an organisational, paternalistic point of view, rather than looking at people as separate entities. People were seen *en masse*. And I think a lot of improvisation was a kind of response to that dehumanising aspect of life.

In sum, the sociological theories at present seem so preliminary as to fit almost any development, even such a relatively small one as the introduction of triplet rhythms across longer units of metrical time than just beats (see Chapter 2), just as well as they might fit the larger changes such as free jazz's demolition of conventional jazz harmonic repetitive structures, and fixed emphasised rhythmic pulses. Conversely, they do not obviously lead to valuable predictions, and they are certainly not supported by quantitative information which could convince any empiricist. They reduce to two simple, possibly unrelated sets of descriptions: that of the musical entities, and that of the coincident social patterns. There may be no need or justification for the two to be forced together as yet.

the music of any period is heterogeneous and follows its own laws. It is only coincidentally related to the society in which it exists ... We could postulate ... that ... music is divorced from the realities of daily existence, for it is a man-made abstraction guided by its own rules, shaped by its own creators, and understood only by the members of the society whose ears have been trained to hear it (A151, p. 318).

I have therefore adopted this conclusion, that musical development is primarily autonomous, in the majority of the text, and applied musical analysis and description independently of sociopolitical interpretation. However, I have a small positive contribution to offer in the area of sociopolitical interpretation, which hopefully will be subject to the fuller scrutiny of others later.

Modernism and postmodernism in improvisation since 1960

It has recently become common to argue that two strands, modernism and postmodernism, can be usefully distinguished within the recent arts, and that the common succession from the first to the second has a significant connection with the development of capitalist consumerist society since the second world war (A60). Nanry (A95) has also discussed industrial and social functions in jazz and modernism, but does not make clear what he means by 'modernism' nor mention postmodernism. Modernism can be briefly characterised (after Jameson) as the search for the highest ideals of an art, embodied in the expressive directness of the creative individual, and for technical novelty. Postmodernism, in contrast, rejects such overtly high aspirations and emphasises the more commonplace, by means of technically familiar means. Postmodernism also stresses the role of the audience in the cognition of a work: art depends very much on its recipients, and not solely on the artist(s) producers (and hence the phrase the 'writerly text'). Postmodernism thus largely avoids elevating the artistic product to the status of personal expression. Technical familiarity is often developed by means of quotation, pastiche and recreation of previous styles in some considerable degree.

In musical composition, the strand from Schoenberg and the second Viennese school through to Boulez, Stockhausen and Henze, can be taken as the main modernist strand. The postmoderns would, in contrast, include Cage, Feldman, and systemic (or less aptly, 'minimal') music such as that of Reich, Glass and Nyman.

Can such an analysis be usefully applied to the development of improvisation in the twentieth century? If so, then the arguments for a sociopolitical basis to changes in improvisation could perhaps be sustained, by applying Jameson's view that the modernist–postmodernist transition depends on the developments of capitalist consumerist society. If we concern ourselves primarily with the period since 1960, then in jazz, bebop and hard bop (see Chapter 1) were initially the predominant styles, the outcome of the establishment of an idealist, technically advancing style of improvising (bebop) and its consolidation (hard bop). The conventional description of Charlie Parker, Thelonius Monk and Dizzy Gillespie, among the pioneers of bebop, as 'turning their backs to the audience', delineates a stereotype of the artist, in other words of the creator of an expression-intensive, modernist music, paralleling modernism in other arts. Thus there are 'parallels between the evolution of jazz and the other arts' and 'these developments are related to a large cultural configuration' (A153, p. 54, referring to bebop). Note however, that this configuration could be seen as one of cultural autonomy rather than as socially derived.

To what did this line from bebop and hard bop lead? Clearly to Miles Davis's early work, to John Coltrane, Cecil Taylor, Ornette Coleman and the development of free jazz: another modernist movement.

What might be termed postmodern within improvising developments? There seem to be three such waves. First, the movement of Third Stream (see for example, R114), in the 1950s and early 1960s, in which classical compositional techniques and orchestration (from serial compositional techniques to use of French horns, flutes and cellos, etc.) were allied with conventional and more abstruse jazz improvisers (from Davis to Eric Dolphy and Coleman). With this wave can be associated the west coast 'cool' jazz school of Bud Shank, vibes player Teddy Charles, Buddy Collette, Chico Hamilton, etc., whose penchants were in a similar, though less grandiose direction (see A19; A151). Also part of this first wave are the groups which emphasised oriental influences (John Handy, Paul Horn, Joe Harriott and Indo-Jazz Fusions, Charlie Munro in Australia, etc.). These activities are postmodern in several of the senses indicated initially, particularly in their use of older techniques in a new amalgam, which is overtly referential toward the old (and, as it happens, also implicitly reverential).

The second postmodern wave, chronologically, would be the work of some of the European (for example, AMM, New Phonic Art) and American (for example, Pauline Oliveros and associates) free improvising ensembles which, among other features, elevated the status of environmental contributions (or at least of factors external to the performance, deriving from chance or outside events) to an improvisation performance. This feature has much in common with some of John Cage's compositional work. It can be construed as postmodernist in that it avoids the elevated ideal of the self-driven creator producing an autonomous work, and emphasises instead that of the creation of a work of music by an interaction between performer, environment and listener.

The third postmodernist wave is then that of the recreators, prevalent in the 1970s and 1980s, and of the jazz-funk movement. The recreators produced a slightly updated version of the hard bop style of the late 1950s and early 1960s – for example, in America, the successive groups of Art Blakey, the Donald Harrison–Terence Blanchard group, much of Wynton and Branford Marsalis, etc., in other words both older musicians who had an involvement with the original period, and young musicians born since it finished. Thus, for instance, Howard Riley, innovative improvising pianist in the 1970s and early 1980s (quoted in *The Guardian* (UK), 28 October 1988):

> I'm trusting myself to let new things come out ... I'm not purposely looking for change the way I used to ... But that's very different from revivalism ... The mainstream of jazz today is post-modern to use the current term and that might be a polite way of saying nobody's doing anything new.

Similarly, and particularly striking, is the recent 'new jazz' movement in the UK, in which young musicians such as Courtney Pine and the Jazz Warriors (R79), Loose Tubes (R85), Andy Sheppard (R116), and Steve Williamson have emphasised styles from the same 1950s–1960s period, but with more emphasis on recreating the early work of John Coltrane. They have had far more work, media exposure, etc., than their older, modernist colleagues. This case could form a plausible late example of Jameson's description of the consumerist relationship of the transition to postmodernism. Thus in relation to some consumerist force, the development of these musicians could be taken as a responsive event, economically driven (however indirectly).

The jazz-funk and jazz-rock movement of the late 1960s and 1970s, some complex (R48; R50; R51; R95), others simpler (as with the Crusaders), can also be taken as within the third postmodernist jazz wave, in its tendency to withdraw from the rhythmic complexities which had been introduced in hard bop, and expanded by Coltrane–Coleman–Taylor. This withdrawal is intrinsic in their tendency to emphasise the first beat of every bar (in contrast with the greater flexibility of other jazz), as discussed in a later chapter. They were also postmodernist in their emphasis on the most simple of harmonic progressions, and exceedingly tonal ones, at a time when other strands of improvised music were breaking these limits. Finally, it was within the ambit of these musicians particularly (for example, John McLaughlin and the Mahavishnu Orchestra, and Miles Davis), that another system of reference to the great historical past of oriental and particularly Indian music was most pronounced: in the names, in the use of sitars, tablas, etc. This system of reference was also present within the first of the improvising postmodernist streams I have identified, but in a less pronounced way (John Handy performing with the Indian tabla player Shankar Ghosh; Paul Horn using an Indian temple for recording, and Indian instruments; as did Charlie Mariano, etc.: see A19 for a listing of these Indian influences).

As the diversion to describe the particular case of 'new jazz' and media presentation in the UK illustrates, sociopolitical features influence strongly the presentation and availability of postmodern and modernist improvisation (see also A35). Are such factors also influencing the generation of such music? Or its impact upon the listener? These possibilities cannot be resolved yet.

Although I have proposed this outline interpretation of the development of improvisation constructively, in so doing I have evaded the fundamental problem of any such an interpretation: even if there is a correlation between the modernist to postmodernist progressions of the different arts, is the correlation sufficiently close to indicate that any common factors might be acting upon the different arts? And if so, is the timing of the different postmodern waves within each art, and in the several arts, sufficiently well placed in relation to the timing of the development of the capitalist and materialist trends that Jameson emphasises as the possible origin of the artistic developments? How could this argument survive the consideration of the different countries and different societies in which such a modernist to postmodernist transition would be shown to have occurred: for example, again, eastern Europe versus western Europe, in turn contrasted with the USA? Or is the argument again too great a contortion, so that at the most only the development in one society is susceptible to the interpretation that sociopolitical pressure were involved, while that in the others becomes more an example of the transmission of technical ideas within the art to other practitioners; in other words, an example of the more autonomous development of that art? And how would any plausible sociological interpretation be distinguished from the possibility I believe particularly important with a self-referential system such as music, that the main developmental forces are autonomous and function independently of the social structure and its alterations in time?

I cannot resolve these problems here, nor does it seem that the literature satisfactorily resolves them elsewhere, I offer the modernist–postmodernist outline for further analysis in these sociological terms by others, and will turn to summarise the conclusion of Appendix 1, which discusses the range of possible approaches to analysing musical entities. This forms the approach applied in the rest of the book.

The analytical stance and organisation of this book

In the preceding sections (and further in Appendix 1) I argue in detail for a key conclusion: that autonomous development is at least important in music in general, and equally in improvised music. By this I mean that musical devices and their usage may evolve largely independently of social change, but in a manner rather dependent on the available musical production of other musical practitioners. But I emphasise some of the unique psychological and social features of the production of improvisation, and the interactions that occur during such production.

I am therefore proceeding to apply some of the analytical approaches discussed in Appendix 1 to illustrate the emergence of new techniques of improvising during the period under discussion. I will do this largely by selecting specific examples from the recorded literature, transcriptions of which will reveal the point addressed. I will give few illustrations of the structure of whole works, but rather more of the changes in the component techniques in rhythm, pitch, harmony, and timbre/texture. Thus Section 1 of this book will concern music as object, and virtually pretend that nothing is relevant outside the recorded or audible sound.

In contrast, in Sections 2 and 3 I will turn to the improvising event, with discussion of instrumental sound production, interactions between participating musicians and their roles, and how each of these aspects has changed in the period under consideration. In Section 4 I will also make comparisons, and illustrate the continuities, with the other arts: for example sound–text, text–image.

It is obvious that I can present only a small sample of examples. Thus the selection is rather arbitrary, and cannot hope to demonstrate priorities or depths of pursuit of particular techniques; I have accepted idiosyncrasy. Even in the case studies of individual musicians or movements which I have included in Section 3, it is not possible to discuss more than a small portion of the recorded works of these musicians, so the same limitation remains. Nevertheless, I hope I have succeeded in at least identifying from a much larger survey, and defining by means of the small sample illustrated, some of the musical and technical devices which have appeared in improvisation in the period. While I will eschew further sociological discussion of the signification and origins of the works I consider, I make a small contribution to the ethnography of the composer–improviser interaction by means of the interview between myself and my composer-colleague and friend, Graham Collier.

I finish the book with a series of predictions and suggestions for the development of improvisation in the near future, which in a sense complement the analyses I have offered. If this book transmits any sense of the way that only a limited selection of the boundless possibilities within musical improvisation have been explored so far, and yet how rich this exploration has been, I will be very well rewarded.

Improvised music as object and evolution

1 The evolution of improvised and composed music in the 1950s: a synopsis

In this chapter I am offering a very brief survey of jazz in the 1950s and some comparisons with events in composed music to set the background for the developments I will consider later. My comparisons with composed music will be cursory, since considerable published material is available on this (see, for example, A49a; A49b; A82; A140).

I have indicated already that this book will distinguish evolving strands of musical change, in the application of particular musical techniques (such as rhythm), in the work of groups of musicians, and in the work of individuals. 'Evolution' is used in a general sense, with no implications of improvement or increasing adaptation, in contrast to Darwinian usage of the word. Nevertheless the evolution is often directional, in that some feature (usually complexity) shows change in a consistent sense over some significant period. In the case of complexity, this is mostly a consistent increase. Sometimes, as with rhythmic developments, such consistent change was also almost continuous, in that most of the possible steps along the route were used for some time. This can be contrasted with discontinuous change, which involves large jumps along the route.

The phases of continuous and consistent change can conveniently be termed 'progressions', again with no implication of increasing Darwinian fitness, nor of sociopolitical improvement. Such an almost linear phase of evolution in music is followed usually by a reaction: an abrupt (rather than continuous) change of ideas and techniques. Many evolutionary strands coexist at a time, at least in the period under discussion, and hence in relation to several strands development may be in a phase of reaction, while in relation to others it may still be in one of progression.

Most of the new composed music in the 1950s involved either extremely complex organisation of pitches, rhythms, and timbral elements ('integral serialism') or developing electronic or taped sound control. Thus Stockhausen and Boulez, somewhat influenced by Messiaen, were concerned with increasing control of all the elements of composition, by serial techniques. At the same time Schaeffer and Henry, in Europe, and Babbitt and colleagues in the USA, were beginning in their different ways developments which would lead into electronic music as we now know it.

I shall not detail the techniques involved. It will suffice to point out that serial composition (see A139) involves treating a number of musical elements (such as the twelve semitones of the mean tempered octave) as equal, and reusing them repeatedly in a fixed sequence (the primary 'series', or, in the case of pitches, the primary 'note row'), and in alternative sequences rigorously derived from it. Mathematical developments from this approach would later permit the control of frequency of use of a particular musical element, without regard for controlling the precise sequence in which it occurred in relation to the other musical elements being used. By computerised means Xenakis developed this to a unique status particularly in the 1960s. Computers were also used to control other elements of compositional procedures.

In contrast, the development of electronic music began from the most elementary of techniques, tape collage, which simply means taking taped sound elements, and rearranging or changing them by physical cutting up and resplicing of tape, playing it backwards or at slower speeds, etc. The sounds chosen were also often outside the conventionally musical (for example, environmental sounds in the work of Schaeffer). Stockhausen was involved in both the rigorous compositional approaches and those of tape music.

There were reactions against these two strands of progression. One such reaction, in which openness, and hence scope for the performer's contribution to the creative process, was emphasised over compositional rigour, will concern us later. Many elements contributed to this: for example, the use of chance procedures and the acceptance of environmental input in performance (as in the work of Cage). Cage's chance procedures of applying marks to the surface of a musical score page, led to graphic output beyond conventional musical notation, and such output was also produced by artists interested in musical sound (for example, Tom Phillips) and by composers interested in visual objects (such as Earle Brown, Will Eisma, Lyell Cresswell). These graphic scores were at a peak in the decade after the mid-1960s (see A31). The importance of such graphic scores was again in part that they clearly required of the performer the role of cocreator, rather than only that of interpreter.

In sum, composition in the 1950s had already reached, retained, and reacted against extreme complexity. But the complexity was obtained by simple manipulation of rigorous procedures. For example, nothing could be much simpler than repeating a twelve-note sequence, in the same order; and the process of inversion, or playing in reverse, is hardly more complex. The complexity arises from the simultaneous occurrence of large numbers of such processes.

Western improvisation was hardly alive in 1950 in any sphere except jazz (see A31 for background on improvisation prior to this period). And it was functioning with much simpler structures than composed music. Themes were often familiar popular songs; harmonies were almost what they had been in the popular song version, and were used in repeating cycles, rarely more than 32 bars long. As discussed in Appendix 1, most of the music was diatonic, based in clearly tonal contexts. Modulation (to new key centres) was usually not a major element of the harmonies. Rhythmic approaches were restricted and repetitive.

During the period we will consider, all these basic elements were undermined, and replaced by a greater flexibility of approach, and often by much greater complexity of output. Thus the roles of the rhythm section players (piano and/or guitar, bass, and drums) in 1950 were clearly predictable: limited rhythmic statement, with very great repetition, and clear-cut harmonic statement with continuous recycling through the composed pattern of harmonies over a fixed number of bars. As these roles were gradually expanded or undermined, so the complexity of actions coexisting within the performing group increased drastically. By the time of free jazz (around 1960 onwards) a performance might easily involve as much complexity of event as did the serial compositions of the 1950s. But this complexity had arisen in a different way, and was not the dictate of a rigorous process. Crucially, it was also not normally the dictate of a single musician (the composer) but of several musicians playing together (the improvisers).

One might also say that increasing complexity in improvised music resulted from reduced dependence on the formulaic elements of repetitive harmonic structure, fixed metre and rhythmic pattern, etc. This, as illustrated later, amounts to a total divergence from composition in the 1950s, whose extreme complexity had been reached by the application of largely (and sometimes entirely) formulaic approaches (as in integral serialism).

However, improvised music had converged in one sense with composition. The jazz of the 1950s had been an 'intensifying' music in which actions are based on a common ground (the chord sequence and rhythmic structure) but produce affect by 'intensifying' elements of it (for example, increasing harmonic subtlety, or rhythmic diversity within the framework: see also Appendix 1). But it had later become a music of 'extension', like composition, in which new musical elements could be introduced, while at the same time musical continuities could be retained if required. The input into this development from improvisers outside the jazz tradition was also significant, and, not surprisingly, quite distinct. Particularly in the last decade, the improvisers from outside and from inside jazz have increasingly collaborated.

What was the nature of jazz improvisation in the 1950s, prior to the period we shall address later? At the outset, the dominant developing jazz movement was bebop. Such a voluminous literature exists on bebop, and its pioneers, Charlie Parker, Dizzie Gillespie, Thelonius Monk and company, that I shall say only a little about it. Bebop was a jazz style still

5

related to some of the African origins of the music: particularly the pitch elements in blues, and the emphasis on rhythm (A64; A130).

It has been proposed that much African music is based on additive principles, in which different metres succeed each other independently in different instruments; and in which 'bar lines' (or more probably, rhythmic cycle divisions) are of minor importance, and are certainly not in common between all the parts (see A64). This interpretation of African music is now the subject of much debate (see, for example, A112); and clearly it neglects the vast distinctions between different African traditions. African music is probably as diverse as Asian music, and to treat it as one music may not be very helpful.

In any case, bebop and preceding jazz has very limited connections with the specific rhythmic elements of African music, only sharing the emphasis on rhythmic intensity or pulse, though in different ways (A85). Bebop is much simpler rhythmically than African music, usually relying on 4/4 pulse and bar lines in common between all parts. The 'oral' and aural element of the jazz tradition was very important, and shared with African music (A132); the more 'literary' written European music was in contrast to this.

Each pulse in bebop was primarily subdivided into two 8th notes so that there were eight divisions per bar of 4/4; previously in jazz in 4/4 it had not been subdivided. Byrnside (A51) provides motivic descriptions of improvisers at work at the outset of the period, from Webster and Hawkins to Parker and Gillespie. The division of the bar into eight, particularly in the soloists' work, established also a division of the rhythmic flux into two major streams; that of the soloist being well separated and distinguished from that of the rhythm section, since the latter was still primarily concerned with quarter notes. There was a greater freedom of phrase lengths in the bebop soloists' work also: instead of monotonous four-bar phrases, irregular patterns were common.

Harmonically, the beboppers were particularly concerned with the higher intervals of chords, adding sevenths, ninths and elevenths on top of simple chords, using flattened fifths (Fig. 1.1), and exploiting these in the improvisation of the soloists but less in the accompaniment of the piano or guitar (see Harrison in A57). Motivically, Parker's improvisations were complex, and could be quite consistent in their derivation (A51; A65; A151). On the other hand, the motivic material used for the improvisation was often disguised or neglected: hence the term 'silent theme' (A149) characterises improvisations on harmonic sequences de-

Fig. 1.1 Common additions and substitutions in bebop harmonies.

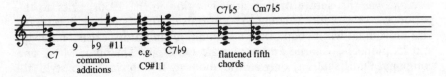

Fig. 1.2 Developments in improvised music.

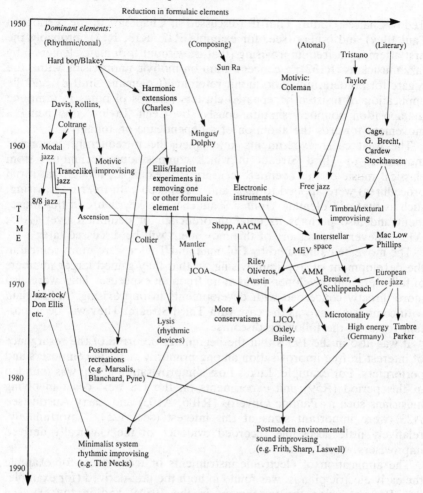

The figure is designed to reveal some key fluxes. The links shown are necessarily very selective and limited; and the choice of individuals and groups to be listed is based on their occurrence in the book rather than an assessment of their importance.

rived from well-known 'standard' themes (popular items), but with little reference to the original theme, and often no serious replacement of it.

Most of the improvising movements in the 1960s which will be discussed in later parts of this book had antecedents in the 1950s. Some are summarised in Fig. 1.2: here the vertical axis represents the progression of time between 1950 and the 1990s; and the horizontal a rough gradient from the most formulaic improvising (left-hand side) to the least formulaic (right). Among the major but isolated events in the development of improvising in the 1950s were harmonic experiments, such as polytonality, and other harmonies which were complex in relation to the jazz tradition; formal initiatives (by the US west coast musicians such as

7

Teddy Charles, Jimmy Giuffre (discussed in Chapter 7 in the section on Paul Bley) and others (see, for example R12; R13; R14); probably the first attempts at free improvising (that is, without formulaic elements) by jazz musicians (R132); a concentration on motivic improvising with little regard for predetermined harmonic referents (Coleman; Giuffre); and the application of insistently repeated clusters (groups of notes in semitone juxtaposition sounded simultaneously) by Cecil Taylor, this being a movement towards the abolition of a dependence on tonality.

The west coast experiments anticipated the infrequently performed movement of Third Stream in which compositional techniques from classical music of the twentieth century (for example, atonal and serial procedures) were applied to jazz, and juxtaposed with freer improvising, such as that of Coleman. Gunter Schuller was a key figure in this movement and also perhaps its chief theoretician, or definition-giver (A65; A131). Several successors of this movement will be discussed later.

The movements initiated by Coleman and Taylor were more central in the development of free improvising, in that they gained larger numbers of followers and developers, and more frequent exposure. They were also more directly concerned with developments in improvising, rather than with composing, as was the case with Third Stream. They will be important topics in the following discourse.

It was also in the 1950s that the beginnings occurred of the resurgence of interest in free improvisation among primarily classical composers and performers. For example, Lukas Foss's improvisation group was founded in this period (R59) and experiments on the US west coast involving musicians such as Pauline Oliveros (R106; A103) and Larry Austin (see A23) were important signs of this interest (see A25). Unfortunately, relatively little accessible recorded evidence of the classically derived improvisers' work exists.

The application of electronic instruments or techniques, for example the early electric pianos, was found in both the jazz-derived (for example, Sun Ra was using the instrument in the 1950s) and in the classical composer-improviser stream. In the latter there was more interest in tape-manipulation techniques springing from the early *musique concrète* experiments of Pierre Henry and Pierre Schaeffer in the 1950s (A49b; A82), though some were applied to environmental improvisation (A103).

It will be necessary several times to refer again later to events in the 1950s, to provide a suitable springboard for the discussion of subsequent events (of which Fig. 1.2 provides an introductory summary). For further musical information on the 1950s music outlined in this section, the reader is referred to A57, A65, A69, A130, and A151, which are virtually the only books with significant musical analysis. There are also a few journal articles with substantive musical analysis; several of these are mentioned elsewhere in this book. In contrast, biographical, critical and discographical books on the period abound.

2 Rhythmic techniques

This chapter will exemplify in the case of rhythm the general thesis of the book, that increasing complexity in usage of particular musical elements can be discerned as a dominant force within improvisation. But as illustrated by the earlier discussion of modernism and postmodernism, increasing complexity does not always characterise linearly the technical usage of music as time progresses. So we will also see reactions against such increasing complexity. It is not practical to present every strand in an entirely chronological way, but I will present part of the evolution of one particular strand (improvised pulse shifts, from one pulse speed to another) chronologically as it occurred in the work of one group. In most other cases I will present the stages of progression without always providing detailed examples (though these are available, space does not permit their complete documentation). In the latter part, I will indicate the nature of the consolidation of rhythmic usage which has occurred towards the end of the period under discussion, and some of the lines of change which are still being pursued (and see also Chapter 11 for possible future developments).

It is necessary first to clarify some terms. 'Pulse' refers to the repeated occurrence of accented sounds at virtually fixed intervals in time. Pulse was an important force in pre-nineteenth-century western classical music. But the emphasis attached to pulse has been greater in jazz than in any other western music (A130). Pulse is also very important in Asian and African music. But until the mid-1960s jazz pulse was nearly always organised into regular metres, whereas this was not necessarily true of Indian and particularly of African music, as already noted briefly. African rhythms may be partly additive, and almost uncoordinated between different instruments. The time line (played by one person) is clearly asymmetric, though repeated: and whereas metre has a hierarchy of accents, the time line (so it can be argued) does not. Metre in western composition,

9

and in jazz, implies the arrangement of pulses into regularly recurring patterns, with different degrees of emphasis, and predicates a concept of generation of rhythmic contrast by divisive techniques. For instance, a metre consisting of four pulses (which are then called beats) per repeating unit (then called bars), involves the accentuation of the first and to a lesser extent the third pulse, and a relative lack of accentuation of the second and fourth pulses.

Free jazz improvisation (from the 1960s onwards) involves a retention of the importance of pulses, but a dissolution of the importance of metre. Nevertheless, in this context the traditional jazz concept of 'swing' can still remain important, though in a modified form (see also Chapter 10). Gunther Schuller (A130) gives a neat characterisation of the special importance in jazz of the rhythmic accentuation which characterises swing, as opposed to any other pulse in Western classical music (see also Byrnside in A51). Schuller points out that swing not only involves enhancing the disparity of accentuation of pulses within metre, but also the slight displacement of sounds in relation to the relatively constant pulse interval, and the alternating distraction from and re-emphasis of the normal positions in time of the pulses. This concept of swing can be applied even when the pulses do not remain constant in length for more than a very short time (or limited number of repetitions); and this is important in free jazz, and to a lesser extent in free improvising in general (see, for example, AMM's *Generative Themes* (R3) which has various clearly related pulses, such as an irregular metronome/clock tick, and elsewhere slow percussion pulses).

Increasing complexity of rhythm in formulaic improvising: the soloist's role

Having laid out the terminology and background, I must reiterate that the evolutionary changes we will discuss did not necessarily occur synchronously in different places, or within the work of different groups of musicians. Nevertheless, there is a surprising degree of chronological consistency in different countries. For example, free improvising which removed the formulaic element of fixed pulse became important in the USA around 1960 with the work of Coltrane and Coleman. But in roughly the same period, it also became apparent in the UK in the work of Joe Harriott, and in Germany, in that of Wolfgang Dauner, Alex von Schlippenbach, and in the compositions of Bernd Alois Zimmerman for improvising ensemble.

As emphasised in Appendix 1 and elsewhere, this cohesion of timing may be most readily explained as consequent on the autonomous nature of musical development, in which musical ideas from one individual or group influence those of another, almost regardless of relative locality and hence of means of transmission of the initial idea.

Fig. 2.1(a) Stan Getz, 'Early Autumn' (1947) modified from Schuller A130, p. 23.

This group was a quintuplet
earlier in the performance

We must first consider improvising within repetitive formulaic structures, such as the jazz chord sequence, where a fixed pulse and metre are retained throughout by the group as a whole. Here divergence and development in rhythm are eminently possible for the musicians undertaking the brunt of the improvisation, and less so for accompanying musicians. As noted already, such a division of labour between the soloist (permitted the greatest freedom of role) and the accompanying rhythm section (in jazz the piano or guitar, bass and drums) was retained by many practising groups throughout the period, and was the norm until at least 1960. A similar division exists in classical Indian improvisation and other musics.

So we will first discuss the changes in the improvisation of the soloist in these formulaic contexts. Such changes are important, but they had limited consequence for the rhythmic stance of the group as a whole, since they normally occurred without greatly perturbing the rhythmic behaviour of the accompanists. In contrast, changes in the latter might be seen as more fundamental, and thus will be discussed in more detail in the subsequent section of this chapter.

It has already been revealed (A130) that a considerable range of rhythmic devices was at work in soloists' playing in early jazz. Fig. 2.1 illustrates some of the rhythmic patterns Schuller has described and notes some displacements of motivic pattern in relation to pulse by Stan Getz, and a superimposition of rhythm by Benny Morton (ten semiquavers in the time of eight, in other words ten notes in two crotchet beats).

What major rhythmic changes had occurred from these stances, during

Fig. 2.1(b) Benny Morton trombone solo on 'Sugar Foot Stomp' based on A130, p. 277.

Fig. 2.2 Lee Konitz playing 'Lover Man' from R103; based on transcription in A86. From first chorus.

the period summarised in Chapter 1, and thus by 1960, at which time this study starts? The key movement had been bebop, and by 1960 it was firmly consolidated as hard bop, and some of its pioneers, such as alto saxophonist Charlie Parker, were dead. Fig. 2.2 illustrates some of the rhythmic devices which were present in Parker's work and not so prevalent beforehand, by means of the work of Lee Konitz a little later. Already the difficulty of transcription of rhythms is apparent (see Appendix 1): when rhythmic patterns are very rapid, and especially when articulation is flexible, it becomes difficult to decide how many notes to indicate, where each began, and hence what the rhythmic structure was. As a result, it is normal to find notations which indicate that the number of notes heard within a pulse were spaced equally within that pulse. This is often not the case, however, as there is usually considerable irregularity of placement, as also found in Indian music. Mehegan's transcription of Konitz, which forms the basis of Fig. 2.2, is exemplary in its practical degree of precision. Fig. 2.2 generally illustrates increased complexity of subdivision of pulses; the main syncopations occur within subdivided beats (for example, beats 2 and 3, bar 1).

In contrast to these irregular divisions of pulses, displacement of regular rhythmic patterns in relation to normal whole pulses has been illustrated in relation to Getz already. But Fig. 2.3 reveals more complex examples in later work of Bill Evans (R56) and much later 1960s playing of John McLaughlin; and these are, of course, simply examples selected from many. The Bill Evans case is primarily one of superimposition of a new pulse speed on the basic pulse: in bar 1 six versus four, thus preserving the pulse at the half-way point of the bar as common to both pulse

Fig. 2.3(a) Bill Evans from 'My Romance' (R56).

Fig. 2.3(b) John McLaughlin, from 'Spaces', bar 20 of solo R35; based on A92.

Fig. 2.4(a) Lennie Tristano, based on A151, p. 298.

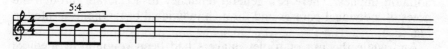

Fig. 2.4(b) Tristano, from 'Crosscurrents' (R132).

Fig. 2.4(c) Chick Corea, 'Inner Space' (R33); an A + B structure where A = 14 bars, and B = 16.

speeds; in bar 2 the new pulse is nine in place of four, so that the half-way point of the bar is no longer accentuated by the new pulse. In the example from McLaughlin the new pulse superimposed is again six against four, but it is displaced by one beat from the initial bar line, so that it occupies beats 2, 3, 4, and 1 of the basic bar, and again does not coincide with the accented third pulse of the parent 4/4.

The superimposition may not be of new pulse, but of new bar length: Fig. 2.4 illustrates this in the work of Lennie Tristano and Chick Corea. Thus in Fig. 2.4a there is no impact on the second beat; and note the similar approach of Fig. 2.4c. This superimposition of new bar length will be considered further later in the chapter.

In general soloists became more verbose in the 1960s, so that besides the evolution of increased pulse superimposition just illustrated, sub-dividing pulses into increasing numbers of notes became more and more common. For instance, a pattern from John Coltrane is shown in Fig. 2.5. His rhythmic patterns often remained very simple, but divided into semi-quavers and demisemiquavers rather than quavers. More complex sub-divisions than this are shown, and they are often more irregular than the notation implies. There is a general tendency to accelerate through the notes of individual phrases and through individual beats (not indicated in Fig. 2.5).

And while the use of triplet quavers had been common at medium tempi in hard bop, Coltrane, possibly largely through his drummer Elvin Jones began also to superimpose a further layer of triplet subdivisions on

Fig. 2.5 John Coltrane, from 'Crescent' (R22), based on M14.

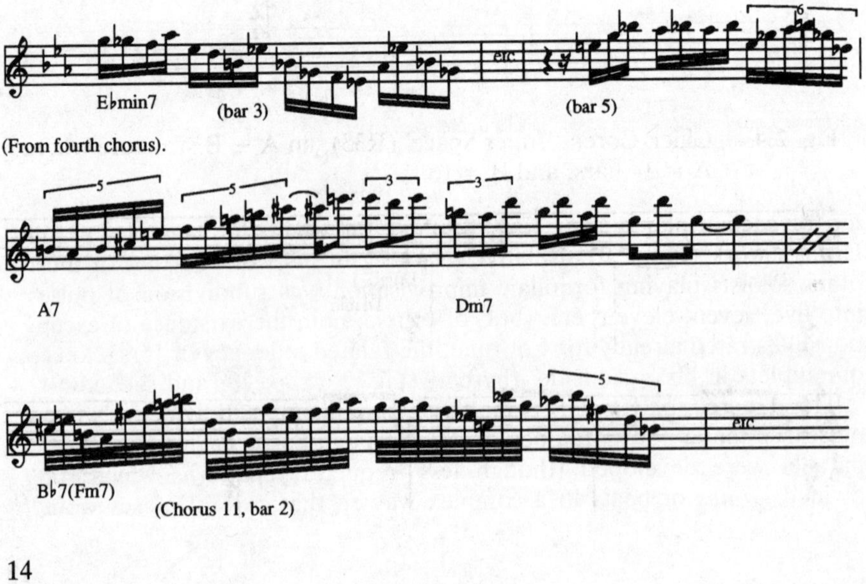

Ebmin7   (bar 3)   etc.   (bar 5)

(From fourth chorus).

A7   Dm7

Bb7(Fm7)   (Chorus 11, bar 2)   etc.

14

Fig. 2.6(a) Elvin Jones drum patterns.

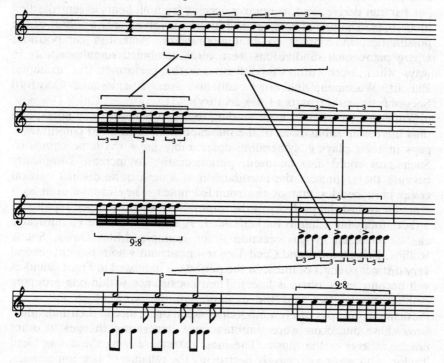

Fig. 2.6(b) Variants of Jones's 'ride' basic rhythmic patterns.

> indicates a small but significant accent, supplementing those on the normally accented beats.

top of each triplet quaver (Fig. 2.6), as shown in the example of Bill Evans's work (Fig. 2.3). Relatively lacking in his work or that of most other soloists playing formulaic improvisation was subdivision of pulses into five, seven, eleven, etc. (but, of course, note the existence of exceptions illustrated already for Coltrane; the related tendency of Jones to use quintuplets in his basic 'ride' rhythms (Fig. 2.6b; p. 29, and see A109).

These increasingly small segments of time mainly subdivide individual pulses, so that a new note does start on and emphasise each pulse. But in parallel were developed (though less frequently) patterns which subdivided *groups* of beats in a complex way so that several pulses would

15

lack newly commencing sounds: Fig. 2.6 also indicates how nine triplets per bar can derive, and so remove accents from all beats except the first in 4/4 bars. The use of complex subdivision involved only a subset of the possibilities, in contrast to contemporaneous American composition, where many such subdivisions were often combined sumultaneously in ways which were ruthlessly difficult for the performer (for example, Babbitt, Wuorinen, Sollberger; and also Ives, Ruggles and Crawford Seeger from earlier parts of the century).

While many musicians were tending to use ever more rapid notes, and thus increasing subdivision of the pulses, a few others used considerable gaps in their playing, generating comparably great rhythmic contrasts. Such gaps could also be used, paradoxically, to increase complexity because they represent the introduction of a new, quite distinct musical component besides that of the sounded notes. They can be seen as a reaction against the prolixity of the improvisers who developed rapidity of attack, following Charlie Parker's lead. A strange mixture of musicians can be included in this reaction – for example, Miles Davis, Sonny Rollins, Eric Dolphy, and Cecil Taylor – musicians who represent several very distinct streams of music in the period (as indicated in Fig. 1.2 and as will become more obvious later). Their coexistence within one grouping emphasises the fact that the evolution of the work of an individual musician or group is rarely a monodirectional one, since in their individual ways these musicians were simultaneously generating changes in other crucial aspects of the music. The most extreme among these was Cecil Taylor, who was progressively destroying the reliance of jazz improvising on tonal harmonies and who was also often a very florid performer.

Within this group reacting in part of their work against extreme profuseness, several improvisers often used simple rhythms (perhaps plain quavers), but placed them in phrases not coincident with bars and varying in length. Fig. 2.7 illustrates this for a Davis solo. Again this device had a counterpart in the work of his own rhythm section, to which we will return. Fig. 2.8 illustrates a similar device from the work of Sonny Rollins.

The use of rests had a complement: the use of long sustained notes in place of the usual flurry of rapid notes, so that a contrast between the continuing motility of the formulaic rhythm section and the solo (sustained line) could be built up (Fig. 2.9). As we will see in the next section, this device encouraged the rhythm section to change their degree

Fig. 2.7 Miles Davis, from 'Seven Steps to Heaven' (R41).

Fig. 2.8 Sonny Rollins plays 'Blue Seven' based on A129, ex.7.

of activity during the sustained notes, often from less to more dense, with correlated changes in rhythmic usage such as asymmetries.

A more extreme case of the use of space, or at least irregularity of attack, was important in the work of Cecil Taylor, and very influential later. This might best be considered as variation in the degree of activity (frequency with which a new sound is initiated in relation to time), but it is combined with irregular placing in relation to the metrical structure of the formulaic background, which produces a strong disjunction then novel in improvising (for example, Fig. 2.10 shows part of an early Taylor performance). In a very short space of time there is a wide range of activity density, which creates just as great a contrast with the pulse statements of the rhythm section (still behaving then in a formulaic manner) as does the work of Davis, even though the bursts of activity often involve very large numbers of notes. Perhaps most important in this kind of improvising is not the number of notes played in a burst, since they are played relatively evenly, but the total time the bursts occupy and their placing in relation to the metre: they can be construed as blocks of occupied time, against which the main metric blocks (bars and groups of bars) are opposed.

This concept also has considerable importance in the work of the rhythm section (to which we will return): contrast the regularity of impacts in the drumming of Philly Joe Jones and Jimmy Cobb (exemplified in R38–40) at the end of the 1950s, with the spacious irregularity of Paul Motian, drumming with Bill Evans or Keith Jarrett a little later (R56;

Fig. 2.9 Miles Davis, from 'ESP', fourth chorus, opening (R45).

Fig. 2.10(a) Cecil Taylor modified from A127; from 'Azure' (R120).

Fig. 2.10(b) Earlier material in same recording.

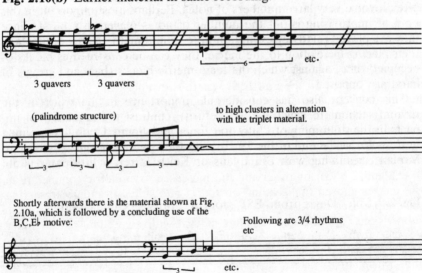

3 quavers   3 quavers

(palindrome structure)

to high clusters in alternation
with the triplet material.

Shortly afterwards there is the material shown at Fig.
2.10a, which is followed by a concluding use of the
B,C,Eb motive:

Following are 3/4 rhythms
etc

etc.

R76; R77). The use of filled blocks of pulses which are not of lengths equal to integral numbers of bars is another example of the juxtaposition of opposing rhythmic blocks: see the final section of this chapter. A further development of this idea is Bill Evans's recorded encounter in 1972 with the drummer Tony Oxley, a pioneering free improviser. Oxley induced both textural and rhythmic irregularity in the performance of the whole trio (R58).

The evolutionary changes in the solo work outlined in this section were clearly influenced by the simultaneous initiation of much greater freedom and complexity in all other aspects of improvising. So we shall now consider the complementary roles of the rhythm section players.

Increasing complexity of rhythm in formulaic improvising: the accompanists' role in fixed metres

We will first discuss the changes in the kinds of metre used in formulaic improvisation during the period under study, and then turn again to the devices used to subdivide, conflict with, or disguise those metres. Of course, the use of new metres involved soloist as well as rhythm section, but the latter were still primarily responsible for maintaining the metrical structure, and hence these metres are appropriately discussed here.

New metres were very important in the period, even associated with popular hits like Paul Desmond's 'Take Five' (R9). But we should ask first what the general significance of metres other than 4/4 might be. Obviously the introduction of a metre which had not been used previously would constitute a new challenge to the improvisers, and might be a liberating influence. But it would also inevitably introduce a different rhythmic complexity from the then present ones. This is particularly so in the case of the asymmetric metres, such as 5/4 or 7/4, where the bar may be divided into parts by the accentuation, but cannot readily be divided into halves or multiple equal elements. For example 5/4 was usually three followed by two beats, with the main accent on the first beat and a subsidiary accent on the fourth. It was thus distinct from 4/4 or 3/4, each having only one main accent and, when subdivided, having two equal parts. If the element of asymmetry were important, then one might expect progressively more complex asymmetries to be built into the metres. We will see that this was the case, by observing the subdivisions of the metres (where, for example, 5/4 was initially 3 + 2, but later both 3 + 2 and 2 + 3); by observing the increased asymmetric complexity in the metres chosen (5/4 leading on to 7/4 and others); and by observing the improvised subdivisions introduced against the initial formulaic subdivisions (for example, dividing 5/4 bars into two equal parts). Later we will also see how this evolution led to the introduction of metres which changed during a piece.

Until the 1950s, nearly all jazz used 4/4. Chronologically the first new

Fig. 2.11 Rhythmic pattern in 'My Favourite Things' as recorded many times by John Coltrane.

metre to be introduced extensively was 3/4, which amazingly had hardly been used in jazz before 1960. It was probably fostered by Rollins, Clifford Brown and their associates in the mid-1950s: an example is given in Fig. 2.11 (R21). 3/4 should involve no internal symmetries, being comprised of an accented first beat and two subsequent unaccented beats. In this lack of internal symmetry it is unlike 4/4. Nevertheless, one of the first rhythmic devices used in pieces in 3/4 was the division of the bar into two dotted crotchets, and thus into halves which are as nearly equivalent as those of a 4/4 bar, because again the second dotted crotchet was accented almost as much as the first. While this effect is not continuous in the early works using 3/4, it becomes almost the predominant rhythm in some of the trance-like, repetitious rhythm section performances in some of Coltrane's music, particularly some of the live versions of 'My Favourite Things' (R21; R25).

'Take Five' is perhaps the best known example of the introduction of a metre (in this case 5/4) which resists conversion into a symmetric struc-ture in formulaic jazz. 'Take five' usually referred to having a break, but it was obvious that playing 'Take Five' was less of a break than most of the pieces in the Brubeck repertoire, and quite a few mistakes occurred in performances. Fig. 2.12 illustrates the repeating rhythmic structure of 'Take Five': it shows that this metre was not a bar of five pulses of which the first was accented, and the following four equal and unaccented, as a 5/4 metre could be. Rather it consisted of alternating bars of 3/4 and 2/4. We will return to this idea of metrical structures with repeated patterns of unequal bars, but first we must consider a few other time signatures which were coexisting in referent-based jazz around 1960, and whether they also involved subdivision of this kind, or whether they formed undivided bars.

6/4 began to be used increasingly around 1960 as in Davis's 'All Blues' (see later). This metre is again symmetrical, with two groups of three equal pulses, with accents on the first and fourth beats, and was therefore hardly different from 3/4, and received the same kinds of treatment, particularly the use of dotted crotchets. Printed scores of this piece often

Fig. 2.12 Rhythmic structure of 'Take Five' by Paul Desmond.

Fig. 2.13 Rhythmic structure of Don Ellis's 'Pussy Wiggle'.

represent the metre as 3/4, which then creates a 24-bar blues instead of a twelve-bar blues. In contrast to 5/4, it was possible for the symmetrical 6/4 metre to be converted back towards an asymmetric one (3/2), and this is revealed again on the performances of 'All Blues'. 6/4 and 3/2 were therefore used as undivided bars.

The remaining metre with crotchet beats which was gradually used later (from the mid-1960s onwards) is 7/4. Like 5/4 this was normally 3/4 followed by 4/4 or vice versa (as in Fig. 2.13). There are some pieces in which other structures like 2/4 + 3/4 + 2/4 are used.

A clear feature of the performances of such pieces is that the first beat of each bar is strongly accented by the rhythm section, presumably to make the pulse and metre secure. Thus the possibilities of superimposing cross-rhythms upon the metrical structure were only pursued in relation to units of one bar, or one part of a bar (perhaps the 3/4 part within a 5/4 or 7/4). To observe this, consider the performance of 'Pussy Wiggle' (Fig. 2.13; R55): there are virtually no first or fifth beats without heavy accentuation in the drum part.

Now let us consider the introduction of metres of the form $n/8$ in which quaver pulses are important (see the listing in A19). One of these pieces (sometimes referred to as 'soul', or 'funk') was another hit, Herbie Hancock's 'Water Melon Man' (R68), which used an 8/8 structure. So this metre was a regular element of jazz materials of the time.

Many other pieces were closely related, including Hancock's later 'Maiden Voyage' (R69; Fig. 2.14) and music by the Adderley brothers, such as 'Mercy Mercy' (R1). A striking feature of such 8/8 metres is that they were treated as flexibly as 4/4 was at the time, in contrast to the 5/4, 7/4, etc., discussed above. In other words, in 8/8 it was found possible to place accentuations anywhere within the bar, and to execute rhythmic patterns which ran over more than one bar (see, for example, Fig. 2.14).

Because of the pressure to retain a clear sensation of the position of each quaver of the eight, even if not literally playing it, the rhythm section tended to accentuate regularly one or other of these quavers. A

Fig. 2.14 Rhythmic structure of Hancock's 'Maiden Voyage'.

Fig. 2.15 Tyner's 'Utopia' (1969).

etc .

syncopated effect was maximised when even-numbered quavers were accented and particularly when the fourth or sixth quavers were accented. This is built into a famous later composition, Ron Carter's '81' (R45; p. 199 in Appendix 1). The evolving rhythmic structures in these pieces and the earlier 'soul' pieces such as 'Sidewinder' later merged into the genesis of what was called jazz-rock, and later fusion. Thus there is clear continuity in rhythmic usage between the works mentioned already, particularly '81', the later jazz-rock work such as that of Davis's 'In A Silent Way' (R48), the music of the groups which emerged from Davis's groups (such as Weather Report: R137), and of many from other streams (see, for example, Fig. 2.15; R135). 8/8 was thus progressively used more in ways which generated asymmetry from symmetry, rather like 4/4 had been.

Let us now consider those $n/8$ metres which are intrinsically asymmetric. Do these also tend to be used as subdivided patterns ($a/8 + b/8 + c/8 + \ldots$ where a, b, c are whole numbers) or undivided? And did they come into use later in the progression of this strand of rhythmic development? It is clear that subdivided metres gradually became the norm as the period progressed. Some pieces in 7/8 were recorded: these tended to be treated as $3/8 + 4/8$ or $2/8 + 3/8 + 2/8$, etc. Similarly the later 15/8 piece, 'Ostinato' (R70) consists of subdivisions (Fig. 2.16); as does the 15/8 material in Ornette Coleman's 'Una Muy Bonita' (Fig. 2.17). But this piece was composed in the late 1950s, before the rhythmic devices we are discussing had gained much currency, and at that time was performed with soloing usually in 4/4 and a rubato rhythmic rendering of the theme.

Fig. 2.16 'Ostinato' by Hancock.

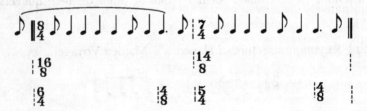

Fig. 2.17 From 'Una Muy Bonita' by Ornette Coleman.

Later on some performers gave precise renderings of the 15/8 section, though it is printed in standard jazz 'fake-books' (printed outline scores of jazz pieces) as if entirely in 4/4 (M12).

In the performances of these *n*/8 asymmetric metres, as with the asymmetric crotchet-based metres, heavy accentuation of the first beat of the bar, and often also of those beginning the subdivisions, was a monotonous and possibly restrictive feature. The technical difficulty of maintaining these metres makes this observation unsurprising; but it does lead one to question whether the restrictions entailed for the improvising, particularly of the rhythm section, were justified by the interests of the rhythmic structure. Their decreasing emphasis (the 'reaction') in the mid-1970s onwards is quite apparent, and concurs with this interpretation.

It is important to note that the soloist is in a very different position from the rhythm players in relation to these asymmetric metres: introspective analysis by jazz musicians indicates that it is quite possible to play some of the time with regard only to pulses (considered independently of metre). Perhaps to facilitate such an approach it was common for the harmonic basis to be simplified, as with 'Ostinato', which is based on one A♭ rooted scale. When harmonic changes are enunciated by the rhythm players, the soloist, if playing independently of metre, could hear and almost instantaneously follow them. The soloist could also follow accented first beats, even if not rigorously following the rest of the metre. So for the soloist these metres are not necessarily a restriction of freedom to improvise. A key role of the rhythm section is, then, to free the soloist from the metrical constraints, while still making the metre(s) patent.

One can observe this in action by counting the frequency with which soloists accentuate the 'down' beat (the first beat), or other metrically accentuated beats within such pieces (relatively rarely) and comparing it with the frequency with which the rhythm section players do (far more frequently). Such a disparity between soloists and rhythm section is quantitatively clear even on the 8/8 piece 'Maiden Voyage'; and more so on the 15/8, etc., pieces. To make the freedom of the soloist secure some of the 8/8 as well as asymmetric *n*/8 pieces simplified grossly their harmonic structure, and did away with predefined lengths of solo: for example 'In A Silent Way' only has one D7 sus4 chord for long periods.

Don Ellis has published a catalogue (A39) of the various metres he and others have used: an impressive diversity. One of his rhythmic and

Fig. 2.18 Structure of the (3⅔)/4 metre as used by Don Ellis; with alternative descriptions.

metrical structures has been illustrated in Fig. 2.13; another, from *Live in (3⅔)4 Time* (R54), is shown in Fig. 2.18. In general the performances of the Don Ellis orchestra (for example, R55) of these works involve less interesting solo playing than musical compositions, and they fall under the description given above of the soloist following the metres loosely rather than being totally in command of them. Some other compositional elements in the work of Don Ellis are discussed in a later chapter.

One of the most interesting of the asymmetric metres was 11/8, which can be a simpler description of 3⅔/4 (Fig. 2.18). But John McLaughlin's 'Arjen's Bag' (R96; Fig. 2.19), consists of 4/4 + 3/8 rather than 3/8 + 3/8 + 3/8 + 2/8 or 8/8 + 3/8, so that we have reached, a decade after 'Take Five', not only an asymmetrical metre, but also one having two different pulse speeds (the crotchet in 4/4 and the quaver in 3/8). The grounds for distinguishing the first part of the bar as 4/4 rather than 8/8 are the relative infrequency with which the rhythm section plays more than three or four quavers within the 4/4 part, and the frequency with which the drums accentuate most of the crotchets. This permits different rhythmic 'feels' to alternate, and at times in the improvisation to coexist. Fig. 2.19 illustrates the simplified metrical nature of this piece and some of the cross-rhythms of Tony Oxley (playing drums). This structure does pro-

Fig. 2.19 'Arjen's Bag' by John McLaughlin.

Fig. 2.20 Mahavishnu Orchestra: 'Birds of Fire' (R95).

'Celestial Terrestrial Communities' (Mahavishnu Orchestra; R95).

duce regular variations in degree of activity within the bar (limited in the 4/4 and greater in 3/8), and also in the rhythmic freedom exploited (greater in the 4/4 than the 3/8). Few rhythms are heard in the 3/8 other than continuous quavers and continuous semiquavers, although Oxley is again more diverse, as illustrated. The accentuation of first beats of both 4/4 and 3/8 remains a predominant feature, but because of the rhythmic structure of the bass riff the second beat of the 4/4 bar can be heavily accentuated.

The idea of having two different pulse speeds successively within a bar has been taken quite a lot further in subsequent developments. For example, in the work of the Mahavishnu Orchestra (for example, R95) there are metres involving $n/8 + n/16$, and others where the contrast between pulse speeds is even greater, of the form $n/4 + n/16$ (Fig. 2.20). Again in 'Celestial Terrestrial Communities' the 7/16 or 3/16 part of the bar (see Fig. 2.20) tends to be treated rather uniformly. The lack of a constant pulse is in some ways disorientating for the listener, but it offers the new sensation of dominant pulses appearing only irregularly, as did the innovations of rhythm in free jazz, to which we will come shortly.

Another way of achieving this sensation is simply to have one predominant simple metre, and occasional bars of different metre. This originated within the stream of improvising which led to free jazz (see, for example, Fig. 2.21); and on Ornette Coleman's 'Congeniality' (R16) metric changes are improvised in relation to instabilities in the group performance as a whole (A128).

The use of a predominant simple metre and occasional bars of a different metre was developed much more in formulaic jazz in the early

Fig. 2.21 Part of Coleman's 'Bird Food' (R15).

1970s, following the other *n*/8 experiments outlined already. This is illustrated in Graham Collier's modified 12 bar F minor blues 'Song 3', which has a single 5/8 bar among varying 6/8 and 9/8 patterns (see also Chapter 10). It comprises sequentially four bars of 9/8 (on F), two of 6/8 (on B♭). two of 9/8 (on F), one of 5/8 (on C), one of 6/8 on B♭, and finally two of 9/8 (on F).

The soloist could be liberated from total regard for metres in an additional way: through the use of irrational metres (such as 4/7) which tend to be too complex for rigorous and flexible soloing, but which could be maintained by a rhythm section. These metres have been used extensively in the composed music of Ferneyhough in the late 1970s, but also in a simpler way in composed pieces which still strive for rhythmic vitality as a particular end (for example, M11). The notation of these metres involves the convention that the divisor (*n*) of the metres indicates a pulse length which is one *n*th of a semibreve. Thus (2/3)/4 can be written as 1/6, and still comprise one pulse of two triplet quavers. This approach does not seem to have been taken in jazz which uses composed metres but it is quite common that free jazz rhythms can be construed in this light (see Fig. 2.22). There is little to indicate analytical awareness of this on the part of improvisers.

A simpler way of liberation which has been exploited occasionally is the use of pauses – most strikingly on Davis's 'Silent Way'. See also the extract from my own 'You Yangs' (Fig. 2.27) for another example which adds a further layer of complexity to the idea: one part of the group pauses while the other continues to build rhythmic pulses.

A converse approach to building freedom of timing within a formulaic music is to have multiple rhythm section players, instead of simply piano, bass and drums. This was a common device in the 1960s and early 1970s (A19). This was apparently not often exploited to produce multiple metres, however; but see the section on Andrew Hill in Chapter 7, for a multiple-metre piece from 1963, just as the *n*/4 and *n*/8 metres were becoming exploited. This piece involved the rhythmic organisation of the whole ensemble, rather than just soloists or rhythm section, and this is our next topic.

Fig. 2.22 Pulse variation in a solo of Humair on 'Body and Soul' from Kuhn (1973) (see Chapter 7 for details of recording; the passage illustrated occurs at 5'11" in the piece).

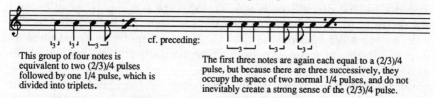

This group of four notes is equivalent to two (2/3)/4 pulses followed by one 1/4 pulse, which is divided into triplets.

cf. preceding:

The first three notes are again each equal to a (2/3)/4 pulse, but because there are three successively, they occupy the space of two normal 1/4 pulses, and do not inevitably create a strong sense of the (2/3)/4 pulse.

Rhythmic extensions in the jazz ensemble as a whole: the development of non-formulaic improvising

The separation above of the roles of the rhythm section from those of the soloist is, of course, arbitrary, and necessarily incomplete, as the discussion itself revealed. Now we must consider the developments which were of such complexity that they necessarily involved all the performers. In rhythmic matters, these included first irregular subdivision and superimposition, and then progressive abolition of fixed metres and of fixed pulses, and hence were an important step in the liberation of the player to free improvising.

Superimposition of metres by aggregating pulses or their subdivisions into extrametric pulse groups

A logical development once a multiplicity of metres was introduced was to attempt their combination. Whereas the metrical devices considered so far in the discussion of the rhythm section have been largely fixed in the compositions, it is perhaps more likely that *improvisation* of one pulse simultaneously with another could occur, than that such a superimposition would be fixed in composition. Some very forthright examples of this occur early in the period under study. Fig. 2.23 illustrates an incipient example of a common device in the playing of Dave Brubeck in which, while the rhythm section plays 4/4, Brubeck plays a quite clear-cut 6/4 whose bar length is the same (the case illustrated is, however, from a recording without rhythm section, and Brubeck uses his left hand to replace it).

Fig. 2.23 Brubeck plays 'The Duke' (R8). Bars 17 and 18.

Related, much more forceful, techniques were evolved improvisatorily by the members of the Miles Davis rhythm section of 1963–5: Herbie Hancock (piano), Ron Carter (bass) and Tony Williams (drums). For instance in 'All Blues' (see Figs 2.30–36) there is a superimposition of a 4/4 metre of identical bar length on the prevalent 6/4 metre. And in Fig. 2.36 we see a 3/2 bass part against the same 6/4 metre as noted already. We will document this progression chronologically and in detail in a later section.

On many of the fast 4/4 modal recordings by the Davis group in this period ('Milestones' on several successive albums – for example, R46, where it is just called 'Miles') there is a repeated superimposition of 3/4 against the 4/4 (Fig. 2.24). The pulse speeds of the 3/4 and 4/4 are

Fig. 2.24 Rhythmic patterns on performances of 'Milestones' by the Miles Davis quintet.

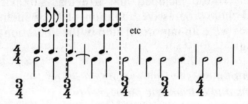

Fig. 2.25 From 'Isotope' by Joe Henderson (R74). During drum solo, Hancock (piano) plays:

Then during the piano solo, twelve-bar units are repeatedly divided into six of piano in 4/4, followed by six bars of bass reconstructed into eight groups of 3/4 patterns:

identical and 4 ¾ units plus a 4/4 are used to fill the space of 4 ⁴⁄₄ bars. In Fig. 2.25 (Ron Carter again playing bass, about six years later) the bass also uses a repeating 3/4 pattern with the same pulse as the prevalent 4/4, so that the down beat of every fourth repetition of the bass's 3/4 coincides with the down beat of every third 4/4 bar. Because the new metre is generated by aggregations of pulses from the basic metre, the pulse is unaffected (cf. the superimpositions discussed earlier in this chapter, whose prime effect was to undermine some of the normally accented pulses within the metre). What is introduced, instead, is an alternative metre, 'extrametrical' to the fundamental metre, and continuous for several bars.

These metrical devices involve stating metres other than the fundamental in simple rhythms closely related to beats of the alternative metre. If these rhythms were heard without the fundamental metre they would seem rather rudimentary. But they form a continuous gradation with those in which cross-rhythms from complex subdivisions of the fundamental beat are arranged so as to occupy spaces other than those which fit integrally into bars: for instance, the patterns deriving from the triplet subdivisions developed by Elvin Jones and from the quaver subdivisions of beats practised by the Miles Davis Quintet. We will briefly consider these devices next, but since they inevitably involve the introduction of new pulse speeds, unlike some of those discussed earlier in this subsection, we will return to them in more detail in the next subsection specifically concerning changing pulse speeds.

The rhythmic patterns developed by Elvin Jones, based largely on triplet subdivisions of beats, have been analysed in a preliminary way by Kofsky (A71–3), and Fig. 2.6 illustrates some of the main additional

Fig. 2.26 Overlaid pulses in drumming by Tony Oxley.

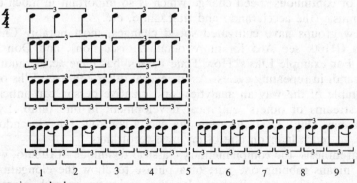

Nine superimposed pulses
in the time of eight beats
(two bars of 4/4).

forms I have noted. The effect of these forms is to provide several alternative pulse rates, and to undermine the constancy with which any particular pulse field has its intrinsic pulses fully accentuated (Fig. 2.26).

It is difficult to document a chronological evolution in Jones's application of these techniques because there are so many recordings over a very short period of time, between 1960 and 1965, in which the whole range of techniques seem to spring to life almost as a unit in his work with John Coltrane. But later extensions of these devices were developed by the percussionist Tony Oxley, who had consciously studied Jones's work. Some examples are given in Fig. 2.26. These often derive from superimposing a second layer of triplet subdivisions on the first, as already mentioned for the playing of soloists. But whereas the soloists tended to use this simply to produce pulses divided into large uneven numbers of notes, Oxley has developed a variety of ways of using the nine-part division of the pulse to assemble other pulses which can coexist with the main pulse.

We will next see how changing pulse speeds were improvised, and harnessed further in the move away from referent-based improvisation.

Changing and coexisting pulse speeds in metrical improvisation
It is normally assumed that the pulse speed in jazz improvising is rather constant. In fact there are significant variations in most performances (for example, in the case of John Coltrane's 'Spiritual', the 12′40″ version on side A of R21 speeds up considerably; it has a much slower starting tempo than the 20′32″ version on side D, which only speeds up slightly). These are not clearly controlled or recognised, just as they are often not fully controlled in interpretative music. Nevertheless, jazz is probably more consistent in its pulse rates than much Indian music, in which the performers are aware of the possibility of dividing a space whose length is thought of as flexible, into a fixed number of pulses (Ghosh, personal communication, 1988; see R61–4). Has jazz simply omitted to exploit the device of continuous speed change which is so important in much composed music (the accelerando and ritardando, etc.)?

A few groups have cultivated speed changes, most notably Charles Mingus (R100; see A65 for more detailed discussion), and Don Ellis (R52). For example Ellis's 'How Time Passes' has huge accelerandi and decelerandi in repeating cycles. As in several other contexts, Ellis offers an example of the way an analytical and creative person can anticipate whole streams of others' empirical development in one jump. Lysis's 'You Yangs' (Fig. 2.27) illustrates the way a controlled accelerando has been used much later on one of my own recordings.

In parenthesis, the complementary classical technique of rubato, which strictly means robbing one part of a phrase to allow the elongation of another so that the overall phrase length remains unchanged, is actually often performed so that the bar length is increased, too. This is also the

Fig. 2.27 'You Yangs', after Fred Williams. By Roger Dean. Arranged for austraLysis 1989.

sax part is transposed

case in solo performances by many jazz musicians (such as R34; R57; R78). The piano trio medium has also exploited such freedom of intermittent slight lengthening of bars (see, for example, R76; R77). An extension of this idea is to move through a fixed chord sequence with an arbitrary length of almost unpulsed time on each chord or with a fixed number of irregularly spaced 'pulses' (such pulses being simply points of unified accentuation). These possibilities are discussed in the subsection on non-metrical improvising which follows this.

We come next to the possibilities of discontinuous jumps in pulse speed within metrical music. Just as the beats of a bar can be subdivided into two (for example, the crotchet into two quavers) or three (the crotchet into three triplets), so the pulse speed can be changed in similarly precise ratios. For instance, a bar which was regularly divided into four beats, as usual in jazz, might for a time instead be divided into six beats. In this case the bar would be of constant duration but its divisions would be of changed duration. However, one might also envisage bars, for example, of seven beats at a speed 6/4, i.e. one and a half times the previous beat speed: in this case not only the pulse speed but also the bar length would change. We have already discussed the alternative case where a changed bar length is produced by keeping pulse speed constant, but changing the number of pulses per bar. In this case, bars of 4/4 might be succeeded by bars of 3/4 with the beat speed constant, and so the bar length would shorten (as in the standard song 'How My Heart Sings' as rendered frequently by Bill Evans). Our subject here is the first two of these categories, where pulse speed is changed.

I will illustrate this concept in a chronological and evolutionary way, in the work of a single improvising group, operating together over several

Fig. 2.28 Bass riff to 'All Blues' (Davis).

Variant of riff:

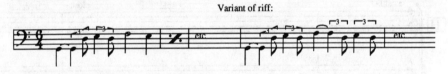

Harmonic sequence of 'All Blues'.

✳ Note that the #9 (E#) is
usually written as F, as here.

Fig. 2.29 Basic rhythms in Cobb's drumming on 'All Blues'.

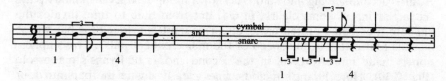

years. The Miles Davis group introduced such devices into formulaic jazz improvising, in their succession of recordings of his theme 'All Blues'. This piece is a blues in a compound metre, each bar consisting of two groups of three divisions. It is often written in 6/8, but the pulse shifts performed upon it are more readily understood if it is taken to be in 6/4. Fig. 2.28 shows the main bass riff which (with slight changes of timing and accentuation) introduces all the performances of this piece. The slightly modified twelve-bar blues chord sequence of 'All Blues' is also shown in Fig. 2.28.

The theme of the piece occupies one chorus of the twelve-bar blues, but is played twice (or more) on the recordings in question. Solos follow, improvised on the twelve-bar sequence, but they are always preceded by an extra four (or some other multiple of four) bars of the G9 riff played by several of the rhythm section. In the first recording of the piece (22 April 1959: R40) the essential rhythmic subdivision of each beat is the triplet, and the tempo slow. The bass riff already shown (Fig. 2.28) reveals this. Fig. 2.29 shows a recurrent pattern in the drumming of Jimmy Cobb on this version, which is also based on triplets.

Fig. 2.30 Evans's rhythms on 'All Blues'.

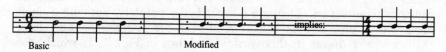

Three notations of Evans's opening phrase in his second solo chorus:

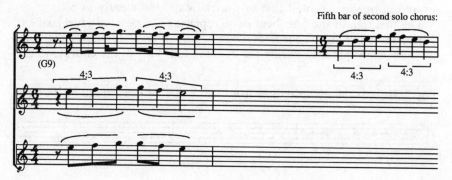

The first implication of a possible pulse shift can be heard in Bill Evans's accompanying and solo. As shown in Fig 2.30 Evans mainly plays accompanying rhythms clearly in 6/4, but from time to time divides the bar into four equal dotted crotchets. This implies a four-beat bar whose pulse is four-sixths of the speed of the main six beat pulse. This implication is made more forceful in the second chorus of Evans's piano solo (Fig. 2.30). Here Evans's melodic lines clearly divide the bar into four equal units, in each of which he plays two equal subdivisions. This can be construed as quavers in a 4/4 bar whose crotchet pulse speed is four-sixths of the main 6/4 pulse.

Four years elapsed before the recording of Davis's next readily access-ible version of 'All Blues' in June 1963 in St Louis (R42). The rhythm section by now was Herbie Hancock (piano), Ron Carter (bass) and Tony Williams (drums), as in all the remaining versions we will discuss. The most important feature of this version is the significantly increased speed of the pulse of the piece. This makes it easier for the musicians to feel large numbers of pulses as single units (and, of course, those units might not necessarily be equal to an integral number of bars). Two tendencies thus arise. One is that of subdividing the pulses not into triplets as before, but into two quavers. This is shown in its most pronounced form during the piano solo on the St Louis version, when Tony Williams drums several bars which consist almost entirely of equal quavers, twelve to the bar.

The second tendency due to the increased speed is to replace the main pulse by a slower pulse. Although this is resisted on the St Louis version, the next recorded version, on *My Funny Valentine* (R44) is even faster, and the tendency can no longer be avoided. The bass riff is now subtly changed to fit with the increased emphasis on quaver subdivisions of the pulses: instead of triplet short notes it contains short notes which are closer to semiquavers. They are not plucked separately, but with a single pluck which also sounds the succeeding longer note. The new basic rhythm in the drums in this version is shown in Fig. 2.31, which also indicates that during the D chord of the sequence, Williams often plays a spacious rhythm which is syncopated (the accented note does not occur on the normally accented first or fourth beats) but clearly in 6/4.

The first sign of the four-beat pulse replacing the now very fast six-beat pulse, is in the fifth chorus of Davis's solo. Fig. 2.32 shows the four divisions Hancock uses during the opening four bars of the chorus, which

Fig. 2.31 Basic cymbal rhythms from 'All Blues' on *My Funny Valentine*.

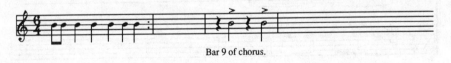

Bar 9 of chorus.

Fig. 2.32 Rhythm section patterns in fifth chorus of Davis's solo on 'All Blues' from *My Funny Valentine*.

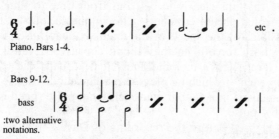

are identical but for their precise accentuation to those used by Evans earlier. Fig. 2.32 also shows the subtlety of this group, in its capacity simultaneously to suggest counter trends in the rhythmic development of the piece. Thus Carter plays during the last four bars of this chorus a rhythm pattern which is unrelated to the four-beat bar, and which can be seen as a syncopated 6/4 pattern, but is felt as a 3/2 pattern, that is, it has three equal pulses in the space of the two pulses of the 6/4 bar.

In Hancock's solo, the second chorus contains the same eight units to the bar (bar 9 of sequence) as Evans used (Fig. 2.33). Hancock's version seems more clearly to be quaver subdivisions of a 4/4 bar than did Evans's. However as Fig. 2.33 shows, this chorus also contains the 3/2 pattern in both bass and drums of bars 11 and 12. Indeed in the second chorus of Shorter's saxophone solo, which follows Hancock's, the bass lays the 3/2 pattern throughout (subdividing the last minim of the chorus into two crotchets).

If the 1964 version of 'All Blues' showed a brilliant polyvalence, oscillating continuously between the six, four and three subdivisions of a bar of constant length, the next (R46) is brilliant in its unanimity. It is yet faster, and starts in the usual 6/4, with the bass riff vacillating between the triplet and semiquaver short note. After one chorus of Davis's solo (in 6/4) the whole group immediately switches to 4/4, with the pulse speed being four-sixths of that of the 6/4, as in the cross-rhythms discussed above. The bar length thus stays constant.

Fig. 2.33 Rhythm section playing on Hancock's second solo chorus on 'All Blues' from *My Funny Valentine*.

Fig. 2.34 Rhythm section patterns on Davis's second solo chorus on 'All Blues' from *Live at the Plugged Nickel Vol. 2*.

Fig. 2.34 shows the main rhythms used by the piano, bass and drums during this chorus and the ensuing 4/4 choruses. It is notable that in the harmonically strongest ninth and tenth bars of the chorus (where the D7 and Eb chords occur, and the harmony changes more rapidly than elsewhere) Williams states the 6/4 pulse briefly, though gently. As Davis's solo progresses, drum cross-rhythms mount in importance, and the seventh chorus in particular has a large space in which Davis is silent and Williams's drumming becomes the leading voice. By the eleventh chorus Williams more strongly states the six pulse to the bar rhythms, but now in bars 11 and 12 of the sequence (see Fig. 2.34). Its position at the end of the chorus emphasises the possibility of the group returning to the six-pulse rhythm for the subsequent chorus, which in the twelfth it does.

Now the drums play clearly in six, the bass mainly divides the bar into

Fig. 2.35 Rhythm section playing in twelfth chorus of Davis's solo on 'All Blues', from *Live at the Plugged Nickel Vol. 2*.

two halves (thus being compatible with both the six and four pulses), while Hancock starts with rhythms feeling like 4/4 (in the first two bars) and then moves towards 6/4 (Fig. 2.35). There are two more choruses of Davis after this, and it is interesting that the band hesitates (and there is some extra time in the linking bars before Shorter's solo) between staying in 6/4 and moving back to 4/4 (which Williams tends towards). Eventually they settle on 6/4 and the brief instability is over.

Several levels of rhythm coexist during the rest of this performance, but the only feature which has not been noted already is the four-pulse feeling in the fourth chorus of the saxophone solo which is precisely twice as slow as the four-pulse pattern discussed already (Fig. 2.36). For this pattern, the apparent bar length is now twice that of the original 6/4 bar. Another hesitation in the performance occurs during the piano solo (which is mainly in 6/4), where Hancock partly moves to 4/4 but the band resist this, so that there is only a part of a chorus with strong 4/4 overtones during his solo.

The flexibility with which the quintet effect these changes of pulse is exceptional, and there is a remarkable tension resulting from the changes. The marked increase of complexity as we progress through these recordings is a very clear case of an evolutionary process generated by formulaic improvisation.

Few examples seem to exist in the recorded literature of improvisation of equally subtly effected changes; and even fewer of pulse shifts in which pulse speeds, bar lengths, or both, bear more complex relationships to each other, as in the compositions of Elliot Carter. However, such shifts are equally potent vehicles, and have a wider range of possible structure. After the mathematically simple pulse shifts discussed it would seem that more complex shifts of pulse could be permitted if the other aspects of the formulaic nature of the music were loosened. Surprisingly this has received very little attention since the efforts around 1970 of Chick Corea and colleagues in the group Circle. These followed a period in which both Corea and Dave Holland (bass) who formed Circle, had worked with the Miles Davis group, and probably experienced all the rhythmic devices they had just generated.

Fig. 2.36 Rhythm section in fourth chorus of Saxophone solo on 'All Blues' from *Live at the Plugged Nickel Vol. 2*. Two equivalent notations.

Fig. 2.37 Some Complex Metrical Pulse shifts.

(a) Bar length constant.

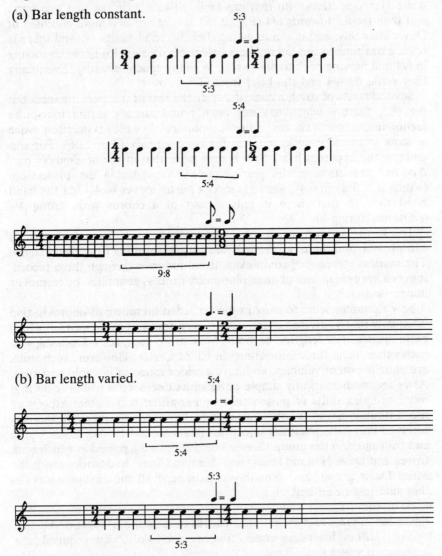

(b) Bar length varied.

Fig. 2.37 illustrates some of the possibilities one can easily envisage, and which are discussed in A31. There are two major categories: those in which bar length stays constant, and those in which it changes. In the former the relationships of pulse speed have to be integral (of the form $n2:n1$). This entails that the metre also changes. In the latter category where bar length changes, the pulse speed could change in any ratio, and in principle the new metre could be the same as or different from the old.

Fig. 2.38 From McLaughlin's 'Pete the Poet' (on R96). This piece follows 'Arjen's Bag' without gap.

Very few of the possibilities in this mode of rhythmic improvising seem to have been exploited in the late 1960s and early 1970s when rhythmic techniques were in the greatest state of flux in western improvisation. Some examples from Circle are illustrated in A31. A few other examples can be mentioned such as John McLaughlin, again evolving from his period of working with Davis (R48; Fig. 2.38) but they hardly extend the range of possibilities exploited.

This area is one that has been developed in the work of my group Lysis in the later 1970s and early 1980s (see Chapter 7; and A31). We found that it is possible to maintain a protracted overlap of the old and new pulses and metres, so that a musical tension exists for the players in which they have to decide to which pulse they will move, and when. With polyrhythmic playing in rhythm sections, as in Fig. 2.35, it could easily be that four different choices of new pulse would coexist for some time, and members might make more than one choice before the group as a whole arrives at a new pulse unanimously. Many of these techniques are illustrated also in a didactic way by Lysis on the tape which accompanies A31.

A parallel line of rhythmic development in composition has been the work of Elliot Carter and the concept of metrical modulation, which is illustrated in a fairly complex example from the duo for violin and piano in Fig. 2.39. The pulse-speed changes used in Carter's music are approached often from (notated) complex subdivisions of a beat (for example, in Fig. 2.39 a septuplet semiquaver becomes the new semiquaver) in a metre of crotchet pulses, producing a pulse speed ratio of 7:4 (new:old). As can be heard even on very expert performances of these works (such as R11), such relationships are usually achieved only approximately by performers.

The metrical modulations in Carter's music are no more complex than can be achieved in improvised pulse shifts in the manner outlined above.

Fig. 2.39 Carter Duo (violin and piano). Clarified piano part only, bars 109–110. With acknowledgements to Associated Music Publishers, New York.

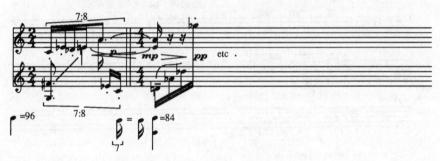

However, introspection and observation suggest that most rhythmic sub-divisions in use in improvised shifts are derived from working with pulses themselves (old and new simultaneously). Fewer are derived by the subdivisions (for example, by seven) of one pulse changing into a different subdivision of a new pulse (though we have illustrated an example of this in Fig. 2.39).

In considering pulse shifts we have reached the concept of coexistence of two or more pulses and metres within metrical music: in other words some musicians could be using one pulse speed and metre, others another pulse speed without having delineated a metre, while a third group might be using both a different pulse speed and a different metre from the first. Such effects have occasionally been used in composition in the period (for instance, in Kagel's *Oral Treason* the percussion section at one point establish a repetitive rhythmic pattern, which continues while the rest of the group commence a totally different metre and pulse speed (R83). Have they been used in improvisation?

In this subsection I will just discuss the usage within pieces which are primarily metrical, and in the next subsection we will return to the concept of coexistence of pulses in non-metrical music. In the case of improvisation on composed structures, some examples of preconceived coexistence of different pulses and/or metres have been recorded: for instance Coleman's 'Lonely Woman' (R15) and George Russell's 'African Game' (R113). In Russell's 'Front 4' a slow line, with mainly crotchet pulses (and both triplet and semiquaver subdivisions) is used as an introduction, but then reappears against an 8/8 rock with different pulse speed. In addition in my own 'Suite: Time' (1979: see A31, pp. 101–9) a long structurally composed section of the piece is concerned with such coexisting metres, and pulses. Examples of improvisation leading to division of the group into two metric parts may relatively easily arise when doubling of instruments is involved (as in R17; R26). I anticipate that these areas of rhythmic development are open to many further initiatives: see Chapter 11.

As noted already African music (and see Appendix 1) may lack co-ordinated bar divisions, that is, co-ordinated metres. And as Schuller (A130) 1968 pointed out, such additive rhythms were not used in early jazz, which was essentially based on divisive rhythms and fixed metres. This remains true until the present, since although additive rhythms may be the basis of the complex metres discussed already, their simultaneous application in different ways in different parts of the improvising ensemble has not been developed in jazz. Nor has it been used systematically in free improvisation, though the distinction between the divisive and additive rhythmic approaches disappears when metre is no longer important, because virtually all rhythms are then additive. The evolution discussed so far, away from the formulaic rhythmic elements, cohering with the movement away from fixed harmonies, etc., can be construed as a move from divisive rhythmic structure (dividing the formulaic elements) towards additive rhythms.

Pulses in non-metrical (non-formulaic) improvising
The separation of rhythmic techniques from pitch control and other musical techniques facilitates analysis, but it also entails introducing kinds of music which developed in the 1960s, such as free jazz, whose characteristics have only been very briefly described in the preceding synopsis (Chapter 1).

As indicated in the synopsis, several thrusts in improvisation colluded in the 1960s to free it from many previous conventions: the chord sequence could be abandoned, or at least treated very flexibly; pulses could be arranged in a non-metred or varied manner; and a linear kind of improvising, in which motivic development was paramount (Coleman, etc.) dictated that harmony was progressively more generated by the motivic improvising, than from preconceived structure.

It is in this context (which will be discussed later in the book) that we need to consider the use of pulses in non-metred playing. This was largely initiated around 1960, and developed into an element of the jazz vernacular by the late 1960s. By then its relation to the free improvisation deriving from non-jazz streams had become apparent, and practical overlaps resulted, such that strong pulses could be re-established in the non-jazz stream, in some of the work of Riley, Oliveros and the groups MEV, New Phonic Art, etc. (see later).

Some of the early documents in this quest are Coleman's *Free Jazz* (R17), Coltrane's *Ascension* (R26) and Joe Harriott's *Free Form* and *Abstract* (R72; R73). Thus 'Shadows' on *Abstract* mostly escapes pulse. Of *Free Form* Harriott says (sleeve note): 'We make no use at all of barlines and there is no harmony or series of chords, but there is an interplay of musical form and we do keep a steady four in rhythm.'

Fig. 2.40 Irregular grouping of constant pulses: a constructed example.

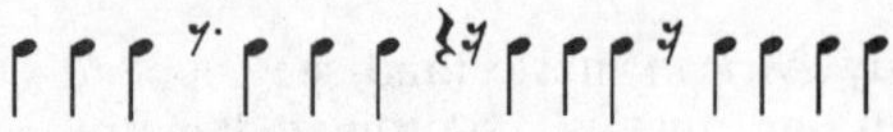

Actually there seems to be a contradiction between playing in 'four' and not using 'barlines', and the pulse is not a 'steady four'. In all of these works of Coleman, Coltrane and Harriott it is clear that pulses are sometimes assembled into metres, but that there are passages in which no regular metre occurs. Instead a space filled with irregular groupings of fairly constant pulses occurs (Fig. 2.40). We can deduce that there was an intuitive rather than analytical stance on the part of Harriott.

For the improvisers this pulse base has the ambivalent feature that rhythmic devices cannot be juxtaposed against a predictable rhythmic framework. That improvisers are led by metrical conventions (among other factors) is obvious from statistics, for example, of positions in the bar on which phrases begin in metred music (as mentioned already). For the group as a whole non-metred pulsed playing offers the possibility of implying many different metres by the juxtaposition of several individual patterns; and it encourages the formation of motivic structures over irregular and non-integral groups of pulses. Fig. 2.41 illustrates some of these possibilities.

The later recordings of Coleman (for example, R19) and Cecil Taylor (R121–9); and the separate developments of AMM (R3–7) and MEV (R97–8) exploited this advance, and led to a further state of improvising in which pulses are not at all obvious much of the time, although they occur intermittently. This is in contrast to many free jazz players, who retain pulse more distinctly and insistently.

We must make clear this distinction: we can take it that pulses are obvious if they recur at a fixed interval of time, and several times over (say, at least three). Thus Fig. 2.42 illustrates a recognisable pulse, and contrasts it with a non-pulsed pattern occupying the same space of time. Now one might ask whether in the sections of free improvising which lack stated pulses there are comparable divisions of time into rhythmic units

Fig. 2.41 Motives occupying irregular numbers of pulses: a constructed example.

The first motive phrase, two minims, occupies four pulses (the pulse being a crotchet). The second motive phrase (a minim followed by a note in spatial notation) occupies four and a half pulses (as can be judged by its relation with the pulses notated below). The third motive phrase is six and a quarter pulses long.

Fig. 2.42 Pulses and impulses.

larger than the short notes played? In other words, might an improviser feel division of time in a way which is just as strong as regular pulses, even when these divisions are irregular in length (as in Fig. 2.42) and sometimes unstated?

In summary of this issue, there seem to be two different stances, for both performer and listener. In the first, there is taken to be a continuing function of the same status as pulse (we can term it 'freepulse' or 'impulse' to distinguish it from fixed pulse) throughout most of the music. These impulses usually occur fairly close together in time – between twice and four times per second. This is apparent in the work of many of the free drummers such as Sunny Murray and Andrew Cyrille working with Cecil Taylor; of Milford Graves with the New York Art Quartet (R82) and with Don Pullen (R65); and of Rashied Ali (R29).

On the other hand, many musicians, including many of my European free improvising colleagues, admit to feeling rather slow impulses, of around one per 1½ seconds, which are fairly regular, but do not quite qualify as pulses, and within which they place irregular groupings of subimpulses. The more serene parts of the late work of Coltrane (such as 'Love' from R27; and parts of R30) are also comprehensible in these terms. The positions of the main impulses are usually not accentuated, but felt to move in relation to the ongoing subimpulses and to change duration in relation to these. The flexibility of approach this allows is useful for the improvisers in giving a sense of space units, which can be taken as appropriate for placing successively contrasting ideas, often one per space. On the other hand, the space units are not necessarily felt synchronously by the other musicians, in fact usually not. This seems to create no difficulty especially as the beginnings of the impulses are not normally accentuated. It does mean, however, that a massive convergence on an accentuation point, out of a grossly divergent structure, is very rare, in contrast to the use of large spaces of time within pulsed and metrical improvising discussed above. The consequence of this approach is that overall activity of a group free improvisation can readily become extremely dense, with events happening many times per second. There is no clear pressure to wait for the beginning of a subsequent impulse (one or more later) for the next action, unlike the situation in pulsed music.

Indeed if as usual the musician is defining the impulse by the activity s/he performs within it, it may become rather difficult to continue to sense an impulse progression when not playing. This is perhaps one of the limitations of impulsed free playing.

Do any improvisers work in what they feel to be an impulseless space? In some electronic music and computer music in which there is absolute continuity of sound, a totally suspended, impulseless state can be achieved. There are some remarkable examples of the achievement of this state in improvisation. They probably spring partly from the late work of Coltrane, but also from the input of improvising composers, and the idea of the Indian trance which was so attractive to many musicians in the 1960s.

The most notable examples are the early work of AMM and, to a lesser extent, that of MEV, as already mentioned, dating from the late 1960s and early 1970s. It seems particularly possible to achieve this state with electronic instruments, or at least with amplification of very soft sounds so that they can be sustained for very long periods. Such a feature is also among the achievements of the amplified percussion kit, such as developed by Oxley around 1970, and the constructed instruments of Hugh Davies (R103): these are discussed further in Chapter 8.

It is interesting that there was a comparable involvement with long notes among composers in the early 1960s (see A103). Thus Lamont Young's *Composition Number 7* of 1960 consists of an 'infinitely' sustained two-note chord of B and *F#* (for further information, see A88; A100). Many of these composers, like Oliveros and Young, were also improvisers, and it may perhaps be because of that experience of the process of producing/performing music (see also Chapter 11), as opposed to that of composition, that they developed this interest in long notes.

In more recent improvising, with the wide availability of synthesisers which can sustain permanently, groups involving other instruments have also begun to be more able to perform such virtually impulseless music: for instance, AMM; Wired (R138); New Phonic Art (R105a and b); and Gruppo Nuova Consonanza (R66); Stockhausen (R118) can also be cited here. This is an example of a clear influence of the availability of technology, but the wide development of circular breathing techniques among improvisers since Coltrane (for example, Evan Parker, saxophonist: R107–8) shows that human devices can overcome the technical problem anyway, and this was a simultaneous evolution in the early 1970s. I have developed this in my own work, and the use of sequencers can be subverted from their normal commercial ends to permit some new initiatives in this kind of improvising. We will return to this possibility in Chapter 11.

In this chapter we have discussed rhythm as a *component* feature of musical development, but it can sometimes be the *primary* motivic feature. On the other hand, western musical attitudes tend to lead to the expectation that other features of a motive (pitch, timbre, texture) are more important than rhythm, and it is difficult to discuss motivic development of a rhythm without realising the effects of the superimposed pitch structures, etc. However, most jazz and much free improvising has concentrated on rhythm, and thus shared the emphasis given to rhythm as motive by some other musics, such as Arabian music (A59), in which rhythmic constancy of a motive may be the important factor, and pitch variation of it quite secondary. We have seen how the evolution of rhythmic techniques in improvisation eventually encompassed the total obliteration of any formulaic role; the creation of new kinds of impulse; and the possibility of continuous, impulseless sound spaces.

A parallel evolution has occurred in composition, at least in regard to the creation of impulseless spaces – for example, in the open, slowly changing textures of Ligeti. There are also crucial related achievements within electronic music, and particularly in newer computer music of the 1980s (of, for example, Risset, Dennis Smalley, and Mike McNabb).

The emphasis on rhythm within composition is still slighter than in improvised music, and it is thus difficult to identify a counterpart in composition to the creation of new forms of impulse in improvisation. However, a postmodern evolution in composition since the 1970s, the 'minimalism' of Reich, Riley and their followers and developers (such as Glass, Mertens, Martland, etc.), has at least re-elevated rhythmic impulse to the primary status it had in baroque music, and used long rhythmic patterns as foreground to slowly moving and rather simple harmonies. A close postmodern improvised counterpart to this is to be found in the improvised 'New Age' recordings on the Wyndham Hill label, with much the same characteristic of simple slow-moving harmonies. However, a key difference between these two postmodern elements, deriving from the improvising and composing traditions, respectively, is that in the improvising traditions, the reaction into postmodernism has produced a decline in the importance of rhythmic pulse, while the converse has been true in composed minimal music.

This is an interesting illustration of converse outputs from rather similar evolutionary patterns, resulting from the initial differences in the importance attached to pulse.

3 Pitch usage in improvisation: motive and harmony

We have indicated already that improvisation until the 1950s was primarily tonal, with very limited harmonic diversity. Yet by then an immense array of harmonic procedures were already in use in composed music. Thus there was composition in tonal, polytonal, atonal, and serial veins; and microtonal elements particularly in electronic music. Improvisation had some catching up to do, and so it is not surprising that some non-linear flights of harmonic innovation took place there, using elements already known from composition. At the same time, it is often impossible to separate motivic aspects of improvisation from harmonic ones, especially as the prearranged harmonic formulaic element was being reduced.

Because of these factors it is less feasible to identify clear progressions within this aspect of improvising than it was with rhythmic change. But some can be noted, and we can indicate how the diversity of harmonic approaches in improvising gradually expanded, so that again the reliance on a particular harmonic referent could be reduced, making way for freer improvising, just as we have seen in the more linear rhythmic developments.

George Russell was one of the few theoreticians of harmony for improvising, and we can start with his provocative, amusing and perceptive description of changing jazz styles in the 1940s and 1950s (A124):

Coleman Hawkins ... [takes] a steamer called 'The Melody (parent scale) inferred by each chord'. This steamer is a local and will make stops at all the towns along the river ... Lester Young takes an express steamer that ... stops only at the large ports ... (the tonic stations) ... the name of the steamer is 'The Melody (parent scale) inferred by a tonic station' ... John Coltrane takes a local ... also. [But he uses] a rocket ship called the 'Chromatic Melody (parent Lydian Chromatic scale) inferred by each chord'. This rocket ... jets off from one small town and soars into the chromatic universe,

then descends upon the neighbouring town ... repeating this ...
for the duration of the trip. [Ornette Coleman uses a] rocket ship
[named] 'The Chromatic melody (parent Lydian Chromatic Scale)
inferred by the overall tonic station' ... The gravity of this overall
tonic allows [him] to concentrate on ... the idea suggested by a
single tone or ... by the preceding idea. These elements serve as
... propulsion of Coleman's rocket ship, whereas the propulsion for
Hawkins and Coltrane is the gravity of the chords. Lester Young's
gravity ... is less rigid.

The intuitive impression these remarks give is potent and relevant. It is
also interesting that Russell makes no effort to justify his remark that
Coltrane and Coleman use Lydian chromatic scales: but we will discuss
this shortly.

Motivic improvising

The conventional formulaic jazz of the 1950s, using repetitive simple
chord sequences with hardly modulating diatonic harmony, had led to a
looseness of melodic improvising which permitted both cliché and in-
genuity, continuity and discontinuity, within the individual solo and
between soloists. This has been summarised already (A149–50) and
discussed in detail in relation to Charlie Parker (A104) and Bill Evans
(A136). Fig. 3.1a illustrates simple motivic displacement by Stan Getz
(derived from A130) together with some transformations. The procedures
of a seminal figure of the 1960s, John Coltrane, have also been analysed
(A68) and Fig. 3.1b illustrates some of Coltrane's motivic work in the late
1950s.

Perhaps the most interesting development in motivic improvising in the
early 1960s was the emphasis on continuity of material being used. This
took two main forms: motivic improvisation, usually against a fixed harmonic formula, in which the initial motive was continuously the basis of
the continuing developments (an archetype being Sonny Rollins: A129);
and what has been described as chain improvising (A65) in which there is
a metonymy between successive motivic entities. The term 'metonymy',
taken from literary theory usage (see, for example, A137–8), indicates
that while there is direct continuity from beginning to end, the final
motivic variants in chain improvising are very much further removed from
the initial material than in the case of continuous motivic improvising.
The category of chain improvising can be closely associated with Ornette
Coleman, and to a lesser extent, Cecil Taylor.

Gunther Schuller (A129) has offered a classic analysis of Rollins's
motivic improvisation on 'Blue Seven'. It is also interesting to consider
this solo in terms of pitch sets, as Pressing (A111) has done for some of
Coltrane's work (see later). This approach reveals further features of the
motivic improvisation in this piece, though in view of the difficulty of

Fig. 3.1(a) Motivic transformation in a performance by Stan Getz (see A130 for more detail).

Fig. 3.1(b) Devices of John Coltrane (see A68 for other details). From 'Kind of Blue' (Davis).

⌐⊥¬ indicates Kernfeld's analysed 8,3,1 motive. x indicates the retrograde, which he does not emphasise. Both are the D triad (minor) and principal notes in the mode used.

Fig. 3.2 Miles Davis: Metonymic improvising from 'Seven Steps to Heaven' (R41). From first chorus, middle eight-bar section.

⌐⌐ indicate variants of the ascending 3 note motive (0,2,4,). ----indicate descending variants.

recognition of some pitch sets (A18), one may question whether such features are perceived. Possibly they are more relevant to the 'off-line' complex computation (in this case by the improviser) discussed in Appendix 1.

Rollins's approach influenced many musicians, such as Hancock (who recorded with Rollins on several occasions), and was shared by Miles Davis, though in a simpler way (see Fig. 3.2). It was not a radical approach to motivic improvising, in the sense that it still permitted the motivic improvising to be subordinated to fixed harmonic structures, or at least co-ordinated with them. In contrast, the development of chain improvising revealed a way out of this particular constraint.

Fig. 3.3 Tristano's 'Descent Into Maelstrom'. Sketch notation (arrows indicate gaps).

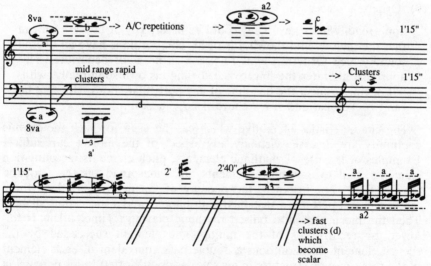

Some timings are shown. a,b,etc are motivic elements; a'->a3 etc are variants. a3 is an inversion of a, while a2 is an extension.

Ornette Coleman was one of the well-publicised initiators of the procedure of chain improvising. However, a clear antecedent of his techniques is to be found in the work of the followers of Lennie Tristano. At first most of these highly motivic improvisers, such as Konitz, Warne Marsh, Peter Ind, Ronnie Ball and Chas Burchell, kept within the bounds of chord sequences, as did their later followers (such as Connie Crothers). But already by 1949, in *Descent into Maelstrom* (R133) these bonds were broken by some. Fig. 3.3 shows some of the motivic elements being expanded and modified in the title work. Many of the members of this school have continued to develop such motivic improvising free from harmonic structures as well as using it within such structures.

Aaron Copland has commented (A26, p. 96): 'Most jazz improvisers are not entirely free ... partly because of the conventionality of jazz harmonic formulas, and partly because of over used melodic formulas. Recent examples of group improvisations by Lennie Tristano ... are remarkable precisely because they avoid these pitfalls.'

Fig. 3.4 reveals the same procedures in the work of Ornette Coleman around 1960, and shows gradations of escape from harmonic structures. In his first albums, harmonic progressions were retained, though often altered rhythmically, for instance having blues-like harmonic sequences with irregular numbers of beats in some of the bars (shown earlier). The early recording of Coleman with Paul Bley is discussed in Chapter 7. Later, as in the Croydon concert (R19), motivic improvising entirely outside fixed harmonic progression was the basis of virtually all the performance.

George Russell has again offered an illuminating comment (A125, p. 9). Ornette's pieces

> don't readily infer key. They could be in any key or no key. I mean that the melody and the chords of his compositions have an overall sound which Ornette seems to use as a point of departure. This approach liberates the improviser to sing his own song really, without having to meet the deadline of any particular chord. Not that he can't be vertical and say a chord if he chooses.

The characteristics of motive which can be used for such metonymic continuity are diverse: virtually any aspect of the motive can suffice. Examples of the use of rhythmic elements, pitch elements, accentuation elements, and even timbre elements are widespread on the Croydon album (R19). For instance, the opening of 'Silence' is based on three motives: a fast pattern; a sustained multiphonic; and a succeeding silence. Then the piece goes into pulsed rhythmic playing ('Time'). This is followed by recurrences of the multiphonic element succeeded by the silence element. Izenzon does a double bass equivalent of each element of the three-motive structure in his solo, as does Moffett in his percussion solo. Ornette later quotes 'Cherokee' in response to audience rudery, and

Fig. 3.4 Ornette Coleman on 'Congeniality'. From first chorus of solo.

The transcription is that of Schuller (A128). Motive 'a' of his description is indicated, together with additional repetitions and variants not noted by Schuller. I give a modified definition of his motive 'b', and additional derivatives.

53

Fig. 3.5

then returns to the multiphonic/silence system. Later he prolongs the multiphonic element so as to defeat the expectation of the silence element on several occasions.

The removal of harmonic frames through the consistent application of metonymic improvising was developed in parallel with Coleman by Joe Harriott in the UK around 1960. This will be discussed later. Although this line of chain improvising leads to the freest approaches present in AMM, MEV (mentioned already), AACM (such as R101a and b) and the diverse ESP discs, we must again sidestep to consider the harmonic developments which ran alongside.

Harmonic developments in improvisation

As noted already, the root of jazz improvising in the 1950s was the formulaic chord progression, which was essentially a simple tonal structure without real modulations. Some other harmonic features had been used occasionally. For example, the superimposition of several keys was implied by some of the bebop chords with high thirds added (Fig. 3.5). This had been used more explicitly in some compositions of Ellington such as 'Rocky Mountain Blues' (1930), although Schuller (A57) points out interestingly how this may have sometimes arisen from improvising errors. And as mentioned at various points there were some very interesting experiments in the early 1950s by Teddy Charles and Jimmy Giuffre and their west coast colleagues (for example, R12–14) in which complex chord superimpositions, polytonality, and formal experiments were involved.

It is difficult to establish the origins of many of the new harmonic devices which became common in the 1960s, in the sense of discriminating between those arising from harmonic consideration *per se*, and those arising from assertion of the predominance of motivic improvising over formulaic harmony. But the introduction of modal improvising was primarily a harmonic issue. 'Mode' is a term used for scales ('a series of single notes progressing up or down stepwise' according to Kennedy

Fig. 3.6 Two Modes.

Fig. 3.7 Dorian chords common on 'Milestones'.

(A67)) other than major, minor, chromatic, whole-tone and pentatonic scales, and includes a variety of scales which were commonly used in European music until about 1600. If we leave unspecified the minimum step size, this definition covers all the scales widely used in jazz (A110) and other contexts: in some cases a step might be larger than the usual one, two or three semitones. Fig. 3.6 illustrates the Dorian and Lydian modes. These modes and their implications and usage are discussed further in Chapters 9 and 10, on composition for improvising, since they were introduced by composers, and earlier as a theoretical construct (A124), primarily as a means of directing motivic improvising. Their relevance here is in the way they influenced chordal accompaniments on the piano, etc.

Fig. 3.7 illustrates some of the commonly used chords constructed from the Dorian mode on G (as in 'Milestones' by Miles Davis). The first group of chords, constructed in thirds, can give an impression of deriving from different keys successively (e.g. G minor, A minor, B♭ major, etc.). The second, in fourths, gives an impression rather of deriving from a single mode based on a pitch centre of G. The latter were therefore adopted as a basis to allow the modal improvising to limit any sense of harmonic progression; in other words, to gain a kind of harmonic stasis, which freed the soloist. This was in contrast to the extreme harmonic motility of bebop, or of Coltrane's 'Giant Steps', which, as pointed out already, tended to restrict the soloists in some ways.

These chords in fourths (also termed 'quartal' harmonies) were predominant in the playing of pianist McCoy Tyner with Coltrane, and in his knowingly titled trio album *Reaching Fourth* (R134). They were also important in the work of most later pianists such as Corea (see Fig. 3.8) and to a lesser extent Hancock. They were prefigured in the 1950s, particularly in the work of Charles Mingus.

Fig. 3.8 Chick Corea from 'Now He Sings, Now He Sobs'.

Fig. 3.9 Conversion of a minor blues into a modal piece, with quartal voicings.

Even a simple minor blues can be virtually made into a modal piece with the tonic being made into the modal pitch centre, and the subordinate chords, the fourth and fifth chords, made into secondary derivatives of the mode (see, for example, Fig. 3.9). Tyner's rendering of the blues with Coltrane is usually an example of this treatment, as is Corea's 'Matrix' (R32). Later jazz-rock ostinati such as 'In A Silent Way' (R48) were often used with modal improvising.

The influence of the quartal harmonies was later expressed forcefully even within jazz playing with very tonal bases, for example in the work of Bill Evans, who also appeared on the initial modal recordings of Miles Davis, the album *Kind of Blue*. Fig. 3.10 illustrates some chord voicings exploiting arrangements of fourths, which he used in juxtaposition to chords in thirds, in highly chromatic but tonal improvising.

When motivic improvising was superimposed upon formulaic harmonies, in a dominating way, it tended to lead to several harmonic responses. First, one should consider increasing chromaticism of the soloist and how it influenced the degree of chromaticism of the accompanying rhythm section players. Players such as Miles Davis and Sonny Rollins, whose motivic improvising was immensely controlled, often with considerable space, had often cultivated the device of introducing occasional emphasised notes which were quite foreign to the harmonies with which they were used (see, for example, Fig. 3.11). This is an interesting improvisation feature which can be extended as a motivic element in its own right (see A31 and the tape which accompanies it).

One of the ways of extending it is to increase the relative frequency of

Fig. 3.10 Bill Evans's voicings from 'My Romance' (R56).

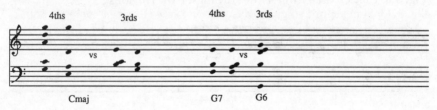

Fig. 3.11 'Foreign' notes within simple harmonies (Davis on 'My Funny Valentine'). First chorus bar 10 onwards.

Fig. 3.12 Frequent chromatic notes: Coltrane on 'Miles Mode'. From bar 141; in seventh sixteen-bar chorus after the 40-bar theme. Bmin or B Dorian is the basic scale.

Transcription based on M14.

the emphasised foreign (that is, chromatic) notes, within the tonal passage. An example of the highly developed use of this procedure is shown in Fig. 3.12. The other initial extension of the technique is to use several non-diatonic notes simultaneously, that is, to move towards polytonality, in which two keys coexist. This was very obvious in the early work of Dave Brubeck (see Fig. 2.23) and may be related to the influence of his one-time teacher, composer Darius Milhaud (see R99).

In a more subtle form the move towards polytonality is also at the root of the chordal developments of Hancock and Corea in the mid- and late 1960s, in which chromatic notes are used in very close voicings, sometimes with several semitone and whole-tone intervals in each chord, rather than spread out as in the Brubeck example, where the two keys whose chords are in use are clearly separated. The close position of the chords of Corea (see Fig. 3.13) and Hancock reduces the disruption of the tonal centre they cause, but produces other equally interesting effects. These chords derived from highly chromatic notes are superficially like those developed by Bill Evans (Fig. 3.10) which again may have both adjacent semitones and tones in the chord, but more frequently these are diatonic notes.

Fig. 3.13 Some chord voicings of Corea on 'Now He Sings, Now He Sobs'.

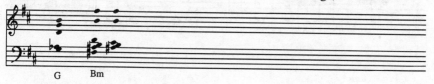

Polytonality was a further logical extension. This is essentially the combination simultaneously of two or more fully stated keys. Bitonality had been used briefly by Ellington (as mentioned already). But while Brubeck superimposed chords and their arpeggiated forms from two different keys, he only occasionally pursued the idea of improvising in one key while having supporting harmony in another. It was left to other adventurous musicians to exploit polytonality more fully. For example, Teddy Charles, as mentioned already, made contributions largely on the compositional level (see below) but his structures also encouraged such polytonal improvisation. It can be found on the early 1960s virtually freely improvised work of Harriott (R72–3) and some of the analytically ingenious pieces of Don Ellis were also directly concerned with encouraging the improviser to use polytonal techniques. Thus 'Tragedy' (R53) uses four tone clusters, to generate a ballad which is 'atonal but improvised tonally', in which the four chords were cued by finger signs. There are some illustrations of this on the tape accompanying A31.

Such techniques tend to give the impression of coexisting blocks of material, which do not completely blend; separate streams perhaps, in the sense of McAdams *et al.* (see Appendix 1). This is a feature which can be exploited; or, of course, which can become predictable and even irritating. It is probably through such occasional sensations of irritation that some improvisers have moved through polytonality in improvising to the state of using all the twelve chromatic tones fluently, whether in a formulaic repetitive harmonic framework or not. The former situation might be termed 'free chromaticism', while the latter leads to atonality, though it may retain tonal elements. An intermediate condition is that of some solo improvisers who use recurrent harmonic bases, but use them freely, with abrupt modulation: one example is Keith Jarrett (R78).

Fig. 3.14 John Coltrane, from 'Expression' (R30). Transcription based on M15.

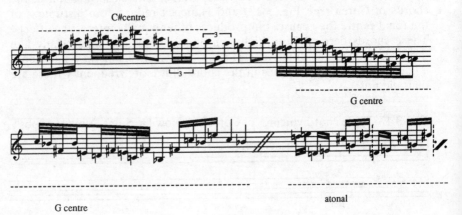

In contrast Fig. 3.14 illustrates highly chromatic playing outside a formulaic structure: now the implications of the motives in relation to tonality are no longer constrained by a harmonic framework, and can be interpreted as needed in their own right. Fig. 3.14 illustrates how some passages might be taken as atonal, while most have implications of a tonal centre. In general it is surprising how frequently the improvisations of members of the American free jazz movement do have strong tonal implications. Such implications are less frequent (except where a humorous stylistic quotation is involved) in the work of the European free improvisers who developed chronologically alongside (for example, Bailey, Breuker, Parker, and AMM). The autonomy of the musical procedure seems to have been more constraining for the Americans than the Europeans. Or a bare sociological interpretation might be that the Americans (particularly the black musicians) resisted such atonal devices in order to maintain a musical autonomous feature which had continuity with their own tradition, rather than let it be subordinated to newer techniques; perhaps this has helped to secure at least a foothold in the European if not American record and work markets for these musicians! Of course, a similar argument might describe the conservatism of the New Jazz of the mid-1980s in the UK, and of most black jazz in the USA in the 1970s, and the requirements for pursuing this kind of analysis are discussed in a little more detail in Appendix 1.

Once free use of the twelve semitones was grasped, it was also obvious to improvisers familiar with compositional techniques that the serial pro-

Fig. 3.15 A series used by Don Ellis (R53).

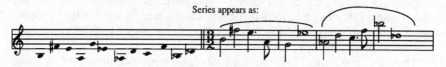

Fig. 3.16 Bill Evans's 'Twelve Tone Tune'.

The twelve notes of the series are indicated (1-12).

cedures originated by Schoenberg in the early part of the twentieth century might be applicable to improvisation, or at least to composition for improvisation. The technique, put simply, involves using all twelve semitones quite equally, and using them in a fixed sequence ('series') repeatedly, so that repetitions of notes are not permitted in a single-line rendering of the motive until all other notes have been sounded (see Fig. 3.15). The 'series' is then used in inversion, retrograde and retrograde inversion. It must be noted that the notes of the series could also be used vertically (that is, in simultaneous harmony) as well as horizontally (in successive notes of a melody); and also several variants of the series might be used simultaneously. Thus the series could be used to generate any note at any time, but this would dictate other notes in the immediate musical space (see A139 for a clear introductory account of serial compositional procedures).

Could this be used in improvising? Some musicians simply arranged chords of the kind they were entirely used to into a sequence derived from the series (Leonard Feather's 'Twelve Tone Blues' and Bill Evans's 'Twelve Tone Tune' (Fig. 3.16); or Laurie Johnson's 'Synthesis' (R80)). These works encouraged very little change in improvising thereon. On the other hand, Don Ellis (R52) gave improvisers serial sequences of notes to improvise on, and allowed them enough freedom of interpretation that they did not become stultified by the difficulties of using the motive in a rigorously serial way. He himself was able to use this improvising technique well and the motivic content of those improvisations was very distinct from that of chromatic improvising at the time.

It has been reported (A19) that serialisation of elements other than pitch was used in a few scores for jazz improvising, just as integral serial composers had done (see Chapter 1); and perhaps it was also used by the improvisers. Works of Lalo Schifrin are mentioned as serialising elements of density and texture (A17) in this respect, but recorded evidence does not seem available.

Thus by 1965 most of the logically possible techniques of motivic development had been introduced within improvisation. Contrast this with the situation in 1955 before Taylor and Coleman entered the jostling match, where chromatic and atonal elements were very limited in extent, and certainly not being applied systematically. Some honourable exceptions exist, as always (such as Tristano, and Charles's first version of 'Boobaloo' (R12)).

So what of the usage since these techniques were introduced? In general, as might be expected in a postmodern world (cf. Introduction), coexistence and recycling have been at work. However, there has been a progressively greater synthesis of the motivic techniques so that elements of all the techniques are combined more freely. For example, Fig. 3.17 illustrates a Cecil Taylor passage: surrounded by the familiar clusters, atonal motives are actually juxtaposed with clearly tonal, almost im-

Fig. 3.17 Cecil Taylor, from *Garden/Stepping on Stars*, side 1. Timings are with reference to the beginning of the side.

The piece begins with a B tonal centre, and uses the DSCH motive of Shostakovich, transposed to G#, A, F#, F natural. There is an intense passage of clusters at 5 minutes; a density in the bass register between 5'20" and 5'40"; and a bass tonal cluster moving F# to F natural to E, around 7 minutes. A cluster passage follows, and then an A centre is asserted at 8 minutes and 8'45". Eb and E natural centres emerge around 10 minutes, followed by dense clusters between 10'25" and 11'30". The material from 11'35" illustrated above, is repeated later in the performance, and may be composed material.

pressionistic materials. It is quite obvious by this stage of the analysis the motivic devices are not always separable from harmonic considerations, and they will be treated together hereafter.

A further development of the use of tonality has occurred to some degree, in that improvised changes of key become workable granted that the formulaic harmonic pattern is removed: it is not necessary, then, to move to atonality or extreme chromaticism. For example, Coltrane's *A Love Supreme* (R23) modulates systematically through all twelve tone centres, mainly as minor keys. In a related fashion, the use of modes (discussed in more detail in Chapter 4) permits a distancing from tonal structures (see Fig. 3.14) but also permits modulation to tonal centres which may be juxtaposed with the notes of a single unchanging mode.

Fig. 3.18 Part of Jeff Pressing's Improvisation A.

From beat 16 to 20 the harmony can be taken as A7#9, with E♭ and B natural as passing notes. In 21 there is A7♭9, but the resolution to Dm is side-stepped. From 26 to 28 we have D7♭9, and this is repeated from 36 to 38, with the addition of #4 (G#) at 38. A, A1 and A2 are triplet rhythmic materials with elements in common also (in the cases of A and A1) in their pitch set structure as discussed by Pressing. The common rhythmic structure of measure 1-2, 3-4 and to a lesser extent 5-7, involving frequent activity resolving to stasis, is also notable.

Thus for example, the Dorian mode, centred on E is compatible with D major, E minor, G major (with the C# becoming a flattened fifth), etc. These implications are often made most clear by the harmonic players in a group: for instance McCoy Tyner with Coltrane playing 'My Favourite Things', which often moves explicitly into D major.

These retentions of elements of tonality even when complete chromaticism and atonality are widespread, and aurally familiar to the musicians, are most prominent in those whose work is also conventional or formulaic in other respects. On the other hand, the free improvisers, who by the 1970s were free of virtually all necessary formulae, have developed a synthesis of all the motivic techniques described above from tonality through to atonality.

A most interesting example to discuss is the case which has been most studied so far: that presented by my colleague Jeff Pressing (A113) in his analysis of two automatically transcribed improvisations he performed in 1985. Let us consider his improvisation A (reproduced in part in Fig. 3.18 in conventional notation only: note that Pressing also transcribed details of timing in microseconds; delays and anticipations; and key velocities, which determined output sound volume on the modified synthesiser being used). This piece was played with a metronome tick sounding every second, and hence was pulse-based (unlike the other improvisation transcribed). Pressing points out several key features of the motives employed. He implies that a tonicisation around D occurs mainly for the reason that sounding of Ds occurs more frequently and for the longer time than any other pitch and its octaves. But as Dunsby and Whitall (A34) point out, the tonic is not necessarily the most frequently sounding note even in Brahms. I would argue that alternative tonal centres are equally plausible. Pressing indicates the importance of the motive F#–C–F and its set related motives. He chooses not to comment on some more obvious points which are relevant here. For instance (see Fig. 3.18), his improvisation clearly reveals momentary tonal centres and at other points chromaticism in relation to them. And at other points there is clearly an atonal harmonic structure. In other words, a flux between various extremes of motivic improvising device is in action, juxtaposed with a similar flux in harmony.

Pressing is also quiet on the subject of rhythmic elements in the motives and how they are used. But there are several rhythmic motives whose derivatives appear several times even through this short improvisation. Fig. 3.18 indicates some. Such short rhythmic motives are very common also in the playing of Cecil Taylor, partly because of its episodic nature, with significant spaces between actions, as illustrated already. Quite often the rhythmic elements in Taylor's improvisation are the only metonymic elements of a motive retained through the improvisation. Indeed one could argue that they are shared by most of his improvisations. So perhaps such rhythmic devices are very important in a music which, like Taylor's and this example of Pressing's, involves a considerable emphasis on pulse, whether regular or irregular. They can by now coexist with a continous flux of other motivic techniques.

The comparison of this situation with that of the newly emphasised rhythmic component of minimal music is illuminating. It can be argued here, too, that the rhythmic component is the main metonymic element – for example, in much of Reich and Riley's work.

Disruption of equal temperament: clusters, microtonal playing and instrumental timbre

The discussion of motives so far has been like that in most western music analysis books (for example, A14; A34) in which no reference is made to the fact that the use of twelve equally spaced semitones as the pitch basis of music is not widespread in the world, and is arbitrary and unnecessary. In Appendix 1 I have argued the case that such a pitch organisation is not necessary from any point of view of structuralist interpretation, signification or affectiveness. It is interesting that the most widely known western music which has made significant use of pitches other than the twelve semitones of the piano, is improvised music. Of course, since the mid-1950s microtonal music (using smaller intervals, and pitches outside those specifications) has been gradually cultivated within electronic and computer musics; but it has been more widely heard within the improvising context, though often used less consistently within a piece than in composed works. I will illustrate next its development in improvisation, and show how, surprisingly, its usage in improvisation now lags significantly behind that in digitally synthesised or encoded music.

Microtones related to other fixed pitches, such as those of the Indian raga or of the western diatonic scale, have been common in improvised music, though relatively rare until the 1960s in composed western music. For example, in jazz, 'blue notes' were usually mild distortions of pitch of minor or major thirds, and minor or major sevenths, in the key in operation. In playing on fixed-pitch instruments such as the piano, the tendency in early jazz to play almost simultaneously the minor and major third and seventh was the nearest equivalent manageable on these instruments. Similarly, in Indian music, many instruments, notably the sitar and the veena, base their whole usage upon microtonal fluctuations of pitch around the notes of the rag in use. This has to be distinguished clearly from vibrato on string and wind instruments in western classical music: the latter is a symmetrical fluctuation of pitch around the central pitch (above and below in pitch), whereas that in the other contexts is a unidirectional slide toward the core pitch.

Let us consider how these microtonal elements have been developed. Whereas a few theorists and practitioners of western composition have proposed and used microtonally tuned instruments (which had fixed pitches other than those of the piano) – for example Ives, Cowell and, most extensively, Partch (A106) – the usage of such instruments in improvisation in the jazz context has been very restricted. In jazz it is extremely difficult to find microtones being used outside a diatonic frame, though such usage can be extremely effective.

One of the paramount practitioners in the period in question, developing from the simple blue note tactics already outlined, was John Coltrane. By developing many fingerings for single notes, Coltrane was able to produce both multiphonics, including the note as one of several important

Fig. 3.19 Microtonal fluctuations in Coltrane's performance of 'Leo' from *Jupiter* (R31).

∿∿∿ = microtonal variation

apparent pitches sounding simultaneously; and microtones around the note, often three or four different pitches sounding in rapid succession. Fig. 3.19 illustrates the occurrence of some microtonal fluctuations in a short passage from 'Jupiter' (R31). These fluctuations are interesting not only because of their pitch changes but also because of significant timbral changes that result: inevitably the harmonic and non-harmonic partial content of these pitches also vary.

It is interesting that certain composers with experience in the jazz tradition but working also outside it have developed a notation and fingering system for some wind instruments directed toward the same objective, the production of microtones whose crucial differences include timbral structure (A12; A55; etc.). An example is *Cool → Warm → Hot* (M10), a remarkable piece for clarinet by Darryl Runswick, a jazz musician, avant-garde singer, and composer.

Microtonal improvising which goes beyond the usage of Coltrane is rare. One line of development, that of Evan Parker, clearly departed from that of Coltrane: Fig. 3.20 illustrates some of Parker's phrases at the opening of a record with Greg Goodman (R107). They share the modal elements of Coltrane's work, as illustrated in the example for R30, but also, and far more, a concern for continuous microtones. Parker's work has led progressively to a style (R108) continuing today in which long sustained (circular breathing) multiphonic and microtonally fluctuating timbres are employed extensively. It is very difficult to represent this appropriately in transcriptions, but fortunately quite a few Parker recordings are available. Even in this work, perhaps partly because Parker often plays with musicians using equal tempered instruments (for example, Schlippenbach playing the piano) tonal references are quite common. Nevertheless, some pieces or passages for long periods use only microtonal and multiphonic elements removed from equal tempered pitches, as in the example shown. When he works in more clearly tonal contexts (for example, in R109; or with the Ken Wheeler Orchestra (see Chapter 9)) equal tempered pitches are quite evident in his playing.

Perhaps the purest early examples of microtonal improvising, free from

Fig. 3.20 Evan Parker and Greg Goodman: 'The Fly-hag replied with a lisp---' (R108).

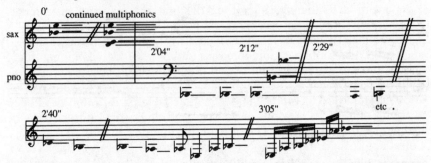

equal tempered influence, are the AMM records (R3; R4). In contrast, even work of the later improvisers using synthesisers, which in principle are easily capable of continuous pitch flux, has rarely escaped from the bounds of equal temperament, again often partly because of juxtaposition with equal tempered instruments (for example, Paul Bley: see Chapter 7) but also presumably because of a lack of interest in asserting this independence on the part of those who performed on the continuously pitched instruments.

It is interesting that contemporary synthesisers, since around 1980, have been increasingly based on digital synthesis techniques, and although there is no necessity for this, they have also tended to emphasise equal temperament in the way they are designed. For example on the original DX7, for a long time the leading synthesiser for the professional, it is quite difficult to play microtonal scales unless they are simply microtones based around the equal tempered scale. This situation has changed recently, in that several of the later DX derivatives, such as the DX7IIFD, are designed to permit a range of microtonal scales to be played from a normal keyboard; and so are some of the cheaper synthesiser modules such as the Yamaha TX81Z. Microtonal improvising is again very accessible, just as it was in the 1960s to Emil Richards, a percussionist collaborator of Harry Partch. His record with the Microtonal Blues Band (R111) is an example of improvised use of the microtonal percussion instruments designed by Partch, a use anticipated by the composer (A106).

Nevertheless, recorded examples of improvisation using microtonal principles as a dominant force and outside the context of mean tempered instruments are very sparse; this has been developed within my own work recently, and quite coincidentally in that of Jeff Pressing, but seems not to have been generally pursued. In contrast, the AMM work remains an imposing example of a microtonal flux, and computer composition has also developed this line (see, for example, R113; R139). It is to be hoped that improvising techniques using this crucial aspect of pitch organisation will soon become codominant with the (western) culturally-entailed equal tempered improvising in Europe and America, as they for a long time have been in eastern cultures such as India and Japan.

As mentioned already, microtonal fluctuations on wind instruments particularly, but also on others are associated with timbral changes. This has rarely been a device clearly and extensively notated within composed music, but performance freedom has often included exploiting these effects to some extent. In contrast, in jazz individual players of a particular instrument, such as the saxophone, have nearly always cultivated an idiosyncratic tone (or timbre) and sometimes related it to, but developed it from, that of a previous hero (be it Rollins, or Coltrane on the saxophone, or whoever). The use of fluctuations in timbre has since Coltrane also become an important part of motivic improvisation, often with a similar relative disregard for the microtones *per se*. This topic will be discussed in more detail in Section 2 on 'Process', concerning performance of the instruments and the music. For the time being, we can just mention again the case of Joe Henderson (see Chapter 2) whose personal timbres are readily identifiable, and who uses controlled fluctuation very frequently. The repetition of a single pitch centre, with minuscule microtonal fluctuations of relatively little importance, but with substantial changes in timbre, is characteristic. These fluctuations may be sufficient to define a motive, and are certainly an important part of Henderson's motivic development, and one which has been widely adopted by other players operating within the formulaic branch of jazz in the 1970s and 1980s.

Textural improvising

The importance of timbre can be such that textural improvising supervenes over improvising based on single notes and their successions. The distinction is an arbitrary one made within a continuous gradation, but at the extreme a texture may be taken as a musical structure with few discontinuities (unlike a succession of single notes) in which many different elements are sustained by their regular recurrence. This might be continuously sustained complex (multiphonic) sounds, changing very slowly or hardly at all; or it might be one or more instruments playing a pattern of separate notes very rapidly and repeatedly so as to give the impression that all the contained tones are present continuously (as in some of the music of Ligeti and Penderecki). Quite often these rapidly alternating notes are played with the conscious realisation that a variety of other tones will also be sounded during the articulation of the improvised or composed tones; such effects are built into much of the work of Ferneyhough, when the demands made on the instrumentalist border on the impossible. In A31 I have discussed procedures for generating and controlling timbral improvisation in some detail.

In the 1960s, increased volume and increased textural density of jazz groups was generated by electronic additions, by doubling the instrumentation (more drummers, more bassists) and by adding exotic (that is, non-western) instruments such as the Indian instruments used by Miles Davis (listings in A19). More fundamentally, several developments in improvising in the 1960s pushed the group performance towards group texture rather than soloistic improvising with accompaniment. Trumpeter Freddie Hubbard said to Robert Rusch (A123) of his efforts on *Free Jazz* (R17): 'I couldn't depend on any of my old clichés'. What he did not mention was that very often even the clichés were partially submerged into a texture anyway. This was even more true of *Ascension* (R26), on which Hubbard also appeared. There the performers formed a circle (unlike the normal jazz lay out prioritising the saxophone and trumpet) which submerged the piano, bass and drums: and correspondingly group improvisation of massive dense textures occupied a large part of the recording, from which only occasionally did solos emerge. The density of these slowly changing textures in the group sections was emphasised in several later recordings (such as R10; R130).

Textural improvising was certainly not dominant throughout on *Ascension*, even if it was on the later recordings, but by 1967 recordings of totally textural improvising by AMM and others were emerging. Similar densities of construction to those in R10, R26 and R130 had been achieved in 1966 by Schlippenbach ('Sun', 1966) and Breuker (1966), which are discussed in Chapter 9. However, an important distinction has to be made, that these two major works arose from motivic composition, and instructions for mass motivic improvisation, rather than from group textural improvising with no motivic direction as in the case of *Ascension*. The AMM music, however, is from the period which most foregrounds the concept of textural improvising: the texture is the primary objective, and not at all a secondary consequence of mass group improvisation (where each individual might still be working in a conventional motivic way, as is the case with Freddie Hubbard's efforts).

As Eddie Prevost of AMM comments (A23):

> What is certainly perplexing, though, is that really, apart from Musica Elettronica Viva, there have been few manifestations of the kind of group which use, to use Evan Parker's term, a 'laminal' approach; layered textures. In the European free jazz side there's still been this emphasis on individual statements in juxtaposition to each other.

The context makes it clear that Prevost is indicating that AMM was one of the groups which used the textural, 'laminal' approach (as one can hear from the recordings) which was somewhat apart from the 'European free jazz side'. Even more was it distinct from the American developments, where since the work of the American expatriates in Europe (Terroade, Burrell, etc.) mentioned already, the concept of textural improvising was virtually absent but for the work of Braxton, to whom we will return later.

4 New structures in composition for improvisers

Because this is a book about improvisation, I shall give rather less emphasis to composition, even when intended for improvisers, than to improvisation. But in this brief chapter I will outline aspects of composition which may have had a significant effect on improvisation. We will return to composition later, particularly in Chapters 9 and 10.

It is often quite impossible to decide whether certain technical features in improvisation arose in the improvising process or rather in compositions for improvisation. Thus several aspects of those features have been discussed already, in the sections concerned with improvising *per se*, when they might alternatively have been placed in this chapter: for example, issues of polytonality. And similarly, instrumental sonority expansion will be discussed in a later chapter even though it might be argued that some aspects of this were introduced into improvisation through the experience of composers (as in the present day work of Ferneyhough, who avowedly asks for technical achievements he does not expect absolutely fulfilled, in the hope that the other sounds resulting will be as he anticipates, and, in any case, novel).

The decision to include technical features in this chapter will be based on two of the possible criteria: that the feature would have been unlikely to arise in a group of improvisers and yet would have required co-ordinated mutual performance (unlike the introduction of polytonal elements by a single improviser such as Brubeck); and that the element is susceptible to complete control in slowly conceived music, but hardly so in simultaneously conceived music such as improvisation. An example of fulfilment of the former criterion would be the case of the use of modes; of the latter, serial construction. We will consider first rhythmic devices; and then pitch devices, thus paralleling Chapters 2 and 3, respectively.

Rhythmic devices in composition for improvisation

Probably the most notable of these devices was designed to allow a fixed progression of harmonies to be followed, but with *variable* numbers of bars on each. This was the case in Miles Davis's 'Flamenco Sketches' (R40; see Fig. 4.1; and A65). Similarly, Don Ellis (R53; and sleeve note) says that he directs the progress through his 'Imitation'. It seems unlikely that this method could have arisen without prearrangement, since the sudden indication by a soloist that a chord was to be held for longer than expected would have been difficult. Nevertheless, some elements of the spontaneity (for example, some of the expected mistakes: see also Appendix 1) remain even in the studio recordings of such Davis pieces, where the group does not always succeed in moving to the next harmony together (as in Fig. 4.1). On the larger scale, Coltrane in the several versions of 'My Favourite Things' improvises for protracted periods on a single harmony, the E minor (Fig. 4.2: this can also mostly be viewed as E Dorian) and then initiates a change to other modes and harmonies at around the time the piano solo begins (R28). Similarly on several performances of 'Spiritual' (for example R21) the piano introduces a change to the previously static harmony at the beginning of the piano solo.

Fig. 4.1 Elements of 'Flamenco Sketches' (Davis).

Five modes are used sequentially during each solo, with variable numbers of bars, chosen during performance, on each mode. The modes used are : I, C Ionian; II, A♭ Mixolydian; III, B♭ Ionian; IV, D Phrygian; V, G Dorian.

Bars taken by each soloist with specified mode:
Evans: I:4;
Davis : I:4; II:4; III:4; IV:8; V:4. On the second bar of V, the bass plays C, anticipating the return to I, which follows 2 bars later.
Coltrane: I:4; II:4; III:4; IV:8 (and on bar 4 the bass plays G in anticipation, while in bars 5-8 Coltrane also anticipates the G Dorian, though C remains the root).
This analysis differs significantly from that given in A65.

Fig. 4.2 Harmonies in Coltrane's 'My Favourite Things' live at Antibes.

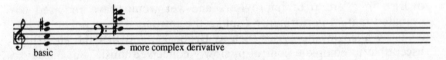

Introduction of changing roots to the harmony, on the same performance.

These techniques prefigured some more extensive freedoms, outside metrical playing, as where an improvised progression without pulse through pre-existent harmonies occurs. On the other hand, the techniques of metrical modulation which were introduced in the process of improvisation itself do not seem to have met much parallel usage in compositions for improvisation, exceptions being in some of my works, such as 'Suite: Time' (see A31, pp. 102–9). Similarly lacking in compositions for improvisation has been the idea of using multiple metres or pulses simultaneously in different parts of the group: a notable case though is in *African Game* by Russell (R113); but the necessary flexibility and independence to achieve freedom in the use of this device is difficult to reach, and the performance occasionally falters (see Chapter 9).

Motivic and harmonic devices in composition for improvisation

It is probably in those compositions where irregular progression through a harmonic pattern was permitted that the isolation of motive from a predictable harmonic frame was initiated. Thus Charles Mingus noted during the 1950s (A19):

> My present working methods use very little written material. I 'write' the compositions on mental score paper, then I lay out the composition part by part to the musicians ... They are given different rows of notes to use against each chord but they choose their own chords except where a particular mood is indicated.

But the removal of such motives from fixed harmonic reference points was probably a subsequent feature in the 1960s, exemplified in the work of George Russell, Bill Dixon, the Jazz Composers' Orchestra, and Graham Collier: see Chapters 9 and 10. It was almost contemporaneous with the introduction of modes, as opposed to harmonies, as an improvising basis, on Davis's *Kind of Blue* album (R40).

The distinctions between the modal approach, and the use of a single conventional chord, are quite fine in purely technical terms, but in practical terms for the improviser they are very substantial. Thus a harmony for improvising, such as Cm7, is a group of notes, usually spaced in thirds (later in fourths, as already discussed) based on a fundamental note (here C). Similarly, Cm7/G is again based on the fundamental note C, but the root sounded is G, so that it is rather like the second inversion of the chord. There can be several different chords on C, such as Cm(maj7) (B natural instead of the B♭ of C7) Cm6 (A instead of the B♭) etc.; and the chord C7 has the clear tonal implication of sooner or later being succeeded by an F chord, of which it is the dominant.

In contrast, the same notes are present in the mode (G Dorian) on which much of 'Milestones' is based as are present in C7. But the notes are arranged in a scale (of which, as already noted, a mode is a special-

Fig. 4.3

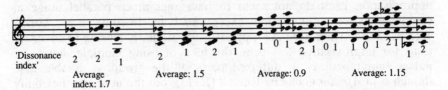

(a) 3 note voicings of C7.　　**(b)** C9/6; 4 note voicings.　　**(c)** G dorian, 3 note chords.　　**(d)** G dorian, 4 note chords.

Commonly used voicings are indicated. Note that not all the voicings of C7 or C9 unambiguously define the parent chord; but the same is true of the modal voicings. The 'dissonance index' shown is the number of semitone or major seventh intervals formed between the chord voicing shown, and an added B natural (a note extremely removed from the chords and mode in question).

ised kind, not tonal but commonly implying a clear pitch centre). And because of that specialisation, the G Dorian mode gives no impression of needing a resolution on to another mode. In fact in 'Milestones' (R39) another Dorian mode, a tone higher is used in alternation with the G mode, and the players create a sense of harmonic progression therefrom in a 40-bar structure (G: 16 bars; A: 16; G: 8; repeating).

From the point of view of the improvisers the modal situation is drastically different from that of chord sequences. Thus there is far greater time to use the scale, and no note played seems as extremely removed from it as say, B natural from C7. This latter point is illustrated by Fig. 4.3, which compares the range of three- and four-note chords likely to be used by the accompanists in the two situations, and shows that there are several chords which give negligible dissonance with a B natural in the modal situation, but none which do this in the tonal situation. This modal approach has been practised extremely frequently subsequently, and has become almost superimposed on most slow-moving harmonic playing now, so that both techniques coexist. Only when harmonies move very quickly has a largely tonal approach remained dominant in jazz.

The interest in modes was partly a response to the theoretical book by composer George Russell, *The Lydian Chromatic Concept of Tonal Organisation for Improvisation* (A124; apparently first published around 1953 judging by a critique published with the 1959 edition). This is discussed further in Chapter 9. One can see modal techniques and the introduction of 'foreign' notes (for example, the B natural discussed in Figure 4.3) in many of the extended improvisations by Coltrane on E minor roots, such as the repeatedly recorded 'My Favourite Things'. The compositional element here is one of simplification of a tonal piece into a modal one; as another composer, Giorgio Gaslini (A44; p. 152) has pointed out, and as mentioned above, the same simplification of structures like the blues harmonies into near-modal pieces has been effected, and he cites the

Fig. 4.4 A serial jazz motive: Coltrane's 'Miles Mode' (opening).

In the subsequent improvisations on this piece, both B Dorian and serial elements are widely used by Coltrane.

example of Coltrane's 'Mr Syms'. This achieves a comparable end to that improvised with quartal piano chords (see Chapter 3). Gaslini goes on to point out the possible use of polymodal compositional devices, which could readily produce a condition of twelve-tone atonality when certain modes are combined (cf. A44, p. 162).

From the use of modes it was a small jump to introduce motives without reference to any external pitch system. This was essentially the approach in the seminal *Ascension* (R26). Similarly other composers, such as Bill Dixon and Graham Collier (see Chapters 9 and 10) have employed this approach extensively. It is interesting that perhaps because of the flexibility they wished to leave for the improvisers, these composers have often used rather few of the systematic devices for modifying motives which were important in composition outside improvisations, such as transposition of the motive.

In contrast, these elementary motive modification techniques such as transposition, remained present in the few serial compositions for improvising which broke out of the conventional jazz mould (for example, R53; R94; R114). Schuller's 'Abstraction' (R114) contains a complete retrograde of the opening section, with Ornette Coleman improvising *between* rather than systematically *with* the serial elements. I have discussed the difficulties of improvising serially in A31. It is virtually impossible to achieve this with precision unless the motive is chosen carefully for the purpose. But as in most aspects of motivic improvising (serial or not) literal precision is probably not required or important; rather contour relationships are likely to be more important, and more practical to obtain. Thus a serial motive (see Fig. 4.4) may still have an impact on the progress of an improvisation by removing the performer from the patterns and facilities of the instrument being used, and on to the pattern of the series. Even when contour is transposed or varied, these patterns may still predicate a motivic development which escapes the routine more than usual.

The composers of the late 1950s writing for jazz with a wider range of techniques than previously used were gathered together under the banner of Third Stream by Gunther Schuller. The music combined 'basic elements of jazz and Western art music – the two mainstreams joining to form a "third stream"' (Schuller in A69). The compositional techniques and formal devices used by these composers were more closely linked to the European tradition than the name would imply, but they were more diverse than just the serial techniques emphasised here. Judging by the main recordings of their works the impact of the compositional procedures upon the improvisers was not comparably diverse; rather the improviser was often left free to employ a normal improvising style, and the improvisers were chosen for their styles, expected to be compatible with the composition. For example, Schuller has commented (liner notes to R114): 'there are many parallels between the playing of Ornette Coleman and so-called serial music, parallels which Abstraction tries to isolate and underscore ... Ornette's choice of notes [is] sufficiently freed to function against an atonal, serialised background'.

This indicates how Coleman's playing (meaning his previous work) was appropriate for addition to a Schuller score (implying addition without particular modification in playing style). Thus these works do not require extensive attention here, but we will return briefly to them in Chapter 9.

Perhaps the extreme examples of compositional procedures which might avoid the individual musician improvising routinely can be found in text scores and sound-text pieces.

Extra-musical symbols and instructions for improvising

The composers' ability to influence improvisation went beyond that in notated composition, since they could in principle interact with the improvising process and its procedures instead of simply providing musical material for improvisation. We can consider this in terms of the gradient of precision of notation in these compositions for improvisation. The problems of the prescriptive effects of notation are mentioned in Appendix 1. Composers who wished to avoid being so limiting in their output developed less definite notations. There is a gradation from conventional notation with pitches and rhythms specified, through spatial notation (where pitches and rhythms are only dictated relatively and approximately), to completely graphic notation. By graphic notation we mean curved lines, geometric shapes, and areas shaded in various densities. There are also purely verbal signs (again precise or completely ambiguous or anywhere in between). The ways of using these instructions are discussed in detail in A31 (and the devices themselves are categorised in A140). Note that as soon as we reach the spatial notation system, the implication of equal temperament, specific scales or modes, etc., disappears, and if one is playing a microtonal instrument, in which pitch is determined by a movement which is also spatial, then microtonal patterns can be simply generated in response to the spatial pattern of the notation, if so wished.

This needs further explanation: the position on which a string of a string instrument is stopped, providing it does not have frets, does bear a spatial relation with the resulting fundamental pitch. Thus stopping a note high up (low down) the string of a bass or violin produces a high (low) pitch. These notes can perfectly well be microtonal rather than equal tempered, and of course in practice they always are. Similarly a keyboard instrument whose keys have been established (as with some synthesiser configurations) to be microtonal, usually gives high pitches to the right and low to the left; the piano does the same, but unless mistuned, mainly generates equal tempered pitches. The woodwind and brass instruments (except the slide trombone) are in an intermediate position: there is little directional or spatial relation between the fingering patterns used for high or low notes, although there is a physical relation in the shape, as well as sometimes tensions, of the embouchure. The most completely spatial improvising is possible on synthesisers which can be driven by a 'mouse' moving in two dimensions on a flat surface. With a microtonal (or, better, a continuously variable) pitch generator this gives a complete spatial parallel to the pitches generated. Thus movement in one dimension can control pitch, and in the other it can control dynamic; and alternative control systems are possible.

The point for the improvisers was that such scores permitted consideration of physical aspects of the instrument and the music, rather than of normal technical conventions, long imbued by practice. Thus in response to a graphic motive, such as a line with many inflections, it might be easier for a trained string player to produce a microtonal, or at least unorthodox, motive, than in response to a fully notated one. And it is certainly easier to improvise on it. It is surprising that microtonality has only rarely emerged as a force in improvising, in spite of these possibilities.

After spatial compositions one comes to purely graphic structures (see Fig. 4.5) in which little or no relationship is specified between a sign on the page and the required musical output. This may leave the improviser feeling that a free improvisation is in order, and have little effect. On the other hand, it may also lead to a decision to devise, usually instantaneously, an interpretation system for the material, which then can be used for improvisational development. It is this last system which, of course, leads to the composer exercising a directional influence. Christian Wolff's 'Edges' (R88) is one of the many American scores for improvisation from the 1960s and early 1970s which might have had this kind of effect. Similarly, in an improvisatory part of Theo Loevendie's *Music for Contrabass and Piano* (M7) motive and graphical sign are combined and there is an instruction about density of performance.

We could consider next the instructional score, which uses conventional words with intended musical instruction (for example, Chapter 9, in A31, pp. 69–80; R91). Here again the improviser is directed towards process, and it can be process of playing the instrument; or process of interacting with other musicians. The objectives in the first case are rather similar to

Fig. 4.5 The opening page of Lyell Cresswell's 'Organic Music' for three instruments, or three groups of instruments. Each performer plays one part (1, 2, or 3) and has to imbue whatever instrument used with characteristics implied by the tree, the animals, and the metal objects. The performers have to extend their ideas of how to use their instruments: thus a string player might use the surface of a metal string, or of a music stand, to generate 'metal' sounds, and so on.

those of the other notations discussed in this section, that is, to free the performer from technical conventions built into playing the instrument. The objective of the instructions related to interaction process are more fundamental, and more crucial for improvisation.

As already pointed out, perhaps the most important feature of improvisation lacking in compositions is the possibility for interaction at any chosen musical level, between several musicians. Whether simultaneous as in improvisation, or not, this potential is virtually lacking from composition. Thus instructional scores could seek to direct the kinds of interaction achieved. We have already discussed the interactions in terms of dialogic problem-solving: this common approach implies an attempt to reach a consistency of direction on the part of the interacting players. In other words, though they might start with very different materials and processes, their interaction would tend ultimately to bring a coherence, a fusion between these materials and processes. So a verbal score could in contrast specify that groups of improvisers should interact in other ways: perhaps continuously in a negative sense in relation to material used. This implies the establishment of a gradient of musical properties in relation to pitch, dynamic, timbre or whatever, and the modification of the usage of this parameter so as always to maintain a position oppositional to the other group of improvisers. An illustration of this and a discussion of the relevant issues is presented in A31. The effects obtained by these procedures are quite strikingly different from most free improvisations, in that a rapidity of flux density change and a continuity of contrast within the music result, instead of the frequent slow change of texture and the lack of gross internal contrast at any one moment which characterise much free improvisation (for example, R10; R26; R130) and equally many compositions.

These technical instruction scores have only become much used since around 1975. On the other hand, another category of verbal score has existed since the 1960s in which, rather than instructions about the processes, instructions about the result are given; this category is exemplified by some of Oliveros's *Sonic Meditations* (M8), and Stockhausen's *From the Seven Days* (M13). This may again lead to unusual action on the part of individual improvisers, as, for example, they seek to cohere with an instrument or environment of totally different nature.

A final category of texts for sound production exists, in which letters are used, but may or may not form words; and the phonemes and words resulting are to be used themselves as sounds, and perhaps to be translated (systematically or otherwise) also into pitches (see Jackson Mac Low examples in A31, A81a, A81b). Kostelanetz (A74a) offers many examples of such work; and some of Mac Low's sound texts have been recorded (R93). Other examples of such sound-texts are discussed in A31 and A138; see also Chapter 10 of this book. As John Cage has written (cover of A81a):

asyMmetries

Are

typewriting transformed into musiC

siLences

sOunds

Words

Verbal elements had probably hardly been used as improvising bases outside the world of the conventional jazz singer in western music until these scores stimulated such usage. The jazz singer had used rearranged phonemes, as in scat singing, in normal jazz contexts. And a line of singers had developed the techniques of such articulations, and of multiphonics and altered timbres (see later), within improvising and in relation to composers. Nevertheless, the idea of developing new sounds from arbitrary combinations of letters, so that many do not correspond to words in any language, and may not even be normal substructures of words, had been used little, and was encouraged by these sound-text scores (see A156).

Thus while there were only a few consistent lines of progress in composition which influenced improvisation, there were many individual compositional ideas which did. The diverse impacts contributed vastly to the healthy range of improvising approaches available by the 1980s.

SECTION 2

Improvised music as process

5 The organisation of the improvising ensemble since 1960

15 Make a found sound lost.
16 Make a lost sound found.
. . .
45 Make a communal sound solo.
46 Make a solo sound communal.
. . .
61 Make a foggy sound clear.
62 Make a clear sound foggy.
63 Make a floating sound land.
64 Make a land sound float.
. . .
71 Make a free sound captive.
72 Make a captive sound free.
. . .
79 Make a public sound private.
80 Make a private sound public.
. . .
83 Make an urban sound rural.
84 Make a rural sound urban.
. . .
87 Make an owned sound shared.
88 Make a shared sound owned.
. . .
107 Make any sound now.
108 Make now any sound.
    (Pauline Oliveros in A23)

In Section 1 we discussed musical elements and how their usage has changed in improvisation since 1960. In so doing we treated the musical output, the improvisation, as a rather static entity. But the essence of improvisation is process and event. So we now turn to the organisation of the improvising process and event. We shall consider first the organisation of the improvising group itself, and then the kinds of organisation which can be imposed from outside the improvising process, mainly by composers. Some of these organisational aspects sprung upon improvised music like some of the compositional elements: in an uncoordinated rush to exploit procedures already available elsewhere. But others developed gradually, in the kinds of progression we have discussed in relation to rhythmic techniques. We shall consider both kinds.

New modes of organisation of the improvising ensemble from within

The issues here are partly predictable from the consideration of the changes in technical usage already discussed. For example, a percussion player might have a restricted role in some formulaic jazz, which would imply that in a sense the percussion was subordinated to some of the other instruments; but once the complex polyrhythmic devices discussed earlier were in operation, that role was inevitably rather less restricted.

Let us consider the self-imposed roles of the various musicians in a jazz group of the 1950s, performing a bop-derived music (and equally their roles in many of the recreative jazz movements since). There was an acceptance of the concepts of rhythm section and soloist. Thus the bass, drums and piano (or guitar) were taken as primarily responsible for statement of the pulse, metre, and chord structure; while for much of the time the 'front-line' instruments (such as saxophones, trumpet, and occasionally trombone) were responsible for the freer part of the performance, the 'solos'. It is apparent that the term 'rhythm section' was not a sufficient description since that section was responsible for the presentation not only of the rhythmic structure but also of harmonic structure. And further, the piano in nearly all pieces would step out of the rhythm section to become the soloist for some of the time, then taking on the dual role of soloist and harmony-stater. The bass, of course, would have a rhythmic and harmonic role, although very few bass lines stated the harmonic basis of the music in any detail: they usually established the fundamental note of the chord in operation, and perhaps one other note of the chord, but were largely constructed as scalar patterns (moving in tone and half-tone jumps). It is partly because of this relative simplicity that Johnson-Laird (A63) was able to programme a computerised 'bass-player' that he 'would not sack', although the performance of the player was clearly suboptimal!

We will consider the developments in playing individual instruments in a later chapter, relating this to the functional roles they played. Here let us consider the differentiation of roles within the ensemble with only secondary reference to the individual instrument roles. Speaking crudely, the formulaic jazz group lacked equality, particularly in flexibility of operation. The rhythm section suffered deprivation, while the soloists enjoyed the fruits of this. Of course, all the instruments became soloists occasionally, and all at least very occasionally became accompanists; and the soloists had periods of silence, while the rhythm section rarely did, so that the rhythm-section players had at least the advantage of being busy.

One of the corollaries of this organisation of the jazz group was that the various musical elements employed were not all exploited comparably: rhythmic and harmonic devices in jazz were initially much more limited than they later became. Perhaps only the melodic and motivic devices were extensively used. And even in the case of pitch employment, our discussion of tonality and microtonality again indicates a considerable restriction of usage in comparison with the apparent possibilities.

What of the contemporaneous arrangements in improvisation outside jazz? Until the early 1960s there seemed to be little activity, with a few interesting exceptions. One was a group of improvisations recorded in 1927 by the English composer Edward Elgar. These reveal the expected performance errors, but are closely harnessed within Elgar's normal compositional style: in other words, they are intensely formulaic. Later works included some Third Stream pieces, and the limited improvisations requested in some works of Cage, Lutosławksi, etc., which are discussed in A31, and mentioned briefly later in this book. We will come to the subsequent developments in free improvising shortly.

What of the changes in roles concurrent with the rhythmic and pitch-usage changes already analysed? The trend was towards equality of role, so that each member of a group might take any or all of the roles of rhythm provider, harmony provider, or motivic provider, as were in use. And these roles were modified so that each ultimately had comparable range and import; though, of course, it was not expected that the whole range of each would occur in use in every piece. For example, the work of Coltrane led to an acceptance of the possibility of rhythmic impact being coequal with motivic, as evidenced by the extended duets of Jones and Coltrane and ultimately the duo recordings of Coltrane and Ali (R29). Similarly in the free jazz development, initiated by Taylor, Coleman and Coltrane, the importance of rhythm was accentuated, and some recordings function as if there were no separation between rhythmic impulses and motivic impulse; for instance, in both the grossly active works (R10; R130) and some of the more open spacious work (such as some works of Don Cherry discussed in Chapter 9).

By the time of the establishment of free jazz in both the USA and Europe, around 1967, there were also improvising groups arising from outside the jazz tradition, which avoided the emphasis on regular pulse that was the main residue of the jazz tradition. And the groups such as AMM, Spontaneous Music Ensemble (SME), Mangelsdorff, Dauner and Kuhn (see Chapter 8) which arose from within jazz, at times moved in a similar direction. They again asserted the equality of roles of every performer, and hence the equality of all the individual musical elements. Such was the equality, for example, within AMM that the musicians recall that not only could the listener hardly be expected to identify the origin of many of the sounds, but equally the performers themselves, during performance, would stop to listen to find out the source of a sound, sometimes only then realising that they were producing it themselves (sleeve notes to R6).

Organisation by composers of the improvising process and of improvisers' relationships

In general the idea of a composition for improvisation is antithetical to that of the equality of the musicians involved in creating the final work, since the more is laid down by the composition the less is the scope of the improvisation. And usually the more is laid down the larger is the number of performers who have defined roles, and the smaller is the number with considerable freedom for improvisation. Nevertheless, there has been a parallel trend in compositions for improvisation towards equality (each performer having the same role potentials). Many of the changes in compositions which reflect this have already been discussed, but here it is necessary to explain their relevance to this trend towards equality in improvisers' roles.

Within jazz-related composition, it has taken a very long time for composers to realise that they need not specify a detailed rhythmic or harmonic framework within which an improviser has to work. Thus many compositions continue to be produced in which the harmonic framework of the whole structure may be complex and varied, and that in which the main improvisation occurs is also dictated, though often less fully: see for example, R113; or Penderecki's *Actions* (M9: see Chapter 9). On the other hand, some composers (such as Mantler, Rudd, Schlippenbach, and London Jazz Composers' Orchestra members, discussed in Chapter 9) have developed means of articulating a composition so that the compositional imprint is present, often even throughout the freest improvising, but in the work of other musicians than the key improvisers. So the improvisers get the maximum possible choice of method and material to juxtapose with that composed environment.

Probably the only kind of composition in which the improvisers are left in the position of potentially complete equality they had reached in free improvisation is that in which no musical material is specified, only procedures for the whole group. These procedures, as summarised in the preceding chapter, may be described in musical, metaphorical or emotive terms. But in any case it is quite possible for a complete equality to arise; and, of course, any of the players in the group might choose any of the separable roles, when these exist. The concept of a group fusing into a unified whole (Oliveros; Stockhausen) is just one possible corollary of the establishment of total group equality.

As mentioned earlier, it is only in western improvisation that such a tendency towards group equality has been important; Indian and most other oriental musics have not moved comparably in this way. Composition has been the one influence on improvisation which has not fostered such equality wholeheartedly, but its effects have not all been restrictive. For as discussed in the last chapter, the technical broadening of several aspects of improvisation, particularly those to do with pitch organisation within equal tempered tunings, have clearly been encouraged by compositional influences.

The composer remains in a knife-edge position in relation to improvisation, and some of the entailed dilemma can probably only be revealed by discussion of the attitudes and psychology of the composer who works with improvisers, and of the improviser who works with composers; this will be among the objectives of Section 3 of this book.

6 Instruments of improvisation

I have already commented that improvisers were responsible for the progressive introduction of an array of new performance techniques on the instruments they used, most of which have also become integrated in the work of interpretative performers (through technical works such as A12; A55). In some cases composers have also pushed technical demands by specifying an end for which no well-known means was available (as mentioned for Ferneyhough).

It is not the objective of this book to discuss the techniques of instrumental playing in great detail. But it is worth considering here how and when the changed techniques have arisen from the process of improvising, and conversely how they may have influenced that process. As in the case of compositional techniques, many different approaches to playing percussion, or woodwind, or brass or string instruments were available at the outset of the period under study; but only a small proportion of these had been considered by the western improviser (and an almost equally small proportion had been considered by the composer). Thus many of the instrumental techniques of Asian musicians (continuous pitch flux on Japanese flutes, for example; taiko drumming) or aboriginal musicians in Australia (circular breathing and sustained multiphonic textures on the didgeridoo) had not been applied in improvisation. So the eventual approach to these techniques was not in the main a linear progressive one, but rather one involving huge jumps by many individuals independently and dependently. The possibility of defining evolutionary strands (unless with reference to an individual musician) in most cases is remote, so we will largely point to technical elements and chronology.

Some technical description is therefore needed, and in this I have received valuable advice from colleagues in my improvising and interpreting ensembles Lysis and austraLysis – in particular, Ashley Brown and Tony Buck (percussion), Mark Lockheart (saxophones), Torbjorn Hultmark (trumpet) and Hazel Smith (violin). I am nevertheless entirely responsible for the ideas expressed, and solely responsible for those on the piano, keyboard instruments and double bass.

Amplification has been applied to most of the instruments, permitting use of sounds otherwise too weak in relation to the normal instrumental sounds, and this will be considered separately in a later section.

Physical aspects of playing an instrument have a significant effect on the kind of playing commonly practised. This is emphasised in relation to developing jazz piano techniques and more generally by Sudnow (A146–7). Movement is one of these aspects, and it has immense influence on the kinds of pitch (and rhythmic) patterns produced on some instruments (Baily in A58). The developing awareness of these factors was necessary for the freeing of improvisers from them.

A brief catalogue and chronology of new instrumental techniques in improvisation since 1960

We can conveniently consider the instruments in the sequence in which they appear on musical scores. The important members of the woodwind family used in improvisation were originally the saxophones, and to a lesser extent the flute and clarinet. The saxophone has always been played by jazz musicians with very idiosyncratic tones. For instance, on the tenor saxophone Ben Webster, Sonny Rollins and John Coltrane can be readily distinguished on the basis of sound alone; John Coltrane and Wayne Shorter playing the soprano saxophone can be equally readily distinguished. In contrast the classical saxophone players, especially those in the French tradition, have cultivated a very limited range of tone production, and cannot so readily be distinguished. They also vary their sound production to a very limited degree. Some improvising clarinet players, such as Bill Smith in the 1960s, have developed a huge timbral and multiphonic repertoire: Smith apparently has more than '750 multiphonics' under control (Eaton in A84; see Appendix 1 for a discussion of the nature of multiphonics).

Thus even in the 1950s the ways in which improvisers were using these instruments were very different from those of interpretative musicians, and in general broader. From this it was not surprising that timbral developments were profuse. Coltrane (M15) was one of the first to use controlled multiphonics, in which several pitches are apparent rather than just one. For example, on the early recordings he sometimes produced quite tonal multiphonics (such as a C and E). Later on he also used split notes where there was no such tonal implication. These became common devices in intense passages (R23; R26) where very high notes at climaxes would often be broken into multiphonic sounds. In later developments it also became possible to alternate the pitch spectrum (as does Adams on

R113). This procedure is necessarily linked with that of expanding the pitch range of the instruments, in this case by increasing the high register. Players such as John Surman on the baritone saxophone (in the late 1960s and 1970s), Dolphy (early 1960s), and later the interpreter Harry Sparnaay on the bass clarinet, expanded the high register tremendously. They were able to develop its use for simple notes, and also as multiphonic elements.

On the woodwind instruments the other devices were primarily directed towards the same end, of maximising the timbral range of the instruments. Thus we have microtonal fluctuations of pitch, not simply by vibrato, but also by the use of multiple fingerings for single notes (exemplified by Coltrane, as discussed previously) where the core pitch undergoes a microtonal fluctuation, but the more important consequence is the timbral (that is, harmonic content) change associated with these fluctuations. This has already been mentioned in relation to Coltrane's playing of the rapidly repeated notes on pieces like 'My Favourite Things'.

An extreme timbral change can be introduced by singing or shouting into the instrument at the same time as playing, and this can be heard in the work of Albert Ayler in the early 1960s. The interactions between the played and sung harmonic spectra can be very complex. Another contrasted timbre can be developed by using the instruments as percussive sources – for instance, by tapping the keys without blowing (as in works of Globokar and Loevendie). And this device is, of course, an inevitable concomitant of fingering normal notes, but can be accentuated.

Vocal developments took place in jazz in the 1960s and 1970s. For example, Abbey Lincoln on 'Freedom Now', performed with Max Roach on occasion, screamed continuously but variously for a prolonged period; while Leon Thomas later introduced an African-inspired yodelling technique (Mokambi: see A19). Fontella Bass (for instance, on the Art Ensemble of Chicago recording for a film, *Les Stances à Sophie* (R8)) has used a technique combining speech with vocals, rather like the *Sprechstimme* of Schoenberg. Few vocal performers have been involved in free improvising, with notable exceptions, such as Christine Jeffery (R103) and Maggie Nichols. But vocal sounds have been used quite extensively by other performers in free improvisation (for theatrical and simply musical effect) – for example, New Phonic Art (R105a and b) and Free Kata (see Chapter 8).

Vocal techniques have probably recently been expanded more by interpretative performers and composers writing for them than by improvisers. This can be observed in the recent work of SingCircle and Electric Phoenix, and of groups like the Swingle Singers from earlier periods, involved with the fringe of jazz and commercial music, and encouraging composers such as Berio to produce works for them. Howell has given a detailed view of the technical considerations in contemporary vocal techniques, relevant to all the applications (A58). We will return later to the juxtaposition of spoken text with improvised music (Chapter 11) as in the work of LeRoi Jones (R82) and Archie Shepp (R115).

I indicated earlier how the layout of an instrument may have a spatial relationship with the layout of pitches in notated pitch space. Thus on the woodwind instruments there are successive cycles in which reducing the number of keys depressed, by first releasing right-hand fingers, then left, causes a gradual rise in pitch. After about an octave, an embouchure change, often together with the use of a key which changes the register (for example, by an octave and a fifth on the clarinet), permits the repetition of the same process in a higher register. Thus within each register, releasing fingers from bottom to top of the instrument leads to rising pitch. Perhaps one of the important functions of the alternative pitches, besides giving multiphonics and microtones, was to begin to dissociate this relationship, so that the normal linearity of playing could be replaced by a more complex configuration. A graphic score with a single direction of movement in a passage might thus originally have led to a scalar pattern of notes, but after these technical developments could in addition have led to a much more complex multiphonic/microtonal motive. Thus one of the important aspects of these techniques is the freeing of the player from the conventional relationships between action, cognition of a motive (as in interpreting a score), and its development.

Moving down a notated score, we come to the brass instruments. Essentially the same considerations apply here as in the case of the woodwind instruments: the developments have been register extension (although this was already extreme in the work of players such as Cat Anderson on trumpet in the Ellington orchestra), multiphonic and microtonal work, and percussive effects. Performers of these instruments often make the statement that the embouchure required for multiphonic playing on the trumpet (lipped multiphonics as opposed to sung multiphonics) is almost incompatible with maintaining the embouchure for conventional trumpet playing (Wallace, personal communication). Nevertheless, several performers (for example, R53; Leo Smith on R104; Hultmark on the tape accompanying A31) manage to achieve both embouchures.

The trumpet and the horn do not have the monotonic relationship between action on the instrument (depressing a combination of three or four valves) and the resultant pitch, which is more crucially affected by the mouth shape and vibration. Thus the dissociation of linear pattern development of pitches from the mode of playing (described above) is virtually intrinsic to these instruments, and the improviser might conceivably develop techniques for establishing such a linear relationship, to constitute an unusual, stimulating approach to playing.

The linear relationship between action and product is inherent in playing the trombone, since the linear slide has just the same relation with the pitch of the fundamental note of the tube: increasing the slide length causes a lowering of the fundamental pitch. Higher notes are played as lipped harmonics above that fundamental. The same developments have taken place on this instrument, but they are more widely practised among performers. For example, Baker, in his book of transcriptions of trombone players' improvisations (A9), has noted multiphonics in the work of Phil Wilson in the 1960s, in conventional jazz formats; but these were virtually restricted to octave and other tonal biphonics. An early exponent of multiphonics, both tonal and microtonal, was Albert Mangelsdorff (see Chapter 8). But many other players (such as Conrad Bauer and Paul Rutherford) have also developed this. The combination of these techniques with electronic support can be heard in Jim Fulkerson's work (R91). It is clear that these players tend to produce tonal multiphonics most frequently, and although the continuous slide should permit free use of microtones, this has not been universally pronounced in their work: this is probably an example of the habituated limitation of playing techniques as a result of conventional training.

Next on the score are percussion instruments. The techniques in use here have differed between interpretative and improvising musicians. For example, the essential concept of jazz drumming is that the four limbs of the body can be used 'independently' whereas there is no comparable concept in classical percussion playing, where an array of instruments may be used, but primarily successively rather than simultaneously and independently. 'Independence' exercises are among the routine practice procedures of jazz drummers, and in principle independence should include the possibility of playing completely different rhythms on each instrument, or at least with each limb. In practice this is achieved by only a few musicians, such as Jones and Oxley, as discussed earlier; while most use rhythmic patterns in which the individual instruments are played by different limbs but such as to form a single rhythmic stream.

Most emphasis has been placed on the development of rhythmic independence, because of the presumption that the drums would be involved primarily in the rhythmic functions of the improvising group. However, with the progressive dissipation of this idea, there has been more scope for developments of newer timbral modifications on percussion. Goldstein (A47) has given poetic descriptions of percussive techniques, emphasising the concept of 'discovery' of new sounds. Again it should be possible for the four limbs to develop independence in mode of timbre production, so that the sound qualities of even similar drums (say, two different tomtoms) might be differentiated by the separate limbs playing them (R90; see the discussion of the work of Tony Oxley in Chapter 8), but this has not been widely exploited within the jazz context.

Outside the jazz context, the emphasis on coexistence of the functions of the different limbs has been slight; rather the performers have adopted a position like that of the classical percussionists, or at least between the two extremes of improviser and interpreter. Taking the untuned percussion first, there has been an increase in the range of timbres, and of tone modification during sound production. The timbral extension has been achieved by use of a wider range of beater and of hand striking techniques (like those used in Eastern music). Beaters may be used with different kinds of attack and this may be progressively changed during a trill on an instrument; at the same time selective damping, or partial clamping of the long reverberating instruments such as cymbals, can be used to cause a continuous change in partial content as the tone proceeds, or to ensure the use of only part of the envelope of the sound instead of its whole envelope (R90).

Turning to tuned percussion instruments, and more to control of pitch structures, the most obvious development has been the introduction of multiple-stick techniques. Thus on the vibraphone and marimba, thanks to the efforts of Gary Burton, Don Friedman and others, it is now routine for players to use four sticks, and thus to be able to develop harmony as well as motive more extensively. Six-stick techniques are also in use, though they are less well combined with scalar or arpeggiated motivic playing, because the extra sticks impede progress and flexibility. The use of pitched percussion does not necessarily require them to have primarily a pitch-orientated role. For example, the African percussion instruments such as the thumb piano, while retaining pitch discrimination, were used in the jazz context as much for their percussive and rhythmic elements in the 1960s (A19).

The general trend towards increased timbral range has also been obvious on the tuned percussion instruments. Al Francis (R53) created a huge range of vibraphone timbres by striking the instrument with metal and plastic objects. He also used various rattles as beaters, thus exploiting the concept of using one instrument to activate another and so getting at least two kinds of sound. Another striking example is given by the vibraphone, where, providing the metal keys are appropriately suspended at two of their nodes, a limited pressure on one end of a key by, for instance, a rubber-headed stick can raise the key slightly off the nodal point and thereby significantly alter the pattern of vibrations: microtonal fluctuations in pitch centre are possible and there are accompanying changes in partial spectrum which are of interest. This effect is not possible on an instrument like the xylophone with almost no sustaining power.

The piano is also a percussive instrument, and can appropriately be considered at this point, for developments in its usage have been along the same lines. The range of available timbres on the piano has been dramatically increased in the twentieth century by the introduction of ways of playing directly on the strings, and ways of altering the impact of notes initiated on the keys by simultaneously touching the strings. These techniques were foreshadowed in a limited way by Henry Cowell in the 1920s but have been further developed since 1960 in the work of improvisers, as well as in that of composers such as George Crumb. The

91

changing pressure on a string at a point other than the suspension points can produce microtonal fluctuations (as on a string instrument), and changes in overtones (and thus of timbre). It is also possible to produce very clear harmonics, as on the string instruments, by fairly gentle stopping of a string at its mid-point, quarter-points, etc.

Besides using the fingers directly on the strings, the nails and external objects are also appropriate. For example, the use of beaters, such as delicate vibraphone beaters or drum beaters, permits another layer of timbral modification which can be very interesting. Multiple beaters allow clear harmonic implication when desired, and because one can choose large or small beaters one can discriminate between cluster improvising, where there are always several adjacent semitones sounding (as in much of Cecil Taylor's playing on the keys), and single-pitch improvising. Freely moving objects such as pieces of wood can be placed on the strings to give additional percussive sounds besides those of the strings, and, of course, this technique relates to Cage's work with the 'prepared piano', in which these objects (often nails) were fixed between strings, but such that they can vibrate. Selective damping, to choose the portion of the sound envelope in use, is again a feature of piano improvising. It is interesting to consider one request of Christian Wolff in his piece '123': that the directionality of a sound be changed. Though this cannot be achieved independently of other effects on an unamplified piano, one can achieve some directionality by physically displacing strings, and by selective damping of groups of pitches. No doubt there are other possibilities also. Several pianists have engaged improvisatorily and by experiment these possibilities of inside-piano sonorities; examples can be heard in the work of Howard Riley, Joachim Kuhn and myself (see Chapter 7). It is notable that many of the improvisers concerned, at least from the jazz stream of improvisatory development, were European. In America the contributions of Paul Bley deserve attention (see also Chapter 7), but there were very few other jazz improvisers using these techniques during the period under study. More of the US improvisers arriving from compositional or electronic backgrounds (such as Rzewski, Teitelbaum and Rosenboom) have shown such an interest.

While the technical features of piano construction have developed in the twentieth century, there has arisen one in particular which offered new improvising possibilities: the third (or selective sustain) pedal. This permits certain notes to be sustained, while others are played either sustained with the fingers or unsustained, enabling even further differentiation of the piano into multiple voices than otherwise (Chapter 7). Perhaps it is worth noting that very few improvisers in the jazz tradition have taken advantage of these possibilities; for example, it is virtually unheard in the work of Cecil Taylor.

It is perhaps because the piano has been central in all kinds of western music that the developments in performance technique on it have been roughly equally shared between composed and improvised music, where-as those on many of the other instruments have probably derived more from improvised musics.

The piano is like some of the large string instruments in that its body is so reverberant that it can be used as an independent percussive source. The sympathetic vibrations of the strings resulting from percussive impacts on the cross-bars or on the wooden case of the piano can then be controlled in all the senses defined above.

So let us move finally to the string instruments. Without amplification many of the effects which have been introduced can be applied on any string instrument, while others are hardly workable on instruments other than the bass and cello. The central development has been to increase the number of simultaneous sounds used. There have been two main ways of achieving this: multiple stopping (where several strings are sounded at once) and multiphonics (where tones with more than one apparent pitch centre are produced). Multiple stopping was, of course, a feature of virtuoso string writing for several centuries, but both in composition and improvisation this has clearly been extended in the period under study. Xenakis in particular, in relation to his concepts of continuous pitch flux and microtones, has required simultaneous performance of two lines on one string instrument, as well as the production of complex chords (M16). Although much guitar playing has been conventional (see A92 for trans-cribed examples, including Wes Montgomery's extensive use of octave doublings in the early 1960s), various kinds of independent two or more part playing have been developed by free improvisers such as Bailey, Chadbourne and others discussed in Chapter 8, and later in more main-stream jazz by Stanley Jordan.

More complex chords than the two or three notes which can be struck almost simultaneously on the string instruments are produced by using both left and right hands as sound initiators. Thus while stopping up to four strings the left hand can play two or more notes while the right hand sounds an additional two or more, which may or may not be stopped notes (in the case of the double bass, see the work of Grillo, or M5). The right hand could attack pizzicato or arco. It is again interesting to contrast the attitude of western and eastern improvisers to a particular technical device: double stopping has remained a 'decorative' technique in Arabian music (A59), as it was in virtuoso string writing in the sixteenth and seventeenth centuries in the West, but it has since become more fun-damental in western composition and improvisation.

Multiphonics on string instruments are often produced by bowing very near to the bridge where a succession of different overtones can be produced while a single string stop is in effect: the balance of the different overtones present can be controlled. Among the components of such multiphonics are often the sounds produced by the string vibrating separ-ately on each side of the point(s) at which it is stopped. While the length of the string between the finger stop and the bridge is normally the source of the sound, the other half usually vibrates, and produces a very slight sound: this can be exaggerated by plucking the string above the point of stopping (between the fingerstop and nut of the instrument). In the same way, pizzicati either side of the stopping point can produce a bidirectional glissando (see, for example, Eaton in A84).

Less workable on the higher string instruments have been percussive techniques using beaters on the strings or the body of the instrument. Hand impacts on the bass produce simple percussive sounds and subsequent reverberations, which can be controlled. Rubbing techniques are also effective (R67) and may be applied to any part of the structure (body, bridge, tailpiece, etc.). Such techniques have been used by the improvisers, and then incorporated into compositions (see, for example, M7).

In using all these techniques on string instruments a general trend has been towards using the two hands independently, rather as the jazz percussionist has striven to use the four limbs independently. So, for example, one hand might be engaged on percussive or rubbing sounds, while the other is using the bow to initiate sound on the strings. Amplification offered a means of applying these techniques to the other string instruments, and was also relevant to the development and enhancement of all the instrumental timbres we have discussed in this section. It will be described in a later section of this chapter.

In summary, all these techniques have two important features in common: the expansion of the sound range available to an improviser, and the partial dislocation of conventional physical movements on the instrument from conventional output in sound. This dislocation is valuable in shaking the improviser away from entirely familiar procedures, and also in introducing some poorly controlled, even chance-driven, elements into the sound. The possibility of reducing control in improvising, rather than maximising it (more common in composition) is psychologically important to many improvisers (see A31 for further discussion).

New instruments for improvisation

Improvisation has also elicited, on the one hand, the use of several instruments previously foreign to itself, and on the other, the generation of several new ones. Even the latter, however, often exploit features not used in western instruments but known in instruments from other cultures. Thus they sprang into improvisation almost fully formed, rather than by a progressive process, as with some electronic instruments.

Let us consider the foreign instruments category first. The clarinet was, of course, a core instrument in early jazz, but somehow fell out of use during the development of modern jazz, in the bebop era. It only re-established itself in the 1960s with the work of Jimmy Giuffre (see the discussion of Paul Bley in Chapter 7), Tony Scott, Prince Lasha (R61) and others. They explored many of the same paths as the saxophonists we have already discussed. For example, they used a broader range of tone-production techniques than their classical counterparts. This was also revealed in the work of the mainstream clarinettist Benny Goodman. The Copland Clarinet Concerto was written for Goodman, and Copland was familiar with at least some jazz developments. Copland had sympathy with the range of timbres Goodman could produce, which depended on his jazz background, and appreciated their distinction from the timbres of the conventional classical clarinet virtuosi.

The developments of Giuffre and others, though primarily in motivic device and matters common to other instruments, nevertheless also resulted in a new enthusiasm for the clarinet. Subsequently this was pursued by very adventurous musicians such as Perry Robinson, Rolf Kuhn, and Tony Coe (discussed in Chapters 7–9) who exploited most of the techniques we have discussed. In some cases (for example, Coe), the players were experts on saxophones as well, while in others (Kuhn, Robinson), they are clarinet specialists.

The oboe had seemed unsuitable for improvising not because of an excessively smooth tone, like the clarinet style of the classical 1950s player, but because of an insufficiency of motility. However, there are always technicians who conquer such limitations, and in the case of the oboe it was pioneered during the 1960s by such as Yusef Lateef and then more widely used in the early 1970s by musicians such as Karl Jenkins (see Chapters 9 and 10) and Mark Whitecage (for example, with Naughton; see Chapter 8). Again timbral variety was accentuated, though the nasal quality of the instrument, and the dominance of odd-numbered overtones has never been submerged. The multiphonic techniques and microtonal devices are fully applicable on the instrument (cf. the brilliant technical developments of the non-improviser Heinz Holliger). Other double-reed instruments like the bassoon were also introduced to some degree, mainly by musicians who were also classical players (for example, Klaus Thuneman, or, in the UK, Lindsay Cooper, who has worked with Derek Bailey's Company). Some very interesting composed sonorities have been obtained by juxtaposing several of these previously unorthodox jazz instruments, in the compositions of the west coast musicians (such as Cooper and Bud Shank) and in certain later European contexts in which restrained compositions for improvisation are preferred (for example, the labels JAPO and particularly ECM). In the freer improvising contexts there has also been slight usage.

Moving to brass instruments, a great enthusiasm for the flugelhorn has emerged, particularly among conventional jazz players (such as Freddie Hubbard and Ken Wheeler; see Chapters 7–9). The instrument is particularly suitable, because of its large bell and related physical factors, for multiphonic work, and Leo Smith has exploited this.

In the percussion world, new microtonal instruments devised in association with Harry Partch were exploited by Emil Richards in the Microtonal Blues Band (R111), and subsequent generations have developed the concept of self-made percussive instruments, as reviewed by the practitioner Hugh Davies (see R103; and the *Grove Dictionary of Musical Instruments*). However, the main thrust of these instruments, as of the keyboard instruments and string instruments, has been to exploit electronic techniques and amplification (see A82), and it is to this we turn next.

One should again ask what significance attached to these developments of new instruments. There are two main elements. The first is an extension of the idea expressed earlier, that a dislocation between playing an instrument and precise expectation of the sonic output is a desirable feature. Clearly new instruments, especially ones constructed for or during individual performances, offer this dislocation.

The second significance relates to new instruments designed to be used over prolonged periods. Many of the new instruments (such as those of Hugh Davies) were designed so as to have fundamentally different characteristics from the familiar ones: for example, to permit microtonal playing, but without offering a full spectrum of pitches; or to generate absolutely continuous sounds which could last as long as desired (contrast the piano). Again these novel features could aid the improviser in moving away from familiar approaches so that rather than just improvising the detail of a structure, they could improvise the structure, pitch language or sound field as well.

Amplification and electroacoustic instruments

Many of the techniques described above were applicable to certain instruments without modification, but could be extended more widely once amplification became available. Thus, for example, the short reverberation time of a plucked note on the violin made it incapable of many of the uses to which a plucked note on the bass (with much longer reverberation) could be put. This could be overcome once the violin was amplified. A catalogue of works involving string instruments with electronics is available (A99), though most are composed works.

Interesting historical surveys of some of the early electroacoustic activities in the USA are available (A49a; A82). Among these were David Behrman and Gordon Mumma's work with the Sonic Arts Union, in which live electronics were involved, and the audience was sometimes used as source of control information to be input to the electronics. Similarly, Alvin Lucier used electrodes to allow brain alpha-waves to control sounds in his 1965 piece 'Music for a Solo Performer'. Robert Ashley was also involved with the Sonic Arts Union, and he produced several pieces for instruments and tape intended for performance by improvisers. Thus his 'Wolfman' (1964) was for the Bob James Trio

(R75) and there were two versions: one for jazz trio and tape, and the other for amplified voice and tape. The jazz trio played only in the middle section of a largely theatrical tape, as was also the case for the new version of this work (premiered by Lysis in 1987). On the same James recording, there was also Ashley's 'Untitled Mixes', in which improvisers had to imitate sounds on the tape. The same procedure was used on Ashley's 'Peasant Boy' (1965). A collaboration with Gordon Mumma was also included on the recording.

These electroacoustic interactions, together with appropriate and convenient contact microphones, developed in the late 1960s and early 1970s, and transformed the playing techniques in improvisation. The improvising musicians always tended to be the most progressive as far as choice of equipment and its use was concerned, and so it is not surprising that improvisers first exploited these techniques of amplification, later giving their findings to the world of composition. For instance, on the double bass the work of Guy and Grillo developed amplification for the instruments, and led to the use of foot pedals within performance, so that rapidly decaying sounds could be caught by the abrupt switching up of amplification to become usable in direct juxtaposition with more forceful sounds. Subsequently both enshrined many of the techniques in their published compositions. These techniques were soon applied on other string instruments – for example, on the violin by Leroy Jenkins, and by Philip Wachsman with the London Jazz Composers' Orchestra (see Chapters 8 and 9). But perhaps most important were the developments of Tony Oxley on percussion instruments, as revealed, for example, on 'Ichnos' (Chapter 8).

It might seem surprising that percussion instruments, some already endowed with great forcefulness, long sound envelopes, and complex timbre, should be an important target of amplification and electronic modulation. But not only did amplification of drums and cymbals permit the same principle, described above, of establishing equality of usage between sounds and timbres which were intrinsically very unequal in potency, but also it encouraged the construction of special frames of metal with strikeable, rubbable and shakeable objects, whose vibration could be amplified by contact microphones to convert them from almost inaudible to very clearly audible. The amplified drum kit thus gave rise to a range of sounds whose origin was very difficult to detect from outside, but whose variety and control were as great as that of a conventional instrument. The advantage, of course, was that these instruments escaped from the in-built conventions of tuning, types of harmonic content, etc., of the conventional instruments and so permitted any vocabulary of musical discourse the player might favour. It has not been a primary concern throughout this book to attribute the innovations described to particular individuals; and in this particular instance it is obvious that there was an overlap of intention and procedure in developing new percussion sounds between Oxley and some of the earlier work of AMM (mid-1960s) and other groups. Such antecedents of new developments can usually be found, but were not necessarily known to the subsequent developer.

Escaping from the previously in-built tuning conventions and timbre characteristics was also possible in principle with synthesisers, which, from analogue origins in the early part of the twentieth century (used for example by Sonic Arts Union and Musica Elettronica Viva (R97)) and in the 1970s (see discussion of Paul Bley in Chapter 7), developed into much more controllable and precise beasts in the digital synthesisers of the 1980s, particularly the Yamaha DX series.

It is interesting that the outlooks of the electrocacoustic groups differed very considerably from each other in the 1960s. Thus Nuova Consonanza tended to favour conventional instruments with tape. But MEV had a wider practice. Thus one of their publicity statements (quoted in A49a) announced:

> Tapes, complex electronics – Moog synthesiser, brainwave amplifier, photocell mixers for movement of sound in space – are combined with traditional instruments, everyday objects and the environment itself, amplified by means of contact mikes or not. Sound may originate both inside and outside the performing-listening space and may move freely within and around it. Jazz, rock, primitive and Oriental musics, Western classical, tradition, verbal and organic sound both individual and collective may all be present.

The advantage of digital control was slightly undermined by the fact that the affordable and widely used instruments were all based around keyboards, whose tuning until recently was equal tempered. This has now been overcome, as already mentioned, and microtonal tunings, using the TX81Z, etc., are readily accessible. In principle the great advantage of a synthesiser, of whatever breed, is that any wave form, and hence any timbre, tuning, etc., can be constructed. In practice, with the exception of sounds specified on a large computer, the range of variation which can be built into the sound is limited, abrupt changes of envelope and timbre in the middle of sounds being impossible to program on some instruments, and difficult on most at present. However, the portable synthesisers do permit systematic subtle variation of timbres in a degree and with a precision impossible on most conventional instruments. Thus real-time (live in performance) timbral improvisation, exemplified by Richard Teitelbaum (see the discussion of Anthony Braxton in Chapter 8) and, more recently, by my own playing on Collier's *Something British Made in Hong Kong* (Chapters 9 and 10) has begun to be exploited. Similarly, the use of sequencers has permitted several new ways of controlling the progress of an improvisation, and the interactions of the improvisers with musical materials, rhythms and other players (see A82). Some future possibilities are also outlined in A31.

In sum, the development of amplification and electroacoustic instruments has made possible the systematisation of many of the ideas of timbral development. Many further openings have yet to be exploited, which are perhaps still out of sight because of the dominance of the equal tempered keyboard, and the wish for simplicity of relationship between the physical action of playing the instrument and the output. The synthesiser distinctly minimises this relationship, in every sense except that of pitch (where there is the usual linear relation between pitch generated and position of key played). For example, the timbre of a note is usually most affected by the programming of the synthesiser voice, and only to a lesser degree by the way in which it is activated; whereas the converse is usually true for the performer on a conventional instrument. Pitch 'mapping' can be used to overcome the linearity of relationship which normally holds with the key position – so that, for instance, middle C might sound as a high F#, while the next 'higher' key (normally C#) might sound as a low E, etc. This mapping could be made probabilistic also (rather than fixed) and has been exploited by improvisers such as Pressing.

Of course, this dislocation is advantageous in the ways already described, such as that it minimises the likelihood that a performer produces only a kind of playing for which his instrumental technique gives facility. But this is only true if the player makes enough effort to avoid the inbuilt conventions of the synthesiser instead; this requires as much application as does the comparable avoidance on the conventional instrument, and has as yet not been much achieved.

SECTION 3

The evolution of improvisation in the work of the individual

In this section I will discuss some interesting musicians who are involved with improvisation and yet not often considered in relevant writing, in order to illustrate and amplify in a more concrete way some of the issues in technical usage which I have delineated so far. Chapter 7 will deal with several contrasting keyboard players, representing both European and American developments. Chapter 8 will concentrate on the furthest developments of recent free improvising, as illustrated by AMM and the Incus musicians, and compare it with the American free improvisers such as Anthony Braxton and members of the AACM. In Chapter 9 I will discuss the position of the composer working closely with improvisers in the recent past, and again compare some of the activities in Europe with those in the USA. I will also consider how composers' work has responded to developments in improvisation techniques, and discuss a few other composers besides the main subjects of the chapter. The chapters in this section each have their own discographies. Records referred to in these chapters are given by date only, unless the leader of the recording (as listed in the discography) is other than the subject of the section.

The main reasons for adopting this approach, and the main kinds of insight we can gain from it are as follows. First, we can see that individual musicians evolve, just as does technical usage in a field at large, or the work of a group. Second, we can see how they reflect developments in the music at large, of the kinds we have already discussed. These two features allow further illustration of the thesis detailed in Appendix 1, that musical development is largely an autonomous cultural rather than sociopolitical matter. But we can also occasionally identify specific outside influences, and this will also be the objective of Chapter 10. Third, we can begin to discuss attitudes as opposed to product; again this can be pursued further in the position of direct contact with a musician, as represented in Chapter 10. Finally, we can indicate how movements in a particular geographic area have occurred, and how they may contrast with those of other areas.

7 Five improvising keyboard players

The subjects of this section are Paul Bley (from Canada), Andrew Hill (from the USA), Wolfgang Dauner and Joachim Kuhn (from Germany) and briefly myself (from the UK). I have chosen these as subjects because they are all musicians in whose work I have been very interested, and because they represent a variety of localities. As mentioned earlier, I am slightly redressing the balance of the literature on improvisation by considering only two North Americans.

We can summarise the important developmental features of these musicians as follows. Bley has been primarily concerned with harmonic devices relating closely to tonality though gradually evolving intense chromaticism, and to a lesser extent with extending timbral devices (on the synthesiser). He has utilised interesting rhythmic devices, but not capitalised on them. Kuhn is in a somewhat similar position in emphasising harmonic matters to the relative exclusion of rhythmic developments, but, in contrast to Bley, he started from extreme atonality used in a highly organised way, and has gradually introduced more tonal elements into his work; at the same time he has used more timbral and textural improvising on the piano, and also on the saxophone and other wind instruments, and developed a greater freedom in improvising. Andrew Hill and Wolfgang Dauner have had far more to do with rhythmic devices, and Hill in particular has composed and improvised multi-layered rhythmic approaches. He has remained close to the jazz tradition in so doing, while Dauner, using electronic instruments, has moved further towards freer improvising methods. While the other pianists have used some textural devices on the piano, including the techniques of playing on the strings directly, these have been particularly exploited by myself, and recently related to textural and timbral devices on digital synthesisers and sequencers. Rhythmic techniques have also been among my particular interests. Thus all the subjects of this chapter have followed

Fig. 7.1 Bley on 'Santa Claus is Coming to Town'.

evolutionary paths in parallel with those indicated for the music at large, but these have never been the sole line of motion for the musicians. Indeed Kuhn has also shown a quite different, almost converse trend in his attitudes towards tonality, moving against the stream of improvised music, but perhaps moving with the reaction against atonality and serial music in composition at the time.

Paul Bley

Paul Bley (born 1932) is unusual among jazz and improvising pianists in the extreme range of his musical experience, from working with Mingus, a 1950s pioneer (on Bley's first trio album) and Rollins, through contributing to the genesis of Ornette Coleman's music, to developing as a lyrical soloist. On the way Bley worked in closely controlled composed contexts, as with George Russell; in pioneering free improvisation with Jimmy Giuffre; and developed the use of the analogue synthesiser. His trio music, with many different musicians as collaborators, developed a whole range of improvising styles. He had studied with the idiosyncratic composer Henry Brant.

Let us consider the broadening of his technical usage in the same terms as we have analysed it earlier. Bley's first record, *Introducing Paul Bley*, was made in 1953 in the auspicious company of Blakey and Mingus. Many of the then unorthodox technical features which permeate Bley's later work (he has made more than 100 records) are already in evidence on this recording. In harmonic and melodic devices there is a tremendous emphasis on major sevenths and minor ninths. For example in chordal passages there is an accentuated B/F/C chord (pitches in chords are indicated in ascending order) representing a derivation of G7 (on 'Opus 1'); and another G7 (on 'I Can't Get Started') has treble voicings of B/F/F# (an octave and a semitone above the F). In 'Someone in Love' there are many eleventh chords with an F/A/B/E construction and Cmaj7 is represented as C/A/B, giving a barer seventh and an adjacent tone. Similarly, the last chord of the piece is C/E/F#/B (an example of replacing the thirds of Cmaj7, normally comprising C/E/G/B, with some fourths). An A♭ several octaves higher is then introduced, giving a minor ninth in addition.

Similarly, 'I Can't Get Started' has an interesting solo introduction with many chords with fourths, seconds and sevenths and sixths. It also has a

Fig. 7.2 Coleman on 'Klactovedeseen': 3/4 with complex subdivisions against basic 4/4.

Dmaj7 instead of D7 in the chromatic progression statement so that a weak minor seventh is converted to a stronger major seventh. Then later D7 is presented with a minor ninth between the resident F# and the added fourth above the fundamental, a G. Similarly Cmaj7 is several times replaced by C7♭9 (i.e. C/E/G/B♭/D♭) in 'Santa Claus is Coming to Town'. Elements of polytonality are present, particularly just after the bass solo on 'Opus 1', and internal scalar motion within chord progressions, causing various degrees of chromaticity, is common (as in 'Someone in Love').

Rhythmic devices in use on this first recording include quavers in repeated 3/4 pattern against 4/4 bars ('Teapot') and a repeating figure over three quavers, again set against the 4/4 pulse (Fig. 7.1). Other motivic aspects are the use of sequences ('Opus 1'), quotations from other tunes ('Split Kick') and pianistic figurations with repeated notes ('Spontaneous Combustion'). In sum, there are many interesting and slightly unorthodox features on this recording and they may partly reflect the breadth of input Bley received from Brant. On the other hand, the record is far from revolutionary in comparison with either Lennie Tristano (R132) or even with the contemporaneous harmonic and structural adventurousness of Teddy Charles.

Let us deal next with rhythmic features in Bley's subsequent work, and then some matters of structural organisation. We can then conclude with the most developed aspect: harmonic and motivic device. Perhaps the most interesting rhythmic devices on Bley's recorded output occur in the record with the incipient Ornette Coleman quartet (Bley 1958). In 'Klactovedeseen' Bley plays a long succession of chords spaced at three-beat intervals, again creating a 3/4 metre, with a first beat accentuation, against the prevailing 4/4. This is extended later as a filled-out repeating three-beat pattern (crotchet, two quavers, crotchet, etc.). There is also a version occupying six beats with double the note values, but this is less disruptive to the metre. Coleman is also using such devices of three-beat pattern against four-beat: for instance, a notable group of rhythms (Fig. 7.2) comprises four roughly equal notes against six quavers, and the number and spacing of the notes in these groups is varied. At the same time the drums play many rhythms based on two dotted crotchets, also therefore occupying three beats.

Bley's most notable rhythmic development in this piece occurs during his free piano solo (unaccompanied) where the two dotted crotchets

Fig. 7.3 Cross-rhythms based on triplets.

(a) On 'Harlem'.   **(b)** On 'Free'.

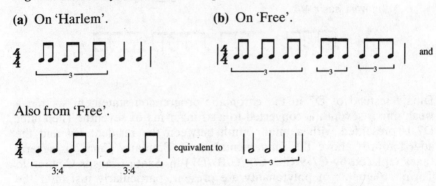

Also from 'Free'.

become briefly crotchets in a new slower pulse which is formed into metred four-beat bars, whose pulse speed is therefore two-thirds of the initial pulse speed. This device is similar to some discussed extensively in relation to the Miles Davis group and Circle. Bley stops playing subsequently when Coleman solos, but Cherry continues the dotted crotchet cross-rhythm. And when Cherry himself solos, Bley repeatedly plays phrases of three quavers' length (comprising crotchet followed by quaver) inside the piano. Coleman later does a ritardando using a repeated dotted crotchet on a single note, and the dotted crotchet becomes a new slower pulse again. So metrical modulation was at least briefly among Bley's horizons.

More important, and more sustained in his works, are the cross-rhythms based on triplets – for instance, in 'Harlem' and variants on 'Free' (Fig. 7.3). It is interesting that a more complex version of this 3:2 pattern is used by George Russell on 'Jazz in A Space Age' (*Chromatic Universe Part 1*) on which Bley appears (see Fig. 7.4). This gives the impression of a seven-pulse pattern above a 5:2 pattern consisting of five equal minims. Bley and Bill Evans, the two soloists, both exploit this pattern in their soloing.

By the time of Bley's next major group of recordings, those with Giuffre (1961), most pieces were played without continuous and consistent pulse, thus reflecting the general movement in improvising towards reduction of formulaic elements in rhythm as in other things. And they

Fig. 7.4 Russell's 'Chromatic Universe Pt 1'.

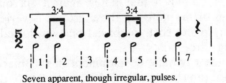

Seven apparent, though irregular, pulses.

Fig. 7.5 Motian triplet patterns.

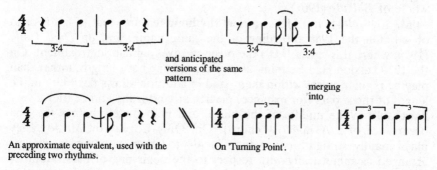

and anticipated
versions of the same
pattern

merging
into

An approximate equivalent, used with the
preceding two rhythms.

On 'Turning Point'.

had begun to take on a characteristic episodic nature, in which each short phrase of Bley, of maybe two seconds, is followed by a space of about half a second, before the next phrase.

Bley made some records as accompanist in this period (1960–5) which involved him in playing in more conventional contexts than those of his own group or Giuffre's. And in these his metrical capacities were used again. For example, with Rollins and Hawkins, Bley was constrained to play conventional pulsed jazz, and 'standard' chord sequences. But most of Bley's subsequent recordings are under his own leadership, and mainly involve music without consistent pulses. On the few exceptions many of the features already noted recur. But a few rarer devices are also found. For example, on the LP *Turning Point* (1964), 'Calls' involves a scalar 5:4 crotchet figure in the piano near the beginning of the piano solo. By this period Bley was often in the company of the imaginative drummer Paul Motian, whose approach (as already noted) to maintaining pulses is rather less orthodox than most – involving, for instance, extensive gaps, and omission of many accented beats (see, for example, Fig. 7.5). Displaced versions of triplet minim patterns occur in Motian's work on 'Turning Point' also (Fig. 7.5) and in this piece it is quite evident that bar lengths are treated as somewhat variable, even though the concept of a fixed number of pulses per bar, and roughly fixed pulse rate, predominate, so that the music achieves a flexibility rather akin to that of Indian music. In pieces such as 'Ictus' the pulses, though inconsistent in length, are very strong (Fig. 7.6). Thus while some of Bley's freer work largely suspends pulse, by working as a succession of phrases followed by pauses,

Fig. 7.6 Pulses from 'Ictus' (as played by Motian).

107

others sustain pulse, though varying it continuously (as on almost the whole of *Ballads* (1967).

'Mr Joy' (1964) introduces a new rhythmic feature: that of 8/8 instead of 4/4. On the 1968 recording of the same name, and on *Dual Unity* (1970, where it is called 'MJ') the piece receives similar 8/8 treatment. On the 1970 version Han Bennink uses spaces of one bar's length, rather than playing regular pulses within them, and in addition allows flexibility in the length of those bars (for instance, particularly after the end of Bley's very florid solo in the middle of the piece, and immediately before the first occurrence of a A♭maj7/B♭ chord). On 'Only Lovely' on *Mr Joy* Bley plays mainly straightforward time in 4/4 together with triplet quavers arranged asymmetrically with respect to the beginning of bars. Another simple variant of the 3:4 pattern, with subdivisions of the 3 so as to create a new slower pulse, as well as a simple cross-rhythm, is on 'King Kong'. More simple time is found on subsequent recordings, including *Fragments* (1986) and no significant rhythmic developments are evident.

Now we can turn to harmonic and motivic aspects of Bley's work. Besides an enthusiasm for sevenths and ninths, already mentioned, Bley relies regularly on the tritone (three tones apart, equivalent to the flattened fifth of the bebop era). For example, the 1958 recording of his own theme 'Harlem' has a succession of parallel tritones. The same interval is emphasised repeatedly on *Ballads* – for example on 'Ending' – and is retained in the solo version of 'Harlem' (1972).

Minor ninths as harmonic elements remain important throughout Bley's subsequent work – for example, the repeated A1:B♭2 interval on 'Harlem' (1958); and chords on 'Gamut' and 'Suite for Germany' (*Jimmy Giuffre Trio Live in Europe Vol. 1*). These minor ninths may be delayed within motives as in Fig. 7.7a (from 'Calls' on *Turning Point*). Sevenths are equally in evidence and they, too, may be delayed, and often in juxtaposition with delayed minor ninths, as in Fig. 7.7b (from 'Pablo' on *Mr Joy*). Fig. 7.7c also illustrates this pair of features at work in *Ballads*. A succession of sixths (for example, E/C followed by G/E♭) or thirds can generate delayed relationships in which an individual note (in this case E) appears with two different accidentals in two different parts successively ('false relations' in classical contexts). Several of these relationships are enclosed within Fig. 7.8 from the Giuffre recording 'Cry'.

Bley is also fond of repeating a single pitch, with a changing sixth to fifth interval played below at the same time and this brings us to the chordal structures he designs from the fifth and augmented fourth, for example C/D♭/G (Fig. 7.9). The first inversion of this chord gives D♭/G/C, in which both intervals are fourths, though unequal ones. This construction, as already noted, was a common feature developed in the Coltrane group and the Davis group of the early 1960s, initially in relation to modal playing, and subsequently used more widely even in the context of conventional scales. Bley also developed this assiduously,

Fig. 7.7 Delayed sevenths and ninths in Bley's motivic work.

(a) From 'Calls' on *Turning Point*.   **(b)** From 'Pablo' on *Mr Joy*.

(c) From 'Ending' on *Ballads*.

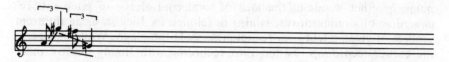

including using the spread version covering a minor ninth: C/G/D♭. In terms of pitch set (see A34 for further information on pitch sets), these all constitute 0, 1, 7 and are equivalent to several other chordal formations characteristic of Bley. Motivic use of these intervals was also common with Bley. This C/D♭/G pattern can be contrasted with the common formation of Dm7 used by Bill Evans, where a third is normally still present comprising D/E/F/B. The latter three notes again comprise the set 0, 1, 7. Chords with pairs of perfect fourths are also used by Bley, particularly in tonal contexts, such as that of the record with Rollins and Hawkins (for instance, 'All the Things') where Bley accompanies almost only with the right hand. The Bill Evans chords are developed by Bley by inversion into chords with a perfect fourth and a minor ninth (for example, E/A/F).

Another important harmonic feature is the insistent use of clusters; and this has a converse (or corollary) in the motivic use of widely spread intervals, far more than an octave apart (Fig. 7.8). The delicate usage of

Fig. 7.8

(a) 'Cry' From *Giuffre in*   **(b)** Parallel motion in 'Dreams' from
    Europe Vol. 1.   *Scorpio*: near end of piece.

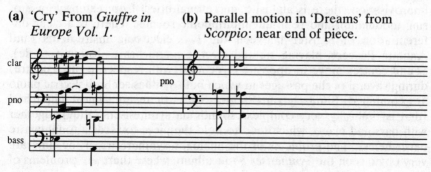

clar

pno

bass

the clusters contrasts markedly with the forceful usage of Cecil Taylor: for Bley they are still harmonic entities, often sustained or arpeggiated, whereas for Taylor the clusters come in very rapid, usually staccato succession, each treated as a single motivic sound, almost as if it were a single pitch, or a multiphonic, rather than a combination of discrete tones. Similarly the widespaced pitches used motivically create a harmonic openness beyond the simpler implications of the pitches themselves when reduced to the closest spacing.

This awareness of the effectiveness of different placings of a given pitch, in other words of the lack of total equivalence of pitch sets repeated at different octaves, is also developed by Bley in using different timbres of given pitches, by techniques inside the piano. While lacking in the earlier recordings, by the 1961 recording with Jimmy Giuffre there are several internal sounds: a progression which can be related to the exposure to the freer improvising approaches in the meantime. For instance, on 'Cry', there is a glissando across damped strings during the bass solo and elsewhere, leading to two resounding notes, usually minor thirds. In addition, Bley rubs the strings at the end, and strikes a mid-register note, probably with fingers. Another huge inside the piano glissando is on 'Gamut'. On 'Suite for Germany' there are double note plucked chords. By the *Turning Point* album Bley is also plucking individual damped notes (as on 'Ictus'), and using selective damping on the *Mr Joy* album (as in 'Touching 1'), where there are also minor third chords at the end of the piano solo, and surface glissandi on individual strings during the bass solo (producing a variety of harmonics and timbres from a single string or group of strings). Harmonics originating from stopping an individual string which is then struck on the keys or activated otherwise were also developed: for example, on 'Ictus' (*Masters of the Modern Piano*), damped strings are used to generate octave and a fifth, and higher harmonics.

By 1970, Bley had also developed an interest in the timbral possibilities of the synthesiser, then analogue (usually an Arp). On some pieces (e.g. 'MJ') on *Dual Unity* Bley uses the instrument as if it were simply a keyboard. But on 'Gargantuan Encounter', which is probably a free improvisation, there is almost a microtonal effect from extensive use of ring modulation and resultant multiphonic sounds. There is a clear differentiation of register between the two electronic instruments (and Annette Peacock playing treated electric piano has a distinctive role). Sound centres move in opposite directions (with respect to pitch centre) during several of the passages in which both synthesiser and electric piano are combined. Similarly on 'Richter Scale' there are almost unpitched (that is timbrally very complex) sounds on synthesisers (Bley) together with bass and piano, which tend to hold the piece towards a tonal centre nevertheless. The problems of the analogue synthesisers of the time are very obvious on the *Synthesiser Show* album, where there are problems of tuning of a low G and A♭ at the bottom of phrases near the beginning of 'Mr Joy'. But the complete pitch flux possible in contrast to the discrete pitch jumps of the piano, is exploited on real glissandi on 'Aelagel'. The use of vibrato on notes, and the choice of time of onset of the vibrato (usually somewhat after the establishment of the note, as with many wind and string players) is a clear feature of the synthesiser, which is not possible on the piano. On 'Nothing Ever Was' there is extensive ring modulation, and some very interesting microtonal fluxes on individual notes, especially near the end of the piece. In Bley we have thus a clear case of the improviser adapting to newly available instruments, and having previously entirely improvised in a chromatically tonal way, gradually introducing pronounced microtonal elements. The timbral sensitivity and diversity remained subsequently in Bley's work with the piano though there was little further exploitation of the synthesiser technologies, at least until 1986.

Finally, we can consider Bley's compositional development. It is striking that most of his recordings since beginning his own groups have revolved around compositions of Carla Bley and Annette Peacock, two of his personal intimates, but hardly around his own. Their pieces have been recorded over and over again, while input of fresh materials from Bley himself has been limited. The style of these two composers, at least in their work for Bley, is inextricably linked with that of Bley himself, particularly from the harmonic and rhythmic points of view. Very few Bley works are on the early recordings: he contributed to the 'Suite for Germany' (jointly credited to Bley/Giuffre and Swallow but obviously extensively improvised); and 'Turning Point' and 'King Kong' are Bley tunes.

By 1970, although instrumentation and ensemble might vary (solo to quartet; piano to synthesiser; and particularly with regard to players), the repertoire remained fairly constant. The harmonic construction and general approach of these compositions is very much in keeping with Bley's own earlier improvised work, and it may well be that these two composers' styles were derived from study of his work. But in any case the congruence of approach they offer is sufficient explanation for his lack of compositional input. Indeed, it is surprising on some later recordings such as *Fragments* (1986) to find several, presumably new, Bley originals (such as 'Memories') appearing in the company of the evergreens of the Bley repertoire. This is perhaps due to the departure of Peacock and Carla Bley to develop their own musical activities independently.

In sum, the compositional input of Bley has been slight. His main developments have been in emancipating a polytonal style based on very large intervals, space within chords, and a few chosen favoured intervals (such as major sevenths and minor ninths). His rhythmic development was little pursued, while his timbral developments were highly effective, though limited. He is thus an example of an individual pursuing primarily one aspect of improvisatory development, timbral control, while obviously sophisticatedly aware of the additional coincident streams of improvising evolution around him.

Andrew Hill

Whereas Bley is clearly most involved with improvising and performance, it is less obvious that the same is true of Andrew Hill. The subtle rhythmic devices he uses might be described as primarily compositional or as primarily improvised: they are important in both contexts, and I have chosen to discuss him here in the context of pianistic improvising, among other reasons, because his compositions are rarely heard without Hill among the performers.

Hill was born in Haiti in 1937 and performed with Charlie Parker at the age of 14. Since then he has worked with an array of musicians, including Roland Kirk. His earliest recordings include some as sideman, in particular for saxophonist Joe Henderson. It is worth noting some of Hill's harmonic and rhythmic devices on this work. On *Our Thing* (1963) the 'Blues Teeter Totter' (in B♭) has Hill accompanying with very sparse chords, often bare sevenths and sixths, or seconds. There are even a few of Thelonius Monk's open major ninths, and some minor ninths. At the same time there are in separate passages chords built around fourths resulting from the modal stream of improvising discussed earlier. On Dorham's 'Pedro's Time' and on the blues, Hill shows a propensity for voicing chords with adjacent semitones in the middle, such as G/A♭ on a B♭ root chord (i.e. between sixth and seventh) and A/D/E♭ on a C root minor chord (i.e. between second and third). But unlike many of the Bill Evans voicings we have considered earlier, the semitones are between the sixth/seventh of the chords or the second and third rather than, for instance, the seventh and the root. There are also the characteristic bare augmented fourths shared by Bley.

But most interesting are the incipient rhythmic devices, such as the 4:3 pattern shown in Fig. 7.9 where four crotchets are placed in the time of three, and then subdivided unequally. Two of these groups occupy six beats and a minim then completes a two-bar phrase, as in the work of the Miles Davis rhythm section on pieces like 'Milestones', but with very

Fig. 7.9 Hill on 'Teeter Totter' from *Our Thing* (Joe Henderson).

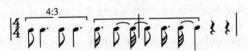

The two patterns are identical, and the second is written so as to indicate where the (submerged) barline occurs.

different nature, because of the more complex subdivision of the three beat phrases.

When we consider larger scale rhythmic devices, we should note that Hill's ideas were not unique in his circle, and some are prefigured by Henderson, for instance in his tune 'Our Thing'. This consists of a repeating structure of eight plus ten bars of 4/4, followed by sixteen of 6/8 (where a semibreve of 4/4 equals a dotted minim of 6/8, or bar equals bar in length), and concludes with ten bars of 4/4 at the original pulse. Within the sixteen bars of 6/8, bars 5–8 are treated as if 4/4 again. But Hill already shows an exceptional flexibility of rhythmic approach by his improvising in the 6/8 sections: in one pattern, starting from duplet quavers, Hill increases the number of notes per 6/8 bar irregularly (as in Indian music) until he reaches a huge flurry of notes, passing through several identifiable approximations to six and nine notes per bar. This indicates his capacity to subdivide bars into any number of notes, equally or unequally, and particularly to group unequal patterns over several bars. Thus in his work as sideman with other leaders, Hill revealed that he had consolidated a fairly individual harmonic approach derived from Bill Evans, and perhaps to some degree from Paul Bley. But he revealed remarkable potential for rhythmic innovation.

In the same year (1963), Hill made several Blue Note recordings under his own leadership. The group of albums he made between 1963 and 1965 are full of inventions in respect of improvising procedures, and particularly in regard to rhythmic approaches. Only a small selection of them can be discussed, so as to illustrate the developmental points. Perhaps the most remarkable of the 1963 recordings is the album *Smokestack*. This uses the unusual instrumentation, on all but one track, of piano, two double basses and drums. One of the bass players was Richard Davis, who has always been reluctant to play repeated crotchets in the familiar walking bass style of the hard bop era. The other, Eddie Khan, was also a flexible player. Roy Haynes, the drummer, had played effectively with

Fig. 7.10 Richard Davis's bass patterns.

Roy Haynes's basic rhythms on 'Smokestack'.

Fig. 7.11 '30 Pier Ave': Andrew Hill.

Slow 4; triplet quaver feel.

everyone from Parker to Coltrane, and has continued to do so ever since. He has always tended to accent a smaller proportion of the normally accented beats than most drummers, and to play triplet patterns over large numbers of beats. Hill delineated several layers of rhythmic function in this group. Haynes sticks relatively closely to the pulse; Davis plays characteristic two- and three-quaver and triplet patterns (Fig. 7.10), rather than crotchets, and usually occupies a high register (the octave below middle C in absolute pitch). Khan oscillates between a conventional bass function (regular crotchets in largely scalar patterns), and a lower register version of the same flexible approach Davis adopts. A lot of the time Hill plays primarily with Haynes, so that a clear rhythmic impulse is provided by piano and drums, and one or two more layers of rhythmic complexity are provided by the two bass players. (This is true even on the piece which is played only by the trio, without Khan.) Fig. 7.10 also illustrates some of Haynes's basic rhythms on 'Smokestack'. Hill's cross-rhythms include 5:3 and 5:4 in crotchets on 'Ode to Vine' (which is in 4/4). On 'Smokestack' he uses 3:4 rhythms (in crotchets as in Fig. 7.10). Besides these rhythms, which are simple changes in frequency of repetition of a note or chord, or simple phrase, there are others in which the rhythm is simple but the pattern of notes within it changes to create the cross-rhythm (see Fig. 7.11 from '30 Pier Ave').

The layering of rhythms is at its most interesting on 'Wailing' (Fig. 7.12). Haynes seems to play a pulse four times faster than Hill, and Davis plays a pattern several times whose pulse is only a quarter as fast as Hill's. Haynes maintains this pattern insistently, and Khan sometimes plays the 4/4 pulse implied by Hill. At the end of the bass solo which Davis also derives from the semibreves he plays at the beginning, and which is accompanied by some clear 4/4 from Khan, the drums move to a triplet pulse which is now only twice Hill's speed, and this is supported by Khan's rhythms.

If the layers of rhythms on 'Wailing' are organised by Hill, they also depend very strongly on their continued improvisation; and on the overlaying within individual parts of cross-rhythms unconventional in their reliance on groupings of 5 and 7 notes and their irregular positioning in relation to bar lines. In a complementary way the clear pulse in 'Catta' (from *Dialogue*) hides a similar complexity of rhythmic layers built into the composition (Fig. 7.13).

Fig. 7.12 'Wailing': rhythmic elements.

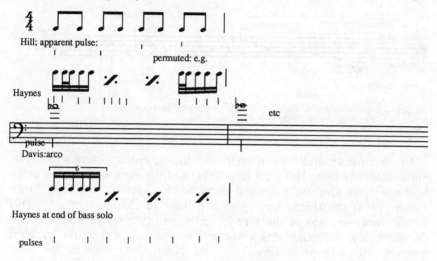

In the piece 'Les Noirs Marchent' on the same record, a simple March rhythm, echoed by Davis's recurring patterns, is used to move in and out of time. Thus although there is a clear 3/4 metre in the middle of this piece, there are parts with no clear pulse, and, interestingly, some use of the continuous sustaining power of the bass-played arco, to generate glissandi round an interval of an augmented fourth (Davis's routine interval) with no clear articulations of rhythm at all. Furthermore, on 'Premonition' (Fig. 7.14) there is essentially no regularly pulsed section. Several other interesting but simpler examples of layering of rhythms occur. For example, a simple pattern of alternating 6/4 and 12/8 is the basis of 'Limbo'.

Fig. 7.13 'Catta' opening rhythms.

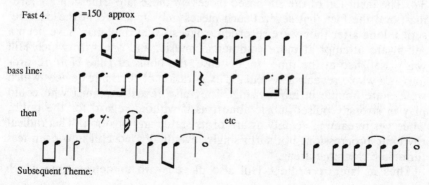

115

Fig. 7.14 'Premonition' from *Compulsion*.

The piece is based on six units of material (1-6 above), which each soloist uses as he will. Note the alternations of semitones E, Eb; D, Db; B, Bb.

The records around 1965–8 seem a slight regression in terms of rhythmic complexity from Hill's earlier works, and the devices are more often of the simpler kind we have just described in 'Limbo'. On *Dance with Death* (1968) the theme has again a pattern of changing metres. This album, however, was in the reissue series, in other words not issued at the time, and although many fine performances, particularly by Hill, probably still lurk to be issued by Blue Note, some such as this have serious mistakes. Some of the themes on this record are very simple, almost recreations of the 'Sidewinder' (by Lee Morgan) patterns of 8/8 rhythm and virtually three-chord harmonic structure, which were part of the jazz soul origins. 'Eutope' (from *One for One*) alternates fast 4/4 with 12/8 bars equal in length to two of the 4/4 bars. Throughout this session Joe Chambers (like Haynes earlier) takes the role of prime pulse generator, while Davis provides the sense of rhythmic freedom by his irregularity of pattern and accentuation. On 'Eris' (from 1969) Hill and Chambers both generate repeatedly 3:4 (crotchets) and 5:4 (minims) group cross-rhythms. This piece has almost no harmonic change, revolving around A/Eb played by Davis frequently. It also has some of the 'Sidewinder' rhythm as in the 8/8 section during Hubbard's solo. Of the 1970 recordings on this record, 'One for One' is really in 4/4, but because of the forcefulness of Ron Carter's playing of the varied bass riff, sometimes seems to be in 5/4 + 3/4, with an occasional apparent 5/4 + 4/4 + 3/4. The inclusion of the 8/8-based pieces on these late Blue Note recordings, and the fact that several such pieces only appeared in the 'reissue' series, long after they were recorded, suggests that they may have been a self-aware attempt at more commercial music, and one with which Hill was dissatisfied at the time. In any case, the bolus of Blue Note recordings as a whole reveals a systematic exploration of rhythmic devices which were quite unique in improvising. They also reveal a pianist who could play in strongly pulsed music almost as if without regard for the pulse, while yet remaining acutely aware of its status and position. This radical rhythmic progression, not surprisingly, eventually led Hill into even less formulaic rhythmic areas.

Thus in later recordings Hill also played with unmetred time which

Fig. 7.15 Elements of 'Verne' from Hill's *Smokestack*.

nevertheless had very clear 'impulses' (as discussed earlier) of between eight and twelve repetitions. For example, with Altschul on 'Spiral' there are several repetitions of each impulse rate; and with Waits on 'Mist Flower' (1980) each particular speed of impulse used by the drums again tends to be repeated between eight and twelve times.

This gives a rhythmic pulse that can be detected rapidly, and then changed for the next pulse every second or so; this is rather different from the routine free jazz pulse discussed already, where two factors often force an impression of continuous pulse change, and continuous overlap of different pulses. These factors are: first, that the notes in a group are usually identical in length for only two or three successive impacts, and then accelerate or decelerate; and second, that several different impact frequencies are usually coexisting all the time, and do not bear comprehensible integral relations with each other so that they do not cohere into a single overall pulse (unlike the situation with Hill's records). As noted, a response to free jazz time on the part of some listeners and some players is to feel pulses of relatively long duration (about one and a half seconds) without particular expectation of accentuation concurring with this. This again is distinct from the impression of Hill's pulses.

His harmonic and motivic sense also developed progressively its unusual initial features. Fig 7.15 shows elements of 'Verne' where there are bare chords (E♭maj7), a very unorthodox progression for jazz (the Fm7 to G# chord), and a brutal example of false relations (the B♭ bar with D and D♭). By *Compulsion*, Hill was prepared to use very limited motivic materials for the improvisation (Fig. 7.16). Almost the whole of this piece is derived from the F and G♭ (motive a) stated near the outset. The

Fig. 7.16 Motivic materials in Hill's *Compulsion*.

117

remainder is derived from motive b. Fig. 7.14 illustrates the whole materials of 'Premonition', in which each soloist uses such elements of this material as he chooses. It is notable that even in this limited material, most of which is in a G minor mode, two cunning juxtapositions are made to force motivic tension: the E natural preceding the low E♭ in the third phrase; and the B natural preceding the B♭ in the final phrase. Also interesting is the way motivic single line material is presented throughout, leading to an avoidance of tonality, but only towards the end is an additional (or alternative) harmonic base for improvising (the A♭ and G♭ chords) offered (allowing a return to tonality). On the *Compulsion* record Hill uses clusters systematically, sometimes only two adjacent semitones, much more often several notes in a range of four tones. This again helps from time to time to dispel any sense of tonal centre, and it depends partly for that effect on its regular intermittent juxtaposition with clear tonal implications. This use of clusters contrasts with that of Cecil Taylor, in whose playing long passages are full of clusters without any intermittent tonal statement; though in his later work tonal statements, reminiscent of the impressionist composers, have also become more frequent. It is interesting that tonal centres seem more important for Hill on his later recordings: for example, on *Strange Serenade*, even though the bass is played microtonally by Alan Silva, the piece 'Mist Flower' has a very clear E tonal centre for at least the last half of its fifteen and a half minutes. Perhaps this is another example of the radical evolution leading to reaction.

Hill was systematically using clusters on the *Compulsion* record not solely in order to undermine tonality but also, as he states on the sleeve, to treat the piano as a percussive instrument. He was concerned with textural devices in music, but in most cases through his compositions and his interactions with other players during performance, rather than through his own playing of the piano. This instance was an exception, and a few other examples, such as the huge glissandi on 'Legacy', occur. Most of the effective textural contrast was built into the performances by the use of contrasting instruments and tones (Dolphy's saxophone tone versus Gilmore; Henderson with Maupin; Konitz versus Kenyatta; bass clarinet and flute in addition to the saxophone; and the remarkable combination of two basses on *Smokestack*). Less successful was the recording with classical string quartet, whose contributions are not integrated, and seem unnecessary. Hill also encouraged the timbral explorations of his collaborators such as John Gilmore by the openness of the structures he offered (for example, 'Premonition' and 'Compulsion', already discussed).

So Hill's profound interest in simultaneous layering of rhythm (as opposed to successive development of rhythmic relationships, which was a subsidiary interest) was combined with unusual harmonic and motivic devices. Textural and timbral development was largely induced in the other musicians playing with Hill, rather than produced by Hill himself. His evolution, and eventual reaction back towards tonality, represent an achievement of an acute intelligence applied systematically.

Wolfgang Dauner

Hill contrasts clearly with our next subject, Wolfgang Dauner, who shares an interest in rhythm, if in a rather different way, but who has concentrated more on timbral and textural devices in his own playing. Dauner (born in Stuttgart, Germany, in 1935) has stated that jazz should swing, but at the same time emphasised that this requires neither traditional roles for bass, drums and piano, nor direct statements of the pulses against which the swing is generated (sleeve notes to his first album as leader, *Dream Talk*, of 1964). Thus he has driven his trio towards a position of melodic and rhythmic equality. For instance, on 'Dream Talk' the melodic line, deriving from an F to B progression, is stated in the bass, and characteristic harmonic voicings in the piano involve the same notes, and also other transpositions of it. There are often adjacent semitones within these chords. There is no stated pulse, but a very slow four is discernible throughout. Even on this early recording Dauner shows signs of interest in extending piano timbres, by strumming chords inside on the same piece. Besides adjacent semitones in chords, Dauner is also fond of adjacent tones, moving in parallel as on the striking left-hand passage of 'Long Night', and of constructing chords with groups of tones and semitones close together, usually over a pitch range of about a fourth.

The harmonic range in the pieces on the *Dream Talk* album is fairly limited, and an F to B motive on 'Dream Talk' even recurs on 'Long Night'. 'Zehn Notizen' has a fast rhythmic impetus, based on sextuplets, and clear-cut rhythms like this also are present on the main recording to be discussed here, the innovative *Free Action*.

Turning first to the title piece 'Free Action', which reveals Dauner's integration of painting and music in having his work on the cover, and using a graphic score (like 'Free Action Shot', Fig. 7.17). The main emphasis is now the textural and timbral uses of the ensemble, with the rhythmic aspects subordinated. As Dauner says (liner notes), he has used instruments in pairs to provide internal contrast: violin and sax/clarinet, cello and bass, two percussionists, and (prepared) piano. Thus the two percussionists may be differentiated by playing different instruments (tabla and percussion on 'Disguise') or by playing successively when accompanying different members of the group (as on 'Sketch Up and Dauner', a simple 24-bar structure). Their different rhythmic concepts are thus revealed and exploited.

In an analogous way the whole of *Free Action* oscillates between clear tonal centres, via clusters, to microtonal and glissando-based playing where tonal centres are at least undermined if not destroyed. These

119

Fig. 7.17 Dauner's 'Free Action Shot', reproduced from the album cover.

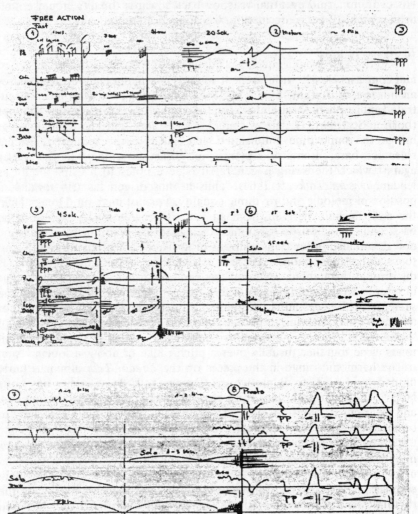

microtonal fluctuations are produced on all instruments: even those not normally associated with pitch change, like the percussion, where changing pressure on the surface of a drum at the same time as striking it can cause a change in pitch centre.

The oscillation between tonally centred and atonal, or microtonal, is most obvious on 'Spanish Disguise'. Mostly the tonal centre is A (A suspended fourth) though sometimes D is used instead as the bass. The piece is in 6/8 though the theme has a 4:3 (primarily in quavers) rhythmic basis. There are several soloists, and each begins freely, atonally, and then moves to a tonal centre, and into a clear pulse. At the outset we hear the prepared piano, where the high piano notes are made to generate differentiated wood block sounds (this recurs at the end). Other prepared piano areas generate clanging metallic sounds (nails, pieces of metal, etc.) but a central area of the keyboard is kept free for normal sounds; another area is simply damped, producing new overtones, but no fresh percussive element. This is one of a handful of recordings which use the prepared piano in improvisation, as compared with the larger number using it in composition, following Cage's 'Music of Changes', etc. Clusters and microtonal pitch flux, glissandi, etc., are used in the free sections by everyone in the ensemble.

Dauner is thus revealing the composer-improviser's capacity to marshal improvising resources, and doing so in a variety of novel and imaginative ways. Perhaps the most interesting piece is 'Free Action Shot' (Fig. 7.17), where a graphic score controls direction of pitch flux, degree of activity, and dynamic, and occasionally suggests the use of harmonics, etc. The score directly encourages the use of glissandi, generating a continuous microtonal pitch flux, and undermining the tonal centres, as Dauner himself mentions on the sleeve note.

Also very interesting is 'Collage', in which Dauner acts as conductor ('while conducting is also the composer' (sleeve note)). His conducting seems mainly to control which combinations of instruments are in action at any time, but also the movement through a sequence of episodes: from free playing, to a rhythmic section in which piano and drums concentrate on a C minor centre, while Dudek (saxophones) uses A♭ G♭ E♭ D♭ as motivic notes: in other words he uses two of the most foreign notes, G♭ and D♭, and two within Cm. He treats these as if they had a common D♭ centre. This semitone conflict of tonal centres is another way of achieving tonal ambiguity and again it is combined with the microtonal work. This is an illustration of controlling the progression of an improvisation by extra-musical signs within it; an interesting process for which there are surprisingly few precedents (such as the limited control exerted during performance by Mingus over his groups, relating to speeds, acceleration, and sections to be played). Although it cannot be deduced from the recording, it is quite probable that Dauner controlled the schism between the two tonal centres to some degree, perhaps so as to maximise their fusion and hence to minimise tonal impression. The psychology of such real-time control for the composer-improviser is discussed further in Chapter 10.

Thus Dauner has particularly emphasised textural and timbral development, and he has followed this up later (for instance, on Mangelsdorff's *A Jazz Tune*). He has used the synthesiser extensively (for instance, on *Output*), and microtonal flux and timbral variety then became more

121

readily large-scale. However, all the fundamental ideas sprang to life in *Free Action*, and were continued. The jazz improviser of *Dreamtalk* had taken advantage, in one large jump, of the compositional variety around him in the musical world. But he had done so in a clearly directional way: like most of the other groups, individuals, and their treatment of particular musical elements which we are discussing, his progression was away from the formulaic. And it was away from the most fundamental of formulae within previous improvisation, the tonal system, not only towards atonality, but further towards microtonality. He paralleled the more intensive developments of this kind in the work of AMM and the electronic groups.

Joachim Kuhn

Next we will consider Joachim Kuhn, another piano player, this time from East Germany. Kuhn's first relatively accessible recording (that is, excluding some made in East Germany) was *Transfiguration* (in 1967): he is a little younger than Dauner. He is distinguished from the other musicians (apart from myself) discussed in this chapter by his initial concentration almost entirely on generating atonal music. Whereas elements of atonality have been commented on in relation to all the other musicians, they have arisen from more tonal contexts and antecedents: conversely, in Kuhn's case they were well formed in the early recordings, and then were diminished in subsequent ones, to be replaced by textural and timbral elements, which were juxtaposed with the new tonality; a postmodern progression.

Thus 'Transfiguration' uses an atonal motive, divided between clarinet and piano (six pitches) and vibes (four new pitches), as illustrated in Fig. 7.18. And Kuhn's improvising exploits this closely, so as to minimise tonal implications. Thus he uses clusters, and pairs of minor ninths (one on top of another, for example, E/F (m9 above) /F# (m9 above again)), which, of course, are just widely spread derivatives of such clusters. There are no defined chords or specified bases for improvisation. Rhythmically Kuhn uses many quintuplets and septuplets, again distinguishing himself from most other musicians discussed so far. Hill had arrived at irregular five- and seven-note groups occupying a given space of time, as we have discussed, but Kuhn springs immediately into a fairly precise, almost equally spaced, usage of the five and seven subdivision. He also

Fig. 7.18 Motive for Kuhn's 'Transfiguration'.

uses sextuplets grouped in fives; and besides these unusual rhythmic features, even for 1967, there are some direct pulse shifts such as a slowing of pulse rate to three-quarters of the preceding.

On the other pieces on the record Kuhn develops many of the same features more extensively – for instance, clusters with two hands rising to the top of the piano in a fast repeated pattern (on 'Lunch Date'). But at the same time he reveals an awareness of the usage of chords in fourths developed by Tyner and earlier in modal playing, as on 'Solo Flight'. Timbrally, he develops scraping of the strings ('Solo Flight') to produce both harmonic and fundamental, but also metallic tones.

The other musicians on the recording reveal a comparable technical development. Berger on vibes plays two lines simultaneously in two registers (for example, in 'Lunch Date'); and uses selective damping of notes (as on the bass solo on 'Solo Flight') so that his instrument's timbre is almost transformed into that of the xylophone. And rhythmically, Berger generates a two-thirds pulse-rate decrease which is supported by the other musicians ('Solo Flight'). Some tonal centres emerge, for example, on 'Stroke of Fall' where an E centre emerges even though the motive has a forceful flattened fifth.

Kuhn thus started work in a European environment, but one certainly not confined to eastern Europe. His elder brother, the clarinettist Rolf, had moved to the USA in the mid-1950s, and Joachim subsequently also went to work and record there. This allows a fascinating comparison of playing styles in Europe and in the USA reflected in the work of one individual. The contrast is emphasised on *Impressions of New York* (recorded in New York in 1967 shortly after Joachim's arrival) where the Kuhn brothers play with Coltrane's bass player, who strums his tonal chords as if playing with Coltrane (for example, A/D/A, followed by A/D/Bb, and then A/D/C). This induces or at least coexists with a set of motivic improvisations which are much more modal in the work of both Joachim and Rolf Kuhn, though Rolf, because of the microtonal possibilities of the clarinet, is more able to undermine them. The same is true of 'Prediction', though the introduction of notes foreign to the C minor centre (usually Bb or F#) and of clusters in Joachim's playing counteracts this somewhat. Piano chords in fourths are common, and Rolf also plays several simple motives based on fourths. The drum solo on 'Predictions' (though played by the Italian, Aldo Romano) is also closer to the simpler rhythmic traditions of the Coltrane environment.

Thus in a European context, Kuhn and his brother Rolf emerged fully formed with an atonal improvising style which was novel. In the American context, working with a more conservative musician, they were able also to adapt, though they were less at ease perhaps, to a modal context, and still superimposed their own idioms. In Kuhn's recording (*Eternal Rhythm*) with another American leader, the American Indian Don Cherry, Kuhn was more at equilibrium. The music was based on relatively simple modal structures, but more unusual rhythmic bases. Kuhn strums the inside of the piano, and plays massive clusters during the collective improvisation ('Autumn Melody'). The sleeve note refers to prepared piano on this album, just as with Dauner in 1967, but this is not readily audible on the recording.

Kuhn's other 1969 recordings (such as *Mad Rockers*) introduce a concept of extremely simple rhythmic devices and equally simple harmonies, against which some free textures ('I'm a Jew'), with funk elements retained, begin to emerge. This they called 'free rock' (a self-aware contradiction in terms), and it is technically rather less interesting than the previous works. But in 'Out of Traffic' there are collage elements at work in that sea and gull sounds are used at the beginning and end of the piece, and intermittently within it, in a more European (and more romantic) equivalent of the postmodern collage of Bob James (where more industrial urban sounds are used: R75). These environmental elements in each case could be taken to reflect the influence of John Cage and his ideas, as mentioned elsewhere in this book. Similarly, there are space launch sounds on 'Rocking Chair to the Moon', together with tape slowing and respeeding. Not only, therefore, is there collage and environmental impact, but also pastiche, since many of the musical elements played live are recreations of earlier styles. 'Going West' again has sea waves.

The simple tonality reintroduced into Kuhn's work in this *Mad Rocker* album has been retained since, but developed alongside an increasing interest in timbral and textural possibilities, including microtonal ones. Thus on *Paris Is Wonderful*, there are themes with very simple major seventh chord progressions but at the same time rapidly moving clusters ('Love Is Here'); and the clusters (cf. Cecil Taylor) are sustained by tremolos and pedalling so that the tones continue coexisting for long periods. In addition, Kuhn plays the alto saxophone as well as the piano, and produces a vast array of multiphonics and glissandi (Fig. 7.19). Again a microtonal effect can be achieved, and several components contribute: for instance, the use of tremolos of several adjacent, or even widespread pitches; or alternatively, the generation of more continuously sustained multiphonics, where several constituent pitch centres, even if not entirely stable, each last for some time.

The rhythmic basis of the 1969 *Paris* album is very free, with little retained pulse. In contrast, on *Open Strings* (1971), with Jean-Luc Ponty

Fig. 7.19 Kuhn's elements on 'Love is Love' from *Paris is Wonderful*.

(violin), Kuhn is placed in a more conventional rhythmic environment, and sounds a little inflexible in his timing ('Part 1'). But the timbral influence is still apparent, and reaches some of the other players (for example, the guitar is played with a bow, col legno on *Open Strings* as is the rhythmic opening on the violin). But it is mainly in Kuhn's own records that the interesting developments are found. On *Sounds of Feelings* Kuhn plays on individual strings of the piano both inside and outside simultaneously. Conversely, he also uses simple pentatonic patterns on the keyboard (on the piece 'Shadows'). 'In the Middle' is the most interesting textural piece on this record, because of its almost continuous pitch flux, generated by shenai (Kuhn, with flute and bass intermingling). There is an interlude in the middle of the piece with bells, and then a simple linear pattern is used to generate a complex texture with singing, glissandi, double stop high harmonics, slides, and arpeggios on bass. After an active alto sax solo, there is Indian-like singing with syllables and phonemes, probably done by Kuhn, while drums play simple triplets. Some of the same elements are apparent on *Monday Morning* (1969) with a larger group, but they are mostly submerged within more traditional devices, such as in 'Oh Grandpa', which is based on a tango rhythm, but juxtaposes it with free improvising.

Kuhn has since made several solo piano albums. These lack much interest in rhythmic matters, as one might by now guess, but they do exploit many of the different conventional and unconventional piano techniques, for example, in *Solos* (1971), tonality (piece 1), Amsus4 with major seventh chords (piece 2), and figurations in fourths (piece 2). But on piece 5, there are tremolo chords, and then very sparse brief bursts, of a kind rarely achieved in group improvising, followed by plucks alternating with on-the-key patterns. After more tremolo chords, there is a dense passage of scratching on the strings which produces an array of timbres and textures.

Kuhn's attitudes expressed on the sleeve of this record are interesting: he comments on his European origins, and states that he played 'free jazz' for two years (distinctly in the past), making the implication that it was no longer for him. Presumably the implied corollary was that improvised music related to the European composing tradition might be more suitable for him. Nevertheless, on subsequent recordings he has retained blues elements and modal harmonies; but still in relation to inside piano damping, and rapidly moving arpeggiated clusters which move from one clear tonality or modality to another (e.g. Dm to Am) on 'Chords'.

Equally, on *This Way Out* (1973), though again stating that he 'plays European music', Kuhn plays some jazz standards, with a rather limited freedom from the basic rhythmic and harmonic pattern employed. Some of the by now familiar rhythmic patterns based on the three-beat structure laid against 4/4 bars (3 + 3 + 2 = 8, i.e. two bars of 4/4) are present but not extended in any way. As noted already, Humair does use triplets to produce interesting irrational structures such as 3(2/3)/4. In later work Kuhn has had many forays into commercial jazz-rock work, while intermittently releasing solo albums with many of the qualities discussed above; there is mainly consolidation, however.

Kuhn's most interesting contributions have thus been textural and timbral, and the emphasis on harmonic devices which was paramount (in avoiding tonality) in the early work has diminished. He illustrates the intense influence of the European movement in the early twentieth century to atonality, and also the overt intention of producing a European improvised music. Perhaps he neglects the possibility that 'free jazz' (as so called by its participants in Europe) might be very different from free jazz in the USA: we will discuss this in a later chapter. Most interesting is that he reached a reaction to tonality early in his career, but continued to exploit with it both atonal and microtonal elements, together with textural, thereafter. Thus the unidirectional or univalent approach is not for Kuhn and the extreme stylistic contrasts within his music are an attractive feature.

Roger Dean

Stylistic diversity is also an objective within my own improvising work. But while pulsed rhythmic flexibility has never seemed very important for Kuhn, for me this has always been among the most appealing possibilities of improvisation. It would not be appropriate, or even perhaps feasible, for me to treat my own work in detail comparable to that above. I will simply mention a few attitudinal aspects of my approaches, such as begin to be revealed in the remarks quoted above from Kuhn. It is probable that a self-analytical stance can reveal more about attitude and ideas than most approaches. Basic biographical information on my musical career is available in A21c, A28, and on my various album-sleeves.

My first improvising objectives when beginning to play with other musicians were to pursue atonal approaches, while developing pulsed playing. Thus for entirely practical reasons (mainly a lack of interest in improvising on the part of musicians involved in contemporary composed music) I first played with jazz musicians (at university) most of whom had come through a conventional background in traditional or early modern jazz. As must be apparent from the existence of this book, part of my musical approach was analytical, and so I realised that to play effectively with such musicians I would need to develop more ability within conventional jazz.

My next objective in improvising, and ever since, was to get the chance to cocreate music, something inaccessible to me as composer of fully notated works. Thus I spent effort on developing modern jazz techniques. At the same time, my long-standing collaborator, Ashley Brown (percussion), starting from a background in traditional jazz, developed a wider range of experience with more contemporary approaches, and knowledge of contemporary composed music.

By the time of our first recording, *Lysis Live* (1976), we had developed both conventional jazz improvising and free improvising, and I had produced compositions for improvising which dictated technical/stylistic approach. Thus the influence of Bill Evans is obvious on some tonal pieces; there is ambitious rhythmic work on others; and the trumpet and piano work reflects an atonal approach. Free improvising, on both piano and double bass, was more extensively represented on *Dualyses*, recorded shortly thereafter. At the same time I remained involved in the mainstream of contemporary jazz in Europe, by being the keyboard player of Graham Collier Music from 1974 until the present, and working with a wide range of jazz musicians from Europe and the USA. Five records with Collier have resulted from this, and some are discussed in Chapters 9 and 10.

Subsequently, I explored a variety of compositional devices which could influence improvisation, first of all in the published literature from other composers, which involved performing Stockhausen in his presence, and working on a range of graphic and text scores. My ensemble, Lysis, broadened into performances of contemporary composed music, making its South Bank debut in London in 1979, and commissioning and premiering many works. From then onwards, Lysis concerts, whether focusing on compositions or not, always included improvised music. Approaches to the text and graphic pieces are discussed in A31.

A fundamental interest was to pursue musical ends which might be specific to improvisation: I assumed this might be achieved by exploiting musical techniques which could perhaps only be developed in that context. In particular, these involved developing, more extensively than previous improvisers, techniques of pulse shift, metrical modulation, overlaying pulses and related devices. These were incorporated in great detail in a long composition, 'Suite: Time' (1980) of which a movement is reproduced in A31 (pp. 102–9). But they were also used routinely in improvising within composed and free contexts, as an important element of pulsed music.

Textural improvising, largely devoid of isolated musical entities, was something I sought in group improvising, particularly when using the members of Lysis most involved with contemporary composed music, but who retained interest in improvisation. This is most reflected on *Superimpositions*. Subsequently, digital synthesisers gave me access to a whole array of such procedures, and, by means of sequencers, to techniques for converting in performance rhythmically defined motivic material into more continuous sound transforming slowly in time.

Textural improvising is one element of improvising which can be harnessed within procedures for improvising. Thus I have constructed schemata for improvising (see earlier) which force the improviser to focus not on musical material, but on how to relate to the progress of other improvising members of the ensemble: a reflection again of my interest in cocreating during improvising. Textural devices and procedural approaches are discussed also in A31.

Although I have not emphasised motivic development much in the above comments, I have taken a strong interest in it, as reflected in my verbal and musical writing. One of my large compositions for improvisers, 'Destructures' (whose title is a postmodern pun), exploits motivic control very carefully, particularly in providing material to be played by Kenny Wheeler (trumpet and flugelhorn) within a composed context, and then to become the basis of his improvising, or to be integrated within it. This large work (around 30 minutes) integrates many other aspects of my improvising interests, such as rhythmic and textural devices.

My compositions and improvising also reflect my intense interests in the other arts. On *Cycles*, the second Lysis album, there is a long work done as a collaboration for a slide show, in which the slides were mostly of industrial objects. While my 1985 work 'You Yangs' (on *Wings of the Whale*) is a response to the Australian abstract painter Fred Williams, and has detailed composed elements, some of which have already been mentioned, another composition, 'The Horses', responds to the contemporary Norwegian painter Frans Widerberg, whose work has strong expressionist elements and involves procedures, and pointers towards effect, rather than any defined musical sounds.

In relation to the evolutionary trends discussed in this book, I stand a little like Joachim Kuhn: interested in progressive lines, now particularly in relation to timbral and microtonal development and the use of live manipulation of synthesisers (for example, in *Something British*; *Wings of the Whale*); but also accepting of a postmodern synthesis of tonal and atonal, and other formulaic elements. American jazz has always been a consuming interest for me, as well as European, and now Australian; and among people active in North America, Bill Evans, Paul Bley (see *Cycles*) and Cecil Taylor (cf. 'Destructures' in parts) have influenced me. Two other pianists whose work interests me are Veryan Weston (for example, *Underwater Carol*) and Chris Abrahams (*Distance* and *Walk*), who come from the UK and Australia, respectively. But in my own work I have always felt part of a rather different development than the American, one which happened to be primarily European (and the composer I most admire is Iannis Xenakis). Very often that development has been heterogeneous, and usually unconventional in relation to the jazz mainstream, though not necessarily in relation to music at large.

Recordings discussed

Abrahams, Chris (1985) *Distance* (with the Benders), Hot HTLP 1015.
Abrahams (1986) *Walk*, Hot 1025.

128

Bley, Paul (1953) *Introducing Paul Bley*, Debut JC-201.

Bley (1958) *The Fabulous Paul Bley Quintet* (with Coleman), America AM 6120.

Bley (1961) *Jazz in the Space Age* (with George Russell Orchestra), Decca DL 9219.

Bley (1961) *Jimmy Giuffre Trio Live in Europe Vol. 1*, Raretone 5018-FC.

Bley (1961) *Jimmy Giuffre Trio Live in Europe Vol. 2*, Raretone 5019-FC.

Bley (1961) (with Giuffre Three) *Masters of the Modern Piano*, Verve CT-2-2514.

Bley (1963) *Sonny Meets Hawk*, RCA RD 7593.

Bley (1964) *Turning Point*, IAI 373841.

Bley (1964/6) *Jazz of the 60s*, Monkey MY 4002.

Bley (1965) *Touching*, Fontana 688 608 ZL.

Bley (1967) *Ballads*, ECM 1010.

Bley (1968) *Mr Joy*, Mercury SMWL 21050.

Bley (1970) *Synthesiser Show*, Milestone MSP 9033.

Bley (1970) *Dual Unity*, Freedom 2383 105.

Bley (1972) *Scorpio*, Milestone M 9046.

Bley (1972) *Open To Love*, ECM 1023.

Bley (1973) *Bley/NHOP*, Steeplechase SCS 1005.

Bley (1974) *Alone Again*, IAI 373840.

Bley (1975) *Quiet Song*, IAI 373839.

Bley (1986) *Fragments*, ECM 1320.

Dauner, Wolfgang (1964) *Dream Talk*, CBS S 62478.

Dauner (1967) *Free Action*, MPS 16017.

Dauner (1967) *Sunday Walk* (with Ponty), MPS 545 112.

Dauner (1970) *Output*, ECM 1006.

Dean, Roger (1975) *Midnight Blue* (with Graham Collier Music), Mosaic GCM 751.

Dean (1976) *Lysis Live*, Mosaic GCM 761.

Dean (1977) *Cycles*, Mosaic GCM 774.

Dean (1978) *The Solo Trumpet 1966–76*, Soma 781.

Dean (1978) *Dualyses*, Soma 782.

Dean (1979) *Lysis Plus*, Mosaic GCM 791.

Dean (1980) *Superimpositions*, Soma 783.

Dean (1987) *The Wings of The Whale*, Soma 784.

Dean (1985) *Something British Made in Hong Kong* (with Graham Collier Music) Mosaic 871.

Hill, Andrew (1963) *Our Thing* (with Henderson), BLP 4152.

Hill (1963) *Smokestack*, BVLP 4160.

Hill (1964) *Point of Departure*, Blue Note CDP 7 84167 2 (CD release of complete session).

Hill (1965) *Dialogue* (with Hutcherson), BLP 4198.

Hill (1965) *Compulsion*, BLP 421.

Hill (1965/70) *One for One*, Blue Note BN-LA-459-H2-0798.

Hill (1968) *Dance with Death*, Blue Note LT-1030.

Hill (1974/5) *Spiral*, Freedom FLP 41007.

Hill (1975) *Live at Montreux*, Freedom FLP 41023.

Hill (1980) *Strange Serenade*, Soul Note SN 1013.

Hill (1980) *Faces of Hope*, Soul Note SN 1010.

Kuhn, Joachim (1967) *Transfiguration* (with Rolf Kuhn), Saba SB 15118.

Kuhn (1967) *Impressions of New York* (with Rolf Kuhn), Impulse A-9158.
Kuhn (1968) *Eternal Rhythm* (with Don Cherry as leader), MPS 15007.
Kuhn (1968) *Mad Rockers* (with Rolf Kuhn), Goody GY 3005.
Kuhn (1969) *Sounds of Feelings*, BYG 529.317.
Kuhn (1969) *Paris is Wonderful*, BYG 529.346.
Kuhn (1969) *Monday Morning*, Columbia SHZE 909BL.
Kuhn (1971) *Solos*, Futura GER 18.
Kuhn (1971) *Piano*, MPS 2121330-7.
Kuhn (1971) *Open Strings* (with Jean-Luc Ponty), MPS 21 21288-2.
Kuhn (1973) *This Way Out*, MPS 88.022-2.
Mangelsdorff, Albert (1969) *Mangelsdorff and His Friends* (one track with Dauner), MPS 15.210.
Mangelsdorff (1978) *A Jazz Tune I Hope*, MPS 15.528.
Weston, Veryan (1987) *Underwater Carol*, Matchless MR 12.

8 Free improvisation: Europe, America, Asia and Australasia

In this chapter I will discuss developments in free improvisation, and how differently they have proceeded in the USA and Europe. I will also comment on developments in other regions of the world, for free improvising has become a world discourse. A diverse range of attitudes to society are held by the participants, and they envisage their music relating variously to sociopolitical influence, if at all.

I start with a quotation (written after the Second World War) from the pioneering Australian composer Percy Grainger, who was a supporter (and, on occasion, an employer) of Duke Ellington:

> Existing conventional music (whether 'classical' or the popular) is tied down by set scales, a tyrannical (whether metrical or irregular) rhythmic pulse that holds the whole tonal fabric in a vice-like grasp and a set of harmonic procedures (whether key-bound or atonal) that are merely habits, and certainly do not deserve to be called laws. Many composers have loosened, here and there, the cords that tie music down. Cyril Scott and Duke Ellington indulge in sliding tones; ... Cyril Scott (following my lead) writes very irregular rhythms that have been echoed on the European continent by Stravinsky, Hindemith and others ... But no non-Australian composer has been willing to combine *all* these innovations into a consistent whole that can be called *free-music* (A41, emphasis in original).

> About improvisation – it's a uniquely American way of making music, just as normal in our society as motets must have been in another (Harold Budd in A23).

In earlier chapters, and elsewhere (A65), it has been emphasised how jazz improvisation in the USA and other countries led to a loosening of the control of rhythmic and harmonic elements in the early 1960s. Fixed metre was abolished by musicians such as Cecil Taylor, and sometimes

131

John Coltrane. Fixed harmonic bases were reduced by Coltrane, and eventually removed by Coleman and Taylor. Motivic improvising was not undermined, however; though in some contexts it was replaced by textural.

As pointed out in the earlier discussion of modernist versus postmodernist views of jazz development, much of the subsequent work in the USA has striven forcefully to retain at least some elements of the preceding jazz convention, however much others might have been displaced. Thus in the discussion of the Jazz Composers' Orchestra Association in a later chapter, we will see how the first and unusual recordings of Mantler are much outside conventional jazz harmonies and rhythms; some, such as parts of the piece featuring Larry Coryell, even undermining motivic continuity in favour of sonic textural continuity (probably using 'distortion' (A35) as primary material). But the subsequent recordings of Mantler, Bley, Rudd and Moncur, the members of the Association, have reasserted rhykhmic conventions, and often brought back even more basic harmonic approaches, and march rhythms, etc. The same is true of most of the AACM musicians, several of whom developed the Art Ensemble of Chicago and elaborated a diverse style with recreations of much earlier music, at the same time as a theatrical presentation, and an ability to push free jazz improvising to the extremes which still allow it to place itself within jazz. Whatever inaccuracies there may be in Grainger's remarks (see A41 for discussion) his basic sentiment is correctly applicable to most of these American developments. In contrast, if Budd's chauvinistic remarks were apt, then this situation would be unlikely to remain.

To quote Bill Dixon (in A123), after he had just strongly praised Archie Shepp's *Four for Trane*:

> Archie Shepp has been PAID to learn how to 'play' and I'm defining this being able to 'play' within the framework of the definition prevalent among the majority of 'listeners' to the music ... Too much ... has been made about ... 'avant-garde' musicians from the 60s and their ... discovery of the traditional.

If the US free jazz improvisers have not logically pursued the openings they exposed in the 1960s, then what of other free improvising in the USA? Undoubtedly there were some very interesting activities in the late 1950s and 1960s. Some of the material is very inaccessible (for example, R59) although Lukas Foss's ensemble is reasonably represented by later performances. But Larry Austin, who also wrote a work of Third Stream jazz, reviews (in A23) some of the activities in the early 1960s of the improvising New Music Ensemble (NME) on the US west coast. In 1963 it was engaged in free improvisation which led into the development of Musica Elettronica Viva (in 1964–5), and it also even performed some works of Cornelius Cardew, a composer and late addition to AMM in the

UK. To quote Austin: 'First, we consciously ruled out any overt jazz expression. That's not to say we succeeded with that conscious exclusion' (A23).

Indeed, Lukas Foss apparently (see A23) thought they did not. The NME became electrified, and this was much extended by MEV (as it was at the same time by AMM, on which some early historical information is also to be found in A23). Thus it can be argued that the major openings of non-melodic continuity (that is, textural and timbral continuity) and of microtonal improvising were more exposed outside the USA than inside. The few exceptions to this statement are eclectic musicians like AACM member Anthony Braxton, and these exceptions often collaborated widely with European musicians, (in Braxton's case with Parker, Bailey, Wheeler and others), and probably worked more outside than inside the USA. Braxton certainly has had periods of poverty, and continued difficulties with US recording companies, in spite of his major stature; and this has no doubt encouraged him to pursue European opportunities. Braxton is not primarily a free improviser, however:

> I'm not interested in only total improvisation because I don't believe existential anarchy is the highest context ... Structure is part of how evolution is arrived at; but I don't mean any disrespect for collective improvisation. I am an improviser (Braxton in A79, pp. 236–7).

> One of the problems with collective improvisation, as far as I'm concerned, is that people who use anarchy or collective improvisation will interpret that to mean 'Now I can kill you'; and I'm saying, wait a minute! ... So-called freedom has not helped us as a family, as a collective, to understand responsibility better. Only the master musicians, the ones who really understood what they were doing and who did their homework, have been able to generate forward motion. So the notion of freedom that was being perpetrated in the sixties might not have been the healthiest notion (Braxton in A79, p. 240).

Perhaps these quotations will suffice to establish Braxton's ambivalence towards free improvisation, and to indicate some of his metaphysical overtones. We will return to him in Chapter 9, where he more fully belongs as a composer for improvisers.

We should note that other fascinating texts and recordings of improvisation arose also on the US west coast from the efforts of Pauline Oliveros and associates. She reviews much of the background and ideals of these activities in her *Software for People* (A103). To quote an interview she gave (A15):

> Improvisation has always been part of my practice, part of my potential, my possibilities. I have worked from conceptions,

schemes, schematics, from strategies and from maps, from signals
... there are all sorts of ways of working ... It has a central and
important role, but it's modified in various ways.

In general, her objectives were usually meditative, and to do with utilising the whole of the sonic environment, as responder and developer. Her
attitudes were clearly related to those of Cage, and converged somewhat
with those of Schafer already mentioned (p. xix). The concern was not
consistently for the development of the specific technical openings we
have outlined above. Nor, of course, was there any reason it should have
been. David Antin, the improvising poet (see Chapter 11) has some
interesting remarks about Oliveros (A5):

> pauline came to the center of the gallery to tell us how to perform
> the piece ... [we were] to listen until we heard a tone we felt like
> tuning to   to try to tune to it and when we were satisfied with
> our tuning we could fall silent and listen   choose another tone
> and try to tune to it and go on like this listening and tuning and
> falling silent as long as we wished ... i ... tried to join a high tenor
> almost beyond my range the history professor nodded and joined us
> there our dark haired neighbour to the left opened a flute like tone
> a fifth above us   all around the room people were crying and
> smiling and singing in waves of sound that throbbed and swelled

Have the European improvisers attempted any more consistent pursuit
of the new openings, that is the dissolution of the pre-existent formulaic
elements applied in improvising? We must first note some of the early
moves within European jazz towards free improvising, which were concurrent with those in the USA. While there seem to have been few
keyboard players in Europe in the late 1950s working with the harmonic
complexity of Cecil Taylor, there were saxophonists developing motivic
improvising in a direction related to that of Ornette Coleman, which
leads to a subordination of harmony, and more flexible tempo and metre.
An example well reputed, though little known, is the work of Joe Harriott, the West Indian saxophonist working in Britain in the period from
the late 1950s, alluded to already. In two key records (R72; R73),
Harriott systematically explored breaking down conventions relating to
each of the major musical materials. His recordings are difficult to obtain
even in Britain. Thus Harrison (A83, p. 92) describes him with no further
qualification as a 'minor figure'; while Ian Carr (A21c) is misleading in
suggesting of the recordings that 'Harriott's abstraction often had no
regular rhythm'. US critics normally write similarly from a position of
concealed ignorance (see A78, in which the description is inaccurate) or
totally omit reference to this work.

Harriott stated that they wished to maintain at least one of the conventional jazz elements in each piece, and categorised these elements as
follows:

Of the various components comprising jazz today – constant time signatures, a steady four-four tempo, themes and predictable harmonic variations, fixed division of the chorus by bar lines and so on – we aim to retain at least one in each piece. But we may well – if the mood seems to us to demand it – dispense with all the others (liner notes to R73).

But Harriott mentioned wishing to exploit the limits of each element separately, providing one jazz element was retained. So he recorded modal pieces with no fixed mode; pieces with no pulse; and pulsed pieces with complex, unconventional harmonic structures. At the same time his two recordings in this mould still retain some very traditional elements and sound not far removed from the atmosphere of 'Kind of Blue' from a year or two earlier. For example, 'Modal' has no set theme, but an alternation of $E\flat$ minor and major. This alternation is somewhat like $E\flat7\#9$, which has the major third (in $E\flat7$), while the $\#9$ is really the minor third raised an octave.

Some more restrained free improvising is on Stan Tracey's *New Departures* album from 1962, which, according to Victor Schonfield (sleeve notes), represents a style of performance which the group had practised for some time. But the piece mostly holds to an $E\flat$m11 harmonic basis, and the recurrent minor ninths in Tracey's piano are common also in composed and arranged pieces by Tracey (such as 'Under Milk Wood'). The *New Departures* recording has no pulse, but still retains the meditative modal atmosphere of the 'Kind of Blue' idiom. Other European musicians, such as Albert Mangelsdorff, were also pursuing aspects of free jazz improvising in the early 1960s, with a greater emphasis on instrumental technical development than evinced by their American counterparts. So, for example, trombone multiphonics, which reach a peak on Mangelsdorff's *A Jazz Tune*, are also to be found in his early CBS recordings; and Wolfgang Dauner's use of prepared piano and Kuhn's use of inside piano techniques in earlier jazz contexts have already been mentioned.

The radical developments in Europe which had little or no counterpart in the USA were in relation to instrumental timbre and texture, and the development of microtonal, multitimbral and multiphonic sounds and their usage in long time units (as with Breuker, New Phonic Art, Vinko Globokar, and Evan Parker and Derek Bailey); and, in parallel, the development of electronic instruments and transformation of normal instrumental sound (AMM, Oxley, Bailey, MEV, Nuova Consonanza). MEV was probably the main American contribution to this development.

On the route to continuous timbral and textural improvising on instruments, was an offshoot of the high density, continuous multiplicity of action achieved notably on Coltrane's *Ascension* (R26), in which the ensemble passages have a remarkable frequency of event, such that most of the ensemble passages congeal into texture, with only the occasional

Fig. 8.1 Tony Oxley, 'Motive of Preparation' from *Baptised Traveller*.

The row is later played at half speed, and as a canon.

motivic element emerging. Some extreme high-energy offshoots followed, such as the BYG recordings of Burrell and Terroade (mentioned already), and some of the work of the Germans such as Brotzman and Schlippenbach. But it was primarily in the work of the Europeans such as Schlippenbach and Breuker, mentioned in the compositional section, and also in Breuker's work as free improviser outside composed frameworks, that these non-melodic techniques were developed.

I use the term 'melodic' here in a restricted sense, to imply a rooting in a motive based on simple, roughly equal tempered pitches, and not with any pejorative overtone. And the compositional influence on Tony Oxley, for example, led to use of simple serial melodic motives to support motivic and textural improvising beyond the equal tempered (Fig. 8.1). Motivic elements involving multiple pitches, and microtonal elements are, of course, melodic in a broader sense. It was such motivic elements which largely replaced equal tempered motives in the work of Breuker (for example, *New Acoustic Swing Duo*, with Bennink). On this recording we find very dynamic rapidity of action, but also long passages of multiphonics changing in spectrum relatively slowly. Similarly, Evan Parker was developing similar techniques in this period (for example, on a 1969 recording with Pierre Favre entited *This Is Free Jazz*) and eventually his range of microtonal and multiphonic control became quite immense. By means of circular breathing Parker could develop a single sustained sound for the duration of a whole piece, perhaps twenty minutes, as on several later recordings.

Arising more from the classical performance side, the composer-improviser Vinko Globokar (of New Phonic Art (NPA)) developed trombone techniques which were applied in free improvisation with NPA: for example, sung and played multiphonics, continuous pitch flux of several coexistent tones, and precise microtonal playing. He also encouraged the use of other techniques involving the vocal cords not necessarily with the trombone. Mangelsdorff, usually in a more conservative context, also developed these techniques. Thus a very slow development of a texture which was itself very complex could be achieved. This was probably unique within improvised music, although, of course, eclectics such as Braxton and Steve Lacy developed related techniques.

It is interesting that Braxton feels pushed into asserting that Europeans were not the source of his developing such techniques (A79), claiming that when he first worked in Europe in 1969 he had already developed such a language, and possibly neglecting that the New Acoustic Swing Duo had already developed and recorded such techniques also. Braxton's first solo saxophone recording *For Alto* is certainly no more diverse or advanced technically than these other performers' work. Indeed, Braxton does note that he learnt circular breathing, by then a fairly routine technique in contemporary classical performance, from Evan Parker (A79). These questions of priority are neither crucial nor our particular concern here. While some of these techniques were simultaneously developed on brass instruments by performers who were not primarily improvisers (Stuart Dempster: see A31), and similarly on the clarinet and flute (see A12; A55) those on the saxophones and double bass were almost entirely the work of improvisers, as already outlined.

One of the earliest examples of sustained microtonal textural improvising is on *AMM Music*. This joins the two technical threads of this section, instrumental versus electronic generation of unorthodox sounds, since both were involved. Electronic amplification of some percussion instruments which otherwise were virtually inaudible, and also of the guitar, used to generate continuous pitch flux, and the cello, when used similarly, also allow the production of continuous sustained sounds. These factors have been described also in relation to a later recording:

> The spread identity which is the basis of instrumental overlap is physically manifested in the architectural groupings of percussion equipment and the extension of the musician/piano interface ... its most extreme example is the guitar which is literally distributed across space as a wired-up instrument at the centre of an orbital system of electronics and wires, gadgets and bits of 'junk' mostly occupying a work table, and for this recording, including a loose spring attached at one end to the bridge of the instrument and at the other, three feet away, to a wall. Among the various transformations undergone by the sounds for which the guitar is the immediate source, the first is multiplication. This effectively means that what we hear is several images of the guitar, skilfully mixed, but leading to ambiguity as to where, or what, the instrument actually is. Plectra for this instrument included battery-driven fans and radio receivers and these, together with other potential oscillators, allow sound constructions to be set into motion and then left to diminish or to function independently as ostinati until the musician decides to introduce a shift. Because it can be detached from the musician as a necessarily immediate energy source and because it rarely sounds like any known instrument (least of all a guitar!) the 'guitar' helps to underpin the sense of environment by its ability to introduce a continuum. Its builder [Keith Rowe] refers to it, not without humour, as a 'continuo' and this usage reveals an underlying similarity of musical function: just as the continuo provides an anchor for the harmonic work built upon it and supports melodic structures,

the continuum of the guitar generates a noise anchor for the entire group, a source and interference, one that can be musically analysed or ignored (Mitchell, in booklet with *AMM Music*).

As the musicians comment (see liner notes; and A23), each of them often had to stop playing to identify the source of a sound, and then sometimes found it was himself.

AMM was and is a remarkable amalgam of social and musical endeavour. For these improvisers were explicitly bound up with social commitment and ideals. For example, Eddie Prevost, in the same record booklet, says, referring to more than music: 'Part of AMM's continuing ethos and aspiring philosophy is enquiry and encouragement of open-ended concepts and consequently we applaud any who enter the fray.' Thus some of their ideas might be seen as a counter-balance to the case argued in the Introduction (and supported in Appendix 1) that sociological interpretations are as yet dangerous and impoverished as explication. But there remains the unexplained and unbridged gap between their motivations and the music: and the question arises why other musicians arrived at similar technical stances at around the same time, even if mainly in Europe. These latter (for instance, Tony Oxley, who developed amplified percussion possibly even further, as already mentioned, shortly after the first AMM recording) did not obviously share the same social commitments. Similarly, while it might be argued that Nuova Consonanza sprung up in a socialist country (Italy, in 1960) and hence might have been involved with socialist ideals related to the ideals of AMM, the Italian-American counterpart group, MEV (founded 1966), who share the 1968 Mainstream recording with AMM (*Live Electronic Music*), only partly supported such ideals.

The technical features permitted by amplifying otherwise inaudible or non-sustained sounds (the guitar; many constructed 'ready made' percussive sources in the work of Tony Oxley; the piano in the work of Howard Riley and others; the double bass in the hands of Fernando Grillo, and Barry Guy in particular) were also shared by the primarily electronic instruments. Thus in MEV Richard Teitelbaum (having previously experimented with his own 'World Band': see Eaton in A84) used analogue synthesisers to develop long sustained complex textures and microtonal elements, complementing the new resources achieved on the conventional instruments in a remarkable way. He has developed this further (for example, with Braxton) and most recently these techniques have become affordable to many musicians through the cheapening of digital synthesisers, and also more efficiently manipulated with computers. As shown, for example, on the Lysis album *Wings of the Whale*, the use of sequencers with digital synthesisers permits control with rhythmic or metrical precision of textures which otherwise eschew pulse: a convergence of conservative and novel techniques. Some of these are discussed in more detail in A31.

Another feature of the European free improvisers which distinguishes them from the US improvisers has been their frequent willingness to work both in conventional jazz and, at the same time, in the freest improvisation. Some examples have already been mentioned. But it is appropriate to list Kenny Wheeler, who plays with Globe Unity Orchestra and at the same time works with Parker, Bailey and Braxton and conventional groups; and Tony Oxley, who retains a capacity for dynamic pulse-based drumming (with Bill Evans R58; Alan Skidmore, *Once Upon A Time*; Wheeler, *Song for Someone*; and more recently with the European Jazz Quintet and SOH), while at the same time playing with the Incus musicians and other European free improvisers and, since 1988, sometimes with Cecil Taylor. Possibly this diversity is simply an economic necessity, though it is one which is largely avoided, for example, by Parker and Bailey.

I started this chapter with a striking statement by the innovative Australian composer Percy Grainger: his challenge has now been met. So we can conveniently ask briefly here whether his challenge has been met not only in Europe and America but also in Australasia and elsewhere. In Japan an early improvising electronic group was the Taj Mahal Travellers (A100), but I have not yet been able to hear any of their work. Yamashita, the pianist who shares Cecil Taylor's high-energy dynamism and reliance on clusters, has gained wide exposure (see *Piano Duo Live at Pit Inn*). He is a most powerful performer, and his work clearly has several individual features, notably, in recent time, an emphasis on clipped repetitive rhythms, akin to some systemic or process music, and very unlike Taylor's rhapsodic rhythmic inequalities.

Australia has had considerable exchange of musicians with the UK, but most of those involved have been in the mainstream of modern jazz, among them several members of Ian Carr's UK-based jazz-rock group Nucleus. Important early adventurous improvisers such as David Ahern are documented (A11; A42), and a survey of more recent jazz improvising and composition is available (A16). The highly multi-cultural nature of Australian society was reflected in one key free improvising group in the 1970s, Serge Ermoll's Free Kata, which made some remarkable records. One (*The New Language of Music Vol. 2*) is mentioned elsewhere because of its improvised speech by John Clare; another (*The New Language of Music Vol. 1*) is largely instrumental, although there are vocal sounds and theatrical elements. The breadth of musical panorama in this work is akin to that of Russian groups such as the Ganelin Trio, which we will discuss in Chapter 9: perhaps Ermoll's Russian origin has some bearing on this. In more recent periods, Ermoll has played more conventional jazz, though his individuality protrudes frequently. A contemporary Australian group, the Necks (comprising Chris Abrahams, Tony Buck and Lloyd Swanton), has produced an interesting form of rhythmic improvising, akin to the systemic minimal music exemplified by the early work of Terry Riley (e.g. 'Dorian', 1957) and operating over comparable time-frames. A compact disc (*Sex*) by this group represents only a small part of their range.

Uncompromising experimentation with instrumental technique, new instruments, theatrical elements, and collaboration with electronic musicians have been the forte of Jon Rose, an Englishman living mostly in Australia. His 1983 recording (*Tango*) with the composer of digital music, Martin Wesley-Smith, improvising on the Fairlight computer music instrument at least partly in real time, is a fascinating example of the possibilities of this medium. It uses one of the most powerful digital synthesisers yet recorded in real-time improvisation. Rose is described, though not with complete sympathy, in A62.

Having briefly discussed developments in Europe, the USA and Australasia, we can return to general conclusions and directions emerging from this chapter. We comment above on the propensity of the European players to participate both in jazz and freer improvising. Improvisers and performers of contemporary music are now also tending to overlap: Teitelbaum, Fredric Rzewski, Cornelius Cardew, and Guy are striking examples. Similarly, my contemporary music ensemble Lysis, and until 1989 the Australian group Pipeline, specialise in both areas. The mingling seems the more inevitable now that most of the conceivable musical elements are in universal use. Future possibilities involving computer interactions and intelligent programs working with the improvisers are essentially a combination of improvisation and composition: they are discussed more fully in the final chapter.

This chapter has shown how different has been the evolution in Europe and America, since the initiation of free improvising. The maintenance of closer connections with the formulaic aspects of jazz within most improvising in the USA, but rather less in that in Europe, is a fascinating phenomenon. I have revealed some of the attitudes involved in the preceding discussion. I have also indicated that my bias is somewhat towards the European; and that, perhaps because of this, I find its products more diverse and more stimulating. The difficulties of sociopolitical interpretation, and to a lesser extent of interpretation in terms of musical autonomy (summarised in the Introduction and Appendix 1), remain, but do not preclude an eventual analysis of deeper structure in these changes. I look forward to further analytic discourse on these issues, when sufficient data and theoretical framework can be obtained and devised to permit valid interpretation.

Recordings discussed

Note that most recordings listed involve musicians mentioned specifically in the chapter, but a few others are given as pointers to areas and individuals not covered directly.

Amalgam (1969) *Prayer for Peace*, Transatlantic TRA 196.
AMM (1968) *The Crypt*, Matchless MR 5 (double).
AMM (1967) *AMM Music*, Elektra EUKS 7256.
AMM/MEV (1968) *Live Electronic Music*, Mainstream MIS 5002.
AMM (1982) *Generative Themes*, Matchless MR 6.
AMM (1974) *To Hear and Back Again*, Matchless MR 3.
AMM (1987) *The Inexhaustible Document*, Matchless MR 13.
Ashbury, Roy (1976) *Fire Without Bricks* (with Larry Stabbins), Bead 4.
Bailey, Derek (1982) *Han*, Incus CD02.
Bailey and Coe, Tony (1979) *Time*, Incus 34.
Bailey (1970) *Solo Guitar*, Incus 2.
Bailey and Holland, David (1971) *Improvisations for Cello and Guitar*, ECM 1013.
Bailey and Bennink, Han (1969) ICP 004.
Braxton, Anthony (1968) *For Alto*, Delmark DS420/1.
Breuker, Willem (1967) see New Acoustic Swing Duo.
Brotzmann, Peter, with Van Hove, Bennink, Mangelsdorff (1971) FMP 0030/0040/0050.
Chamberpot (1976) *Chamberpot*, Bead 2.
Christmann, Gunter (1976) *Solo Music*, CS-5.
Coxhill, Lol (1976) *Diverse*, Ogun 510.
Davie, Alan (1971) *Suite for Prepared Piano and Mini Drums*, ADMW 002.
Davie (1971) *Bird through the Wall*, ADMW 003.
Davie (1971) *Phantom in the Room* (with Daniel Humair), ADMW 004.
Ermoll, Serge (1976) *Free Kata: The New Language of Music Vol. 1*, Kata 002.
Ermoll (1976) *Free Kata: The New Language of Music Vol. 2*, Kata 003.
Favre, Pierre (1969) *This is Free Jazz*, Wergo WER 80004.
Ganelin Trio (1982) *New Wine*, Leo LR 112.
Globokar, Vinko (1969) *Fluide*, Harmonia Mundi 933.
Globokar (1978) *Echanges*, Harmonia Mundi 1C 065-99 712.
Grillo, Fernando Fluvine, *Diverso n. 3* CRSLP 6203#.
Gruppo Nuova Consonanza (1969) *e poi?*, DGG 643541.
Guy, Barry (1976) *Statements V–XI*, Incus 22.
Harth, Alfred (1969) *Just Music*, ECM 1002.
Instant Composers Pool (1971) *Opera*, ICP 009.
Iskra 1903 (1973), New Phonic Art (1973) and Wired (1970), *Free Improvisation*, DGG 2740 105.
Logos Duo (1981) *Improvisations*, IGLOO 011.
Lysis (1987) *The Wings of The Whale*, Soma 784.
Mangelsdorff, Albert (1971) *Live at Dug Tokyo*, Three Blind Mice TBM 5.
Mangelsdorff (1964) *Now Jazz Ramsong*, CBS 62398.
Mangelsdorff (1963) *Tension*, CBS 62336.
Mangelsdorff (1967–9) *Mangelsdorff and Friends*, MPS 68 068.
Mangelsdorff (1978) *A Jazz Tune I Hope*, MPS 0068.212.
Mengelberg, Misha (with Tchicai, Bennink, Bailey) (1970) ICP 005.
Music Improvisation Company (1970), ECM 1005.
The Necks (1989) *Sex*, Spiral Scratch 002.
New Acoustic Swing Duo (Breuker, Willem and Bennink, Han) (1967) ICP 001.
New Departures Quartet (1962), Transatlantic TRA 134.

New Phonic Art (1971) *NPA*, Wergo WER 60060.
New Phonic Art, Iskra 1903 and Wired (1973) *Free Improvisation*, DGG 2740 105.
New York Art Quartet/LeRoi Jones (1964) ESP STL 5521.
Oxley, Tony (1968) *Jazz in Britain 68–9* (with Skidmore, Surman, etc.), Decca Eclipse ECS 2114.
Oxley (1969) *Baptised Traveller*, CBS 52664.
Oxley (1970) *Four Compositions for Sextet*, CBS 64071.
Oxley (1971) *Ichnos*, RCA Victor SF 8215.
Oxley (1972) *Live at The Festival* (with Bill Evans), ENJA 2030.
Oxley-Davie Duo (1974), ADMW 005.
Oxley, with SOH: *see* SOH.
Parker, Evan (1970) *Topography of the Lungs* (with Derek Bailey and Han Bennink), Incus 1.
Parker (1977) *Real Time* (with Andrea Centazzo), Ictus 0006.
Parker (1978) *Abracadabra* (with Greg Goodman), Beak Doctor 2 (Metalanguage 104).
Parker (1978) *Monoceros*, Incus 27.
Portal, Michel (1975) *At Chateauvallon*, LDX 74526.
Prevost, Eddie (1977) *Live Vol. 1*, Matchless MR1.
Riley, Howard (1970) *The Day Will Come*, CBS 64077.
Riley (1971) *Flight*, Turtle TUR 301.
Riley (1975) *Intertwine*, Mosaic GCM 771.
Riley (1977) *Shaped*, Mosaic GCM 781.
Rose, Jon (1983) *Tango* (with Martin Wesley-Smith), Hot 1009.
Schweizer, Irene (1973) *Ramifications*, Ogun G500.
Skidmore, Alan (1970) *Once Upon A Time*, Deram DN11.
SOH (1979) *SOH*, EGO 4011.
Stevens, John with Parker (1976) *Longest Night*, Ogun OG 120.
Stevens (1984) *Folkus*, Affinity AFF130.
Tippett, Keith (1981) *Mujician*, FMP SAJ-37.
Touch of the Sun (*c.*1974) *Milk Teeth*, Bead 1.
Tracey, Stan (1965) *Under Milk Wood*, Columbia E 33SX1774.
Tusques, François (1970) *Pasino Dazibao*, Futura GER 14.
Van Hove, Fred (1972) Vogel 001-S.
Voerkel, Urs (1976) *Voerkel*, FMP 0340.
Wheeler, Ken (1973) *Song for Someone*, Incus 10.
Wired, Iskra 1903 and New Phonic Art (1973) *Free Improvisation*, D99 2740 105.
Yamashita, Yosuke (1974) *Frozen Days*, Crown ZL-27.
Yamashita (1986) *Piano Duo Live at Pit Inn, with Mal Waldron*, CBS/SONY 32DH 360.
Yamashita (1986) *Kodo vs Yamashita Live*, Denon 33C38-7900.

9 Composing for improvisers

I was taught that the Afro-American Tradition placed no limitation on what was possible in art ... My father would have little tolerance for those who let some clouded notion of Blackness interfere with the expansion of our tradition ... The ensemble [Episteme] concerns itself with the central problem which has confronted the music [i.e. Afro-American music] since the advent of Ragtime: the question of the role and function of the composition in what has been a predominantly improvisational music.

If one thinks about the music in this light one might perceive that the revolutions of Be-bop and of the Post-Ornette Coleman Period are in fact reactionary in their conception of form and structure.

In my music the improviser functions within a particular musical vocabulary which is very specific in terms of tonality, tone colour, rhythm, shape and overall design. I have turned more and more toward precise musical notation to insure that the improviser is consciously and physically tuned in to the overall structure of a piece. On first glance this approach would seem to inhibit the improviser. This is a valid criticism, but I believe that this inhibition is now a real necessity when one perceives that 'free' or 'open' improvisation has become a cliché, a musical deadend.

Anthony Davis (sleeve notes to Episteme)

Over the past 15 years many special-purpose notation-systems have been devised with blurred areas in them that demand an improvised interpretation.

An extreme example of this tendency is my own *Treatise* which consists of 193 pages of graphic score with no systematic instructions as to the interpretation and only the barest hints (such as an empty pair of 5-line systems below every page) to indicate that the interpretation is to be musical ...

My most rewarding experiences with *Treatise* have come through people who by some fluke have (a) acquired a visual education, (b) escaped a musical education and (c) have nevertheless become musicians, i.e. play music to the full capacity of their beings. Occasionally in jazz one finds a musician who meets all these stringent requirements; but even then it is extremely rare.

Virtues that a musician can develop.

1. Simplicity ... In 1957 when I left the Royal Academy of Music in London complex compositional techniques were considered indispensable. I acquired some – and still carry them around like an infection that I am perpetually desirous of curing. Sometimes the temptation occurs to me that if I were to infect my students with it I would at last be free of it myself.

(Cornelius Cardew, A20).

In this chapter we will discuss how composition has tried to exploit improvisers in new ways. Thus our prime concern is to ask what influence the composition has on the improvisers and vice versa. How can these interactions be most productive? As a subtext, we may wonder whether any egalitarian or political ideas led improvisers (especially as free improvising developed) to rebel against appearing in any compositional context, in which they might be construed as being subservient. It is specific instances of the general ideas already raised which I want to discuss here. The process of revealing composing and improvising *attitudes* to developments in the music will continue in the next chapter.

These issues are distinct from the central concern of most composers, who are mostly not overtly concerned with improvisers. That central concern might be the construction of appropriate forms, including large-scale ones, in which to embody musical ideas, with the detail of the musical ideas secondary to the larger-scale form. Anthony Davis brings forward the important point that composers writing for jazz improvisers (or at least writing 'Afro-American' music) have been narrow and usually small-scale with regard to form. Thus many still write 32-bar structures which repeat, and merely add decorations to successive repetitions: in other words, structures which are no more than A–A1–A2– ... –An.

In the light of our earlier discussion I counter-argue that what is essentially a composer's view (and thus surprising coming from an improviser like Davis) neglects the complexity of structure which can be generated in free improvising: this may involve far smaller substructures as the fundamental basis of construction than those used by most composers, but does generate a comparable degree of complexity of overall structure, as discussed already (and in Appendix 1). The composer Cardew, quoted above, clearly supports this view to a degree, and has used improvisation to generate extremely large-scale works.

Nevertheless, it is appropriate first to discuss some of the major features of composition for improvisers revealed in works since 1960. I will make specific some of the generalised points raised in the earlier discussion of composition in Chapter 4; and then, by discussion of some European composers in more detail, I will illustrate more directly the attitudes and the interactions involved in the process of composer-improviser creation of music.

Because of the origins of most composition for improvisers from jazz, at least in our period in the West, it is appropriate to consider the composers' stances towards the preservation of jazz elements. Thus one can identify a conservative group who seek to preserve such elements, most often by retaining jazz pulse, usually in a metrical way; and contrast them with a group who are prepared to dispense with any or all of these elements. In general, the American composer for improvisers has fallen into the conservative category, while more Europeans have broken out from it. It is essential to keep in mind that this division into conservative and more flexible is an arbitrary separation of a real continuum, and certainly not to be equated with any particular value-gradation.

Within the more conservative category, it is worth distinguishing compositions which use new or non-jazz techniques to arrive at conventional jazz elements (for example, serial composition to generate simple familiar jazz chord sequences, or the use of canons in the work of the Modern Jazz Quartet and John Lewis's composition), from those which use the familiar techniques in a way which somehow extends them. I will summarise the work of some of the protagonists next.

George Russell and Gil Evans are archetypes of the US conservative tradition. Evans's work is largely that of an imaginative arranger, and his large-scale pieces primarily derive from the control he exerted in performance on his band: we have raised this possibility before, and will return to it in Chapter 10. It is clear that incorrect guesses as to Evans's intention for the next piece or motive are quite an important part of the musical result. Compositional elements are less crucial than they are in George Russell's case.

Russell, as mentioned before, is the originator of the *Lydian Chromatic Concept of Tonal Organisation* (A124), a system of chromatic usage in improvising and composing. This book has a description of procedures for avoiding conventional tonal usage, and using instead the Lydian mode in which the key feature is the inclusion of the tritone above the root. In other words, the Lydian mode includes the notes of a major scale, except for the fourth, which is sharpened. This is one of a large range of scalar patterns often used for improvising (A110). The impact of thinking along Lydian lines is not dissimilar to thinking of a tonal C major scale but using F as the root (which contains the same sequence of intervals). Baker (A8) suggested that the Lydian concept is relevant to Coltrane's music in the early 1960s. This seems a confusion: the modal concept is to use modes for improvising, whereas the pieces Baker mentions, notably 'Crescent' (R22), use relatively complex harmonic progressions as the basis for improvising. The importance of the Lydian concept and modality in general in improvising in general is elsewhere.

Thus many improvisers, such as Konitz and Marsh, have indicated how liberating they found Russell's ideas, and it is easy to envisage how this might have been in the 1950s and early 1960s when styles were more constrained than now. But since the mid-1960s it seems that improvisers can (perhaps should) be aware of a much wider range of scalar and harmonic approaches than they were previously; and that the free improvising environment, and the availability of microtonality, supervenes over limited systems such as Russell's. It is on this basis that I discuss motivic improvising in A31.

So Russell's theoretical contribution was important in interacting with improvisers. And thus the improvising within his own group's performances is often diverse: Fig. 9.1, for example, shows trombonist Brian

Fig. 9.1 Brian Trentham (trombone) on 'Lydia in Bags Groove' from *Sextet at Beethoven Hall*. Transcription based on Baker.

Trentham at work on *Sextet at Beethoven Hall*, and illustrates some extremely chromatic, almost twelve-tone additions to the basic modal structures as well as a great reliance on fourths.

What of Russell's compositions? They extend harmonic usage by means of the Lydian concept, but are fairly conservative in rhythm: simple jazz rhythms are almost always retained (for example, on the Smalltet, the Russell *Sextet at Beethoven Hall*, and the *Electronic Sonata* recordings).

Russell has been extremely diverse harmonically, and has directed pieces on the basis of continually shifting tonality ('Night Sound', on *Jazz Workshop*) or improvising on one material while having accompaniment on another ('Fellow Delegates', also on *Jazz Workshop*). The latter is interesting in that Russell has described it as involving trumpet improvising in A minor with a B♭ minor background: but what is apparent is really only A minor soloing (partly defined) with E♭ and D♭ asserted in the guitar part, so that we really have a Lydian fourth above the A, and a normal third: an example of construction from the Lydian scale. Other clear examples are the recurrent patterns in the piano on *Beethoven Hall* and on *Electronic Sonata*.

Russell has emphasised dissonant intervals, for example generating pieces and soloing from major seconds ('Hypocrite', on *Jazz Workshop*), using minor ninth bass chords ('Billy the Kid', also on *Jazz Workshop*; and *Living Time*), but his motives are also often conservative and use blue notes.

Although he preserves basic jazz rhythm and metres, Russell is imaginative in using it. For example, 'Hypocrite' involves a 6/4 pulse, against which solos use a 4/4 pulse occupying the same bar length. And on *African Game* Russell uses a variety of time signatures, and even at one point divides the ensemble into parts which play rhythmically separate speeds and metres, as already mentioned.

With regard to texture, Russell is again imaginative. He has used tuned drums ('Fellow Delegates'); adjusted to the incorporation of the wide range of multiphonic saxophone playing (*African Game, Electronic Sonata*); and used a 'pan-stylistic' (to quote his own sleeve note) electronic tape (*Electronic Sonata*) which contains collaged verbal and sound elements.

His forms are, however, usually rather simple: characteristically an episodic device, with a recurrent rhythmic and harmonic pattern, separates successive solos (for example, on *Beethoven Hall; Electronic Sonata*). But *African Game* and *Living Time* reveal more complex construction, where successive pieces are integrated harmonically and motivically. The latter is a score to feature pianist Bill Evans, whose own style is no less idiosyncratic than the composer's. Russell notes on the sleeve that Evans's and his own approaches are both modal, but had diverged for a long time before this recording (many years after their previous collaboration on 'Billy the Kid', etc.). Nevertheless, both musicians moulded: Evans plays repeatedly chords which involve a minor ninth construction, with the tonic at the top, in place of his normal version of such a chord with semitones in the middle of the chord between tonic and leading note – for example B/E/G/C (ascending order) in place of B/C/E/G. This, like most of the other Russell scores, is an example of a composition, though conservative in relation to the jazz tradition, encouraging a new response in the improvisers.

The Third Stream composers also fall into the conservative (or later, postmodern) group, in that they sought to use compositional techniques from classical music (for example, serialism) but created an identifiably jazz-orientated music. However, they rarely achieved the creative impact on the improvising practice which we have just met in Russell's work. Examples from Schuller, Lewis and others are on 'Abstraction' (R114). That some of these compositions are essentially conservative is not surprising since the improvising activities of some of the musicians involved were equally so (for example, John Lewis's Modern Jazz Quartet was a postmodern recreation of baroque chamber music within the context of jazz). As already mentioned, some of these compositions in Third Stream, particularly those using atonal harmonic approaches, made relatively little effort to integrate the improvisers (for example, Ornette Coleman) but rather left them to their own devices. In a sense this avoided the possible difficulty of the dictatorial role of the composer, and the negative response of some improvisers to it; but from the point of view of the music as a whole it often seems a limitation.

An even more extreme case of dichotomy between composition and improvisation is that of Bill Smith (improvising clarinettist and composer) and his 'Concerto for Jazz Clarinet and Orchestra' (on *Two Sides*). Although Smith had participated in many conventional jazz recordings (for instance, with Brubeck) he had also developed, in parallel with other wind players, a wide range of multiphonic and microtonal abilities on his

147

instrument (see, for example, 'Variants', also on *Two Sides*). He used a twelve-note series to construct the 'Concerto', but based on the four notes of 'I've got rhythm' (F, G, B♭, C) and two further rearrangements of these notes. The 'Concerto' has a classical four-movement form, and has very simple jazz rhythm section playing almost throughout. The row is used to develop some quite simple harmonies and some more dissonant ones, and the improvising is closely related to the four-note motive, and thus seems far more conventional than the compositional basis. Finally, Smith hardly uses his techniques for microtonal or timbral variation.

These Third Stream examples are thus clearly cases of new compositional techniques being used to recreate familiar styles rather than to expand them. Nor do they encourage expansion in the work of the improvisers. The same can be said of many European composers, such as Johnny Dankworth (for example 'Zodiac Variations' written in collaboration with Mátyás Seiber); Westbrook (for example, *Citadel Room 315* (1975)); and to a lesser degree Tony Coe. Coe's *Zeitgeist* is derived from a row consisting of five plus seven notes, but mainly involves tonal sequences therefrom. It does have some very interesting juxtaposition of contemporary music clarinet playing (Alan Hacker) and singing (Mary Thomas), with improvisatory work, reflecting Coe's breadth of musical experience. As discussed in A31, Penderecki's *Actions* (M9) provides some new stimuli for improvising, and is less conventional harmonically than any of the works just described.

Moving away from Third Stream composing, we next consider the other compositional work in the USA. Most of the works recorded by the Jazz Composers' Orchestra (New York) involve conscious preservation of rhythmic elements of Afro-American music. For example *Escalator Over the Hill*, by Carla Bley, has simple harmonic structure, and pastiches of many styles from rock and jazz to marches, overlaid with an interacting psychological drama. Roswell Rudd's *Numatik Swing Band* (1973), as the title implies, retains jazz swing ('Circulation', based on augmented fourths), and even includes a simple blues ('March for Howard'). Cherry's *Relativity Suite* (unlike his more progressive *Eternal Rhythm*) preserves some simple rhythmic feels, some deriving from American Indian music (for instance, a section in 10/8 preceded by chant) together with simple harmonies. This record is flawed from a technical point of view, in that many of the parts (particularly the string parts) are neither precise nor co-ordinated with the rest of the group: a general difficulty of live recording with limited rehearsal. More successful from a technical point of view is Moncur's *Echoes of Prayer*, which again preserves basic jazz pulses. In comparison with this quite conventional work the relative unorthodoxy of some of Moncur's earlier improvising with his own small group showing superimpositions of chords is quite striking – for example, an A♭7 harmony might have only notes from A(♮)6 with it or mainly notes from Em (as on 'Some Other Stuff'). But an interesting contribu-

Fig. 9.2 Anthony Davis: 'Wayang II' from *Episteme*. There is no improvisation on this piece.

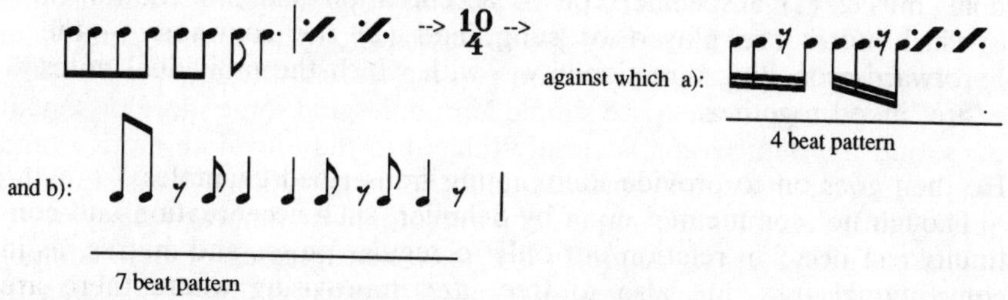

against which a):

4 beat pattern

and b):

7 beat pattern

tion from a dance ensemble moving with sound-generating instruments, as do dancers in some Indian traditions, is included on *Echoes*.

Anthony Davis, whose remarks preface this section, is an improvising American pianist. His compositions, particularly those on *Episteme*, are fascinating rhythmic constructions (see Figs 9.2 and 9.3) related to the work of Steve Reich and the other postmodern 'minimalist' composers who write completely notated music with slowly changing rhythmic systems (A88; A100). These composers may share with jazz an interest in African rhythms.

The composed parts of this particular record by Davis, as his statements imply, offer little scope for the improviser. The improvising rather takes place ouside the metred sections, in less densely composed sections. Undoubtedly that juxtaposition has an influence on the improvisers, and contributes to the overall form of the resulting large piece 'Wayang IV' (Fig. 9.3). As Davis also notes, he depended on the conductor (Mark Helias, an active improviser on double bass and cello) having the 'sensitivity of an improviser'.

Before we turn to the less 'conservative' group of composers, we need to discuss an element of the Afro-American tradition of rhythm, the concept of 'swing'. This is usually much emphasised, but is modified in the work of some of the less conservative group of composers. Swing is an aspect of accentuation of notes, and their placing in relation to pulses, which seems to strengthen the existence of the pulse. As Schuller (A130) says, while admitting the inadequacy of definitions of swing:

> Like the description of a primary color or the taste of an orange, the
> definition takes on full meaning only when the thing defined is also

Fig. 9.3 Davis's 'Wayang IV'.

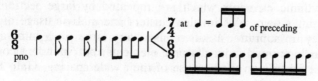

149

experienced ... In analyzing the swing element in jazz we find that there are two characteristics which do not generally occur in 'classical' music: (1) a specific type of accentuation and inflection with which notes are played or sung, and (2) the continuity – the forward-propelling directionality – with which the individual notes are linked together.

He then goes on to provide illuminating transcribed examples.

Though not commented upon by Schuller, such accentuation and continuity can occur in relation not only to regular pulses and metres, as in conventional jazz, but also to free jazz improvising where there are irregular pulses, or limited numbers of recurrences of each successive pulse rate, as illustrated earlier. (Swing within unmetred music is discussed also in Chapter 10.) Swing is discussed here to permit a further distinction among the compositions for improvisers which have dispensed with significant lengths of regular pulse, with which we are next concerned.

This distinction is between those compositions which rely on improvisers who can or do use elements of swing (inside or outside metre and pulse), and those which have no such requirement. We can consider those which do rely on swing first. Several progressive American compositions (such as those of Bill Dixon), and several European ones (such as those of Gaslini) rely on swing elements. Dixon's unusual work on 'Metamorphosis' (on *Intents and Purposes*) expunges any continuous metre. It relies on swing accentuation, and generates sustained chord textures from the ensemble, often quite tonal ones. Fourths and augmented fourths predominate. Almost throughout the record there is some improvising element in progress, though composed elements are also found most of the time. A few rhythmic unisons by the group punctuate the work. Textural variety is present, for instance with the low multiphonics from Dixon on trumpet near the beginning of 'Night for Piece 1'. Similar concerns can be seen on Dixon's subsequent recordings.

Giorgio Gaslini is an Italian composer and pianist, and has produced totally composed music (and theoretical works) beside music for improvisers. His two most important recordings for improvisers are probably 'New Feelings' (on *New Sentiments*) and 'Fabbrica Occupata' (on *Gaslini Meets* ...). The first involves a 6/8 and 5/8 recitativo and aria, and serial motives. There are two basses and two drums so that rhythmic elements are complex, and there is some metred time, but usually slightly countermanded by the other members of that bass and drums team. Some of the pitch motives are heard in a bare form in the bass line and there are some swung rhythmic elements which are repeated by large sections of the band. Gaslini's own solos involve clusters and motivic usage of the material. Lacy on soprano, as often, uses very large pitch intervals in his solos, usually formed from diatonic elements, but sounding compatible with the serial framework because of their wide spacing. Gato Barbieri, on 'Marcia', which is march-like, uses his normal devices of multiphonics and microtonal pitch fluxes in a rhythmic way appropriate for the serial context.

'New Feelings', and the later 'Fabbrica Illuminata' are both works which do not use much fixed pulse, but do exploit the musicians' capacity for swing. Even less fixed pulse is heard on 'Fabbrica'. This is again based on small motivic elements, particularly augmented fourths and major thirds around E♭. Some simple rhythmic patterns recur episodically, punctuating the solo improvising. Motives of Gaslini from 'Tempo e Relazioni' reveal relatively greater complexity of composition, though the work is not for improvisers. The music of both Gaslini and Dixon is progressive in nature, and has positive influence on its interpreters and their improvisations.

As one would hope, there are works which make nonsense of the above categorisations of stance towards preserving jazz elements. An example is *Song for Someone* by Kenny Wheeler. This uses the most extreme of free improvisers, such as Evan Parker (saxophones) and Derek Bailey (guitar) in their own solo and duo contexts, but also juxtaposed with orchestral compositions which are themselves very conservative. A real integration is achieved partly by Tony Oxley (the percussionist who is equally active in both areas); and partly by compositionally defining simple pitch or timbral elements of the surrounding score which can be a starting point for the free improvisers. For example, Parker and Bailey begin without the orchestra on 'Good Doctor', and stop before the written material is presented, but Bailey in particular plays some E naturals, which are emphasised thereafter within the composition, while Parker plays a G to G# movement while an E♭ chord is sustained in the composition. They both participate then in a brief Am6/B improvisation. Similarly on 'Casuesare', the composition is in full flight when an E♭ (#5) chord is established, and Parker uses the B natural implied as his starting point, helped by Oxley. This simple continuity ensures musical cohesion. But the reason for the presence of Parker and Bailey on the record, in spite of their stated wish totally to avoid playing any music involving scores for a long period in the 1970s, is their personal regard for Wheeler (who is a free improviser as well as working in more conventional frameworks). So the musical integration is sought by the improviser, as well as being clearly built in by the composer. This is a much more successful and egalitarian relationship than that of Ornette Coleman with the Third Stream.

Now we reach the progressive group of composers who were prepared to dispense with any of the traditions of Afro-American music, including swing. Among their pioneering works are *Globe Unity* (Schlippenbach) and Breuker's *Litany for the 14th June 1966*. These fascinating works have not received any serious consideration or acclaim since the time of their initial appearance. They are not discussed in A65 (though Jost

Fig. 9.4 Material from 'Globe Unity', by Schlippenbach.

half a 12 tone row   7   9   10   retrograde of notes 2-6,
1-6   transposed up one semitone.

mentions the omission) and not even mentioned in A78. They will be discussed next, but the reader should keep in mind several other examples of progressive compositions (if using smaller forces) already mentioned, such as those of Kuhn and Dauner, from a similar period (around 1966–7).

'Globe Unity' is an extended dense composition by the German Alex von Schlippenbach. It partly develops from his studies with Bernd Alois Zimmerman, who also composed jazz works which were very progressive, such as *Die Befristeten*, and *Musique pour les Souper du Roi Ubu*, which incorporated jazz elements, as did his opera *Die Soldaten*. Schlippenbach was the pianist on Manfred Schoof's recording of *Die Befristeten* (1967). The congruence between Schlippenbach and Zimmerman can be seen from a comparison of the motivic elements in the two composers. In 'Globe Unity' there are some recurrent rhythmic patterns but most of the music is dense and unmetred. Pulses and swing are detectable in the work of many of the musicians, but they are not crucial. In other words, the composition does not depend on swing, though it permits it (as do most!). The piece is written in arbitrary-length bars, cued by the composer, and the material is based on a note row. A clear statement of elements of this row occurs in the tuba in the middle of the piece (Fig. 9.4) and it contains some neat internal derivations. Schlippenbach comments on the sleeve that he always introduces melody in the middle of pieces rather than at the outset even if the melody is the basis for the whole piece.

While 'Globe Unity' with its intensity, rapidity of articulation by all the soloists and emphasis on multiphonics and saxophone shrieks, etc., might give the impression that this compositional style could only dictate extreme activity, 'Sun', on the same record, reveals that this is not the case. This work has a sparseness in places which is a striking contrast; it also uses an array of exotic percussion instruments to produce a wide range of timbres which are probably unique in composed music, and which clearly depend on the ability of the improvisers involved to exploit unfamiliar instruments with a wide range of technique. The same fluency of improvisers in using unfamiliar instruments was noted earlier in relation to Cherry's *Eternal Rhythm*.

Schlippenbach calls the music on this record 'free tonal improvisation', and it is true that some of the soloists reveal tonal centres, but clearly Schlippenbach in giving them tonal centres or limited materials has not *necessitated* that they reveal such centres. There are a few block instrument chords on the record, and some rhythmic patterns, but in general the music breaks away totally from all the traditions of improvised music before 1960. This is at the beginnings of a whole independent European improvising movement.

This break with tradition is a remarkable feat, and one which is also achieved by Willem Breuker in the same year in his *Litany for the 14th of*

Fig. 9.5(a)

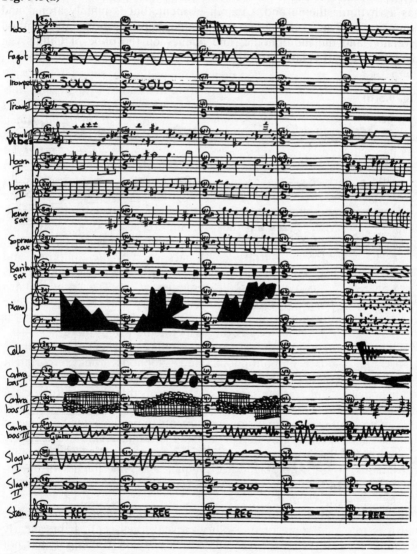

June 1966. It is interesting that a clear continuity of European improviser-composers existed at the time, as now, and Breuker, for example, was one of the performers on 'Globe Unity'. Fig. 9.5 illustrates part of the score from '14th June' (shown on the record cover), and contains graphic elements as well as defined notation. (Perhaps it should be noted that this particular section of the score contains material which is readily audible in the performance (that in Horn I) but the passage as a whole is not readily identifiable on the recording, perhaps because of the recording, or perhaps because it was modified before the performance.) The title work has a rhythmic theme and a march element, but is mainly atonal and non-metred. There are some remarkable improvisations and timbral diversity, and the multiphonics and fluency on the oboe of Gillius van Bergeyk are particularly striking. In 'Time Signal' and 'Sound Density',

Fig. 9.5(b)

Breuker pits two sections of the ensemble against each other, and the resulting 'game' element is exciting and dense, with a sensation of competition leading to a fleetness of musical change which is unusual. Textural variety is again present, with a huge range of percussion used by Courbois, and prepared piano by Misja Mengelberg. These two European records are also near the origin of control of free improvisation by composers, and they exorcised the conventional frameworks which previously controlled improvisation in the West. They can be contrasted with the other works discussed in this chapter, or equally with the fascinating devices of Andrew Hill discussed in the previous chapter.

American composers have been loath to pursue this line, being more conservative in respect of swing and of other aspects: Coltrane's *Ascension* and Coleman's *Free Jazz* can be taken as antecedents, but they both involve extremely simple compositional inputs, which are not in any way comparable with the complexity of organisation of the Breuker and Schlippenbach works. The main notable successor to *Ascension* and *Free Jazz* in the USA was the issue of works by Michael Mantler by the JCOA, such as the series of compositions called 'Communications' (1968). Here we find individual soloists, from Cecil Taylor to Larry Coryell, pitted against a compositional framework involving use of some clearly jazz-orientated devices (for example, in 'Communications 8 and 9', harmonic elements, including pentatonic patterns), but often expunging it. 'Communications #11', featuring Taylor, has motivic patterns in

Fig. 9.6

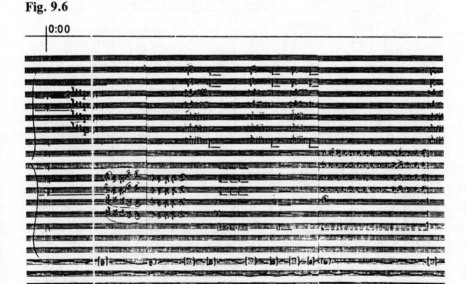

the composed part which are often tremolo chords, but sometimes (Fig. 9.6) articulated gradually widening intervals. Fig. 9.6 is part of the score of '#11' as reproduced in the sleeve notes of the records, which gives an impression of the nature of the work, and the consistent construction of each 'bar'. While the compositional elements are quite simple, the soloists usually proceed in their own characteristic way. It can be seen from the score that no specific demands are made on Taylor. It is probably rather the reverse, that the composer is well aware of the features of the improvising of the soloists and incorporates elements of these techniques in the composition. Certainly the gradually broadening intervals (e.g. F, B; F, C; F, D♭; F, E♭) are a device characteristic of Cecil Taylor's improvising in solos or ensemble. This approach could generate a music removed from the Afro-American tradition; it is perhaps only because of the choice of soloists who retain close connection with that tradition that Mantler's record is less innovative than those of Schlippenbach or Breuker.

Nevertheless, subsequent Mantler records have not pursued this development towards a break with the Afro-American tradition, but rather re-entered it, even while using European musicians such as Jack Bruce (for example, *No Answer*). In this they have converged with the efforts of

Fig. 9.7(a) 'Synchronist Pulse Track Structure'. An example of procedures for rhythmic improvising. Reproduced from A79.

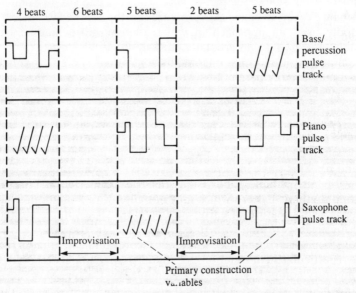

NB: The vertical alignment is not necessarily as strict as it appears, since the tempo or pulse can be different in each of the three strata.

Fig. 9.7(b) Material from pulse track 108A by Braxton (A79).

Pulses: 1   2-5   6   7   8-9·   10-15

This pulse track provides instruction (the notated pulses) and space for improvisation (the pulses without material specified).

the other JCOA composers discussed already (Carla Bley, Moncur, Rudd, Cherry).

Around this period (1967–8) the black American Anthony Braxton, starting out from the Chicago Association for the Advancement of Creative Musicians (AACM), also began accumulating his compositions for improvisers (see catalogues in A79; A118). There is nothing so ambitious or complex in construction in his early recorded works as in those we have just discussed. However, Braxton is a remarkably eclectic composer, and has experimented with an immense array of compositional approaches, from serial to environmental, from precise to imprecise. Some examples of his methods are illustrated in Fig. 9.7.

As pointed out already, Braxton is not committed to total and collective improvisation, nor to compositional control even of every large element, let alone of details. Thus, having been very influenced by Stockhausen and Cage (as evidenced on his first recording, *For Alto*), he also introduced chance elements and arbitrary choices of sequence of performance. And in many performances in the late 1980s, Braxton has repeatedly used an approach in which one or more members of the ensemble are free to interpolate musical material from a completely different composition in the ongoing performance. The interpolated composition may usually be any of several, and the parts used may be taken from anywhere. This procedure is like that of Cage in works such as *Atlas Eclipticalis* and Concert for Piano and Orchestra, works from the 1960s (M1–4); and was recurrent on Braxton's UK tour documented in A79.

This is not to imply that his compositions lack controlled procedures: they do often control pulse by means of what he calls a 'pulse track' (Fig. 9.7a and b). This track involves successive pulses which may be empty or filled with fairly simple subdivisions. The 'gravallic bass' (Fig. 9.7c), a repeating rhythmic pattern which may not align with a metre in which it is played, is also a feature of early works (A118). It is interesting that two of the musicians working with Braxton on that UK tour (A79) found the composed material complex, while the scores indicate that it is quite simple (particularly in relation to rhythm) in comparison with much contemporary composed music (for example, by Carter, Maxwell Davies or Ferneyhough: see also A118); and also that they were surprised to find the degree of freedom of interpretation they were accorded. In most

157

Fig. 9.7(c) The Gravallic Basic in *Composition 23G*. A repetitive pattern used by bass and drums. Taken from A118.

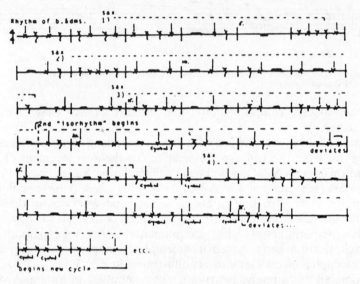

cases the emphasis in Braxton's directions to the improvisers seems to be that individuals function independently: in other words, interaction between improvisers is not emphasised greatly.

In sum, it seems that Braxton is usually not interested in controlling large parts of the musical texture which results in his performances with ensemble. Rather he is simply interested in ensuring that some of his composed elements are present, no matter with what they are juxtaposed. This can be viewed as a collage technique, as he says. This is a curiously intermediate position between control and non-control, perhaps quite appropriate in a composer-improviser. It also indicates that Braxton is not concerned to have great influence on the process of the improvisation *per se*; or to ensure interaction between the improvisers, which I have argued is one of the crucial possibilities of group improvisation.

Braxton is a very interesting musician, particularly because of his willingness to talk and write about his work (A79; A118). However, this verbalising often involves an impenetrable bedrock of mysticism. His statements are not always articulate and comprehensible, though frequently they are; on occasion they are mutually inconsistent. Happily a brilliant study of Braxton's music is available in the thesis of Radano (A118) and it is to be hoped this will become available in book form. There is complementary information in A79. It is partly because of these publications that I have chosen not to devote more space to Braxton. He stands out as a progressive among the American composers for improvisation; and this may partly reflect his participation in the European

Fig. 9.7(d) Line Notations from *Compositions 77A* and *77D* of Braxton. Taken from A118.

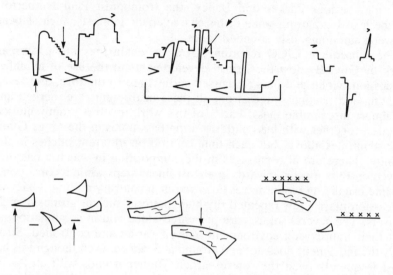

scene, as well as, more fundamentally, his own creative and somewhat analytic mind.

In the aftermath of Schlippenbach and Breuker came a record by Schoof (*European Echoes*) in 1969, which again has an extreme density of action, and many of the same musicians. However, the compositional input on this record seems rather slighter. It involves for the first time some of the key British protagonists, such as Bailey and Parker.

They are, together with Barry Guy, the leading forces behind the London Jazz Composers' Orchestra (LJCO), which could be viewed as the progressive equivalent of the by then traditional New York Jazz Composers' Orchestra. Guy again brought the European contemporary composer's position into the improvised music world, since he is equally active in writing for non-improvisers, for contemporary double bass techniques (some of which leave much to be improvised) or for improvising ensembles. The contributions of Globokar, the trombonist also involved with the improvising ensemble New Phonic Art, can be viewed in the same light. Globokar is particularly concerned with causing improvisation by making technical demands on the performer – for instance, requesting a particular kind of sound from an instrument unaccustomed to making it, either on the score or by prescriptive demonstration to another performer on a different instrument (as on 'Australanghen or *Fluide*, 1969).

The first recording by LJCO (*Ode*, 1972) is of a seven-part suite by Guy. Each movement is inspired by a Surrealist painting. A completely atonal frame is maintained most of the time; metre is largely absent. Guy says that the 'scoring tried to realise the ... area in which the soloist prefers to work' and certainly all the soloists are recognisable. For example, besides Parker and Bailey, the trombonist Paul Rutherford can be heard exploring some of his characteristic interests, such as beats between simultaneously sounded tones.

The subsequent LJCO recording, *Stringer*, again presents a four-part work by Guy. By now the British developments in the use of amplified percussion, violin and bass (discussed earlier) are to the fore, and reverberating and beating sounds from all these instruments are merged into an almost inseparable mass. Part 1 of this work involves mainly musical mobiles, together with bass patterns using bass notes in the range G and four semitones above, but each time centred on different pitches in this vicinity. There are also passages in the composition in which a bass line played on tuba moves upwards in almost linear steps while a corresponding line usually on violin moves downwards in contrary motion. Oxley on percussion plays a few repeated rhythmic patterns such as groups of eight quavers. The several soloists are presented alone and in combination, so that their improvising environment is itself varied and controlled. Strikingly the movement does not end around a G centre, even though this has most frequently been the centre earlier. Rather it ends with an A♭/E♭ combination in the bass. This insecurity of tonal centre then leads well into the second movement where the contrary motion in the tuba and violin begins, with some reversals of step by a semitone during the ascent of the tuba and the descent of the violin.

This section of the argument has so far implicitly assumed that composers would necessarily usually write defined sounds, but, as already indicated, and discussed in A31, improvising procedures can be controlled without defining sounds to be included. Text compositions and procedural devices have been outlined. The LJCO has also used such devices. It has been an intensive force continuing the innovations of Schlippenbach and Breuker, and producing a unique music. The marshalling of improvisational resources by the compositions has continued usually to be efficient and the LJCO remains a significant force (see its *Zurich Concert* double album with a work of Guy, and also several of Braxton).

Just as improvising procedures can be controlled without defining sounds to be included, so can electronic devices. In this manner, Terry Riley worked with the jazz group of Chet Baker (see A88, p. 37); and the electronic collaborations of Bob James with Robert Ashley, etc., discussed earlier, have some elements in common with the others which control improvisation without specifying musical materials.

It is interesting to note an antecedent for such control of improvisation without specifying musical materials, within classical composers' spheres: the Improvisers Chamber Ensemble of Lukas Foss, formed in 1957. A recording of the efforts of this group is on the 1961 record *Time Cycles*, where three improvised episodes are presented juxtaposed with a com-

Fig. 9.8 Braxton improvising with Circle on 'No Greater Love', 1971. Modified from A91.

pletely composed work. Foss says on the record sleeve of this work that in 'Composition all becomes fate, in Improvisation there remains chance and hazard, which can be corrected by the will (of the improvisers)'. He says that he has defined the order and roles of the four performers in the improvisations, and describes the procedures as 'predetermined co-ordination of non-predetermined musical ideas'.

In the event the interludes are very restrained, and no instrumental techniques outside the conventional classical performers' repertoire are in evidence. There is contrast in degree of activity, and in the third improvisation some strong pulses are established. Foss wants these interludes, or rather has designed them on this particular occasion, to give with the composition '2 performance levels' and notes that the interludes ignore the preceding song and relate rather to the previous interlude. The Britons Richard Orton and Jonathan Harvey and the Australian Peter Sculthorpe have also published scores for performance which contain no defined sounds; although Sculthorpe clearly shapes his work overall. Several American composers such as Childs and Schwartz have also included improvised elements in their largely composed works, but mainly in the 1960s. This has not tended to be an evolving line of compositional work in the USA, whereas in Europe it has more so.

Of course, the categorisation of conservative and non-conservative I have given is ultimately inapplicable, and the composers who most cross the boundaries it implies may sometimes be the most interesting. Among these obviously is Braxton, whose extensive composition for large ensemble is hardly represented on record, with a few exceptions, such as the 1976 *Creative Music Orchestra*. This illustrates a huge range of composition for improvisers, from the conservative (the metrical 'Piece 1', with its simple 4/4, and the Ellingtonian 'Piece 5' with its dotted rhythms and triplets in the melodic line); through the march-like parade music of 'Piece 3'; to the balancing of opposing instrumental groups, and the timbral variation of 'Piece 6'. It is clear that Braxton is among the most flexible jazz composers, as he is among the improvisers. Ironically, the element least exploited in his work seems to be the rhythmic, for his own improvised patterns – as on the Circle album, *Paris Concert*, of 1971 (Fig. 9.8) – are rather simple rhythmically, and there is no clear attempt in the compositions on this record to build in extra layers of rhythmic complexity.

161

Another body of work which overstrides the categorisation I have described, and also involves a rare means of control of improvisation, is that of the Ganelin Trio from the USSR, and some from their colleagues (see A40 for biographical and historical background). The trio comprises Vladimir Chekasov (saxes), Vyacheslav Ganelin (piano and other keyboards), and Vladimir Terasov (drums). Chekasin has noted (A40) that the music

> is essentially a part of a chamber work which has already been composed. In principle everything we perform can subsequently be written down, the whole piece is already in our heads. As a matter of fact, our spontaneity is not of the usual kind, our improvisations are a filling-in with textural elements of the space between the main structural landmarks of a piece, which have always been thought out in advance.

Thus the compositions have not been written down (though they could have been); have been arrived at by experiment; but remain a force on the trajectory of subsequent performances of the piece.

Similarly, Sergei Kuryokhin, another Russian improvising pianist (A40, p. 104) says:

> My works have a very formal structure, then I invite those musicians I know, like Derek Bailey does, but he has no structure, his is all spontaneous improvisation, whereas I construct a very exact composition with individual musicians in mind and in my mind I fill out the skeleton, the construction, with improvisations which are characteristic of those musicians.

Thus layers (in time, and in personal improvised input) of conception are involved in generating some of this very large-scale music from the USSR. Now improvisation becomes composition, as well as influencing it. The distinctive ouput of these Soviet musicians is another example of the individuality of European improvised music, and compositions written for use in it. We can only comment again on the complexity of the evolutionary forces at work, their diversity, and their layering together not only of several dominating elements, but also of many residual elements (to redesign Raymond Williams's analysis of literary change).

The concept of layering of music is one close to the ideas of another composer who has operated within both the conservative and the progressive sides of composing for improvisers outlined above. Graham Collier, with whom I have performed since 1974, is the subject of the next chapter, which contains an interview with him. The comments opening the chapter are my own views, and inevitably in the subsequent interview, one between friends and colleagues, I forced Graham to consider some approaches and issues which were not previously important to his work processes. It is interesting how his comments on multiple layers in music parallel the psychological discussion on whether multiple attention is possible: in improvisation the introspective indications are that it is (discussed by Pressing in A27).

Recordings discussed

Bley, Carla (1968–71) *Escalator Over the Hill*, JCOA JT 4001.
Bley, Carla (1973) *Tropic Apetites*, Watt 1.
Braxton, Anthony (1976) *Creative Music Orchestra 1976*, ND86579 (CD RCA).
Breuker, Willem (1966) *Litany for the 14th of June 1966*, Relax 33004.
Charles, Teddy (1953) *Collaborations West*, Prestige 7028.
Charles (1954) *Revelation* (with Brookmeyer), Xtra 5022.
Charles (1957) *3 for Duke*, LTZ-J15119.
Cherry, Don (1968) *Eternal Rhythm*, MPS 15007.
Cherry (1973) *Relativity Suite*, J2001.
Circle (1971) *Paris Concert*, ECM 1018-9.
Coe, Tony (1976) *Zeitgeist*, EMC 3207.
Davis, Anthony (1981) *Episteme*, Gr8101.
Dixon, Bill (1966) *Intents and Purposes*, RCA FXL1 7331.
Ellis, Don (1960) *... How Time Passes*, Candid 9004.
Ellis (1961) *New Ideas*, Esquire 32-183.
Foss, Lukas (1961) *Time Cycles*, Columbia CMS 6280.
Gaslini, Giorgio (1966) *New Sentiments*, EMI QELP 8154.
Gaslini (1976) *Gaslini Meets ...*, Pausa PR-7014.
Globokar, Vinko (1969) *Fluide*, Harmonia Mundi HM 933.
Globokar (1978) *Echanges ...*, HM IC 065-99 712.
Guy, Barry (1972) *Ode*, Incus 6, 7.
Guy (1980) *Stringer*, FMP SAJ-41.
Guy (1988) London Jazz Composers' Orchestra, *Zurich Concerts*, Intackt 004/005.
Mantler, Michael (1968) *Jazz Composers' Orchestra*, JCOA 1001/2.
Mantler, (1973) *No Answer*, Watt 2.
Moncur, Grachan (1974) *Echoes of Prayer*, JCOA J 2003.
Rudd, Roswell (1973) *Numatik Swing Band*, JCOA J 2002.
Russell, George (1957) *Jazz Workshop*, RCA SF-7511.
Russell (1958) *New York, NY*, Brunswick LA T 8333.
Russell (1965) *Sextet at Beethoven Hall*, MSP BAP 5079.
Russell (1969) *Electronic Sonata*, Flying Dutchman FD 10124.
Russell (1972) *Living Time*, CBS S 65010.
Russell (1983) *The African Game*, Blue Note BT 85103.
Schlippenbach, Alexander (1966) *Globe Unity*, Saba 15 109 ST.
Schoof, M. (1969) *European Echoes*, FMP 0010.
Schuller, Gunther (1960) *Jazz Abstractions*, Atlantic 587043.
Smith, William O. (1974) *Two Sides*, CRTI SD 320.
Westbrook, Mike (1975) *Citadel Room 315*, RCA SF 8433.
Wheeler, Kenny (1973) *Song for Someone*, Incus 10.
Zimmerman, Bernd Alois (1966) *Die Befristeten*, etc., Wergo Wer 60031.

10 A composer-improviser dialogue with Graham Collier

Since returning to the UK in the mid-1960s from the Berklee School, and after leaving the ghost Dorsey Orchestra, Collier has led six- to twelve-piece groups, and occasionally a big band. In this chapter I will discuss briefly, from the same stances as I have adopted in the rest of this book, Graham's contributions and methods. Thus I will treat successively harmonic elements, rhythmic elements, etc. My friendship with him and close contact with the music as a long-standing member of his group also permitted a recorded discussion with Collier which revealed otherwise inaccessible psychological and social aspects of the composer–improviser interaction and of the music itself. A small selection from the transcript of this discussion forms the second part of this chapter.

There is a major transition in Collier's work with the composition *New Conditions* (1976). Some of the new elements were anticipated by his *Midnight Blue* (1975), which was also the first jazz record on which I performed. Before this period, most of Collier's pieces were either slow ballads, revolving around major seventh and min7♭5 chords, or faster pieces with modal bases for improvising. So the motivic elements offered to the improviser were either simple harmonies or scalar motives. By the time of *Midnight Blue*, elements of two modes or scales might be combined in a single chord, and there was greater use of 'open' sections of improvising, in which the solo length is not specified.

New Conditions, however, was a seven-part work lasting more than an hour, entirely based on two motives (Fig. 10.1) and the soloists were offered elements of these motives as the basis for every improvised part. The motives consisted of irregular intervals, and might be shown as patterns spread out over more than an octave (see Fig. 10.1). They were derived from chords which the composer constructed in the early stages of writing the work. The first motive was used with two different endings (a and a' in Fig. 10.1) and the two motives shared two pitches (A and G#/A♭).

164

Fig. 10.1 *New Conditions*: Motives.

a   b   spread version of a

a' with alternative ending

Collier's subsequent works have often used a related approach to constructing motives from harmonies, deriving the whole of large works from such a process, so that multiple parts of a complex work are linked by this device (for example, *Symphony of Scorpions*). In later pieces, such as *Something British Made in Hong Kong* (1985), the materials are presented first in a more highly differentiated way rather than in bare motive form as at the outset of *New Conditions*.

Collier's rhythmic devices from an early stage involved the asymmetrical, less conventional metres (such as 5/4, 6/4, 6/8, 9/8, 5/8) often with regular changing patterns, as already mentioned. Collier notes that this was partly conditioned by seeing a score by Karl Jenkins, sometime oboist and pianist in Collier's group (sleeve notes to *Down Another Road*).

Formal devices in Collier's work have also been varied. For instance, after a series of records of short separate pieces, Collier developed a modular form, in which predetermined pieces could be linked in different orders. The relationships between the pieces were often slighter than those between the sections of the later large works like *New Conditions*, but further links were created by improvised cadenzas by individuals in the group, who then chose the subsequent section to be performed (see *Mosaics* and *Portraits*).

A major interest of Collier has been in extra-musical artistic stimuli, such as the abstract Expressionist painters (expressed, for example, in *Midnight Blue*) and the writing of Carson McCullers, Conrad Aiken and, in particular, Malcolm Lowry. Several of his largest recent works have related to Lowry. For example *Day of the Dead* is a work with words chosen by Collier from a large range of Lowry's writing, narrated together with the ongoing jazz score. Collier has collaborated with writers in producing musicals, and would like to produce an opera, and thus to pursue the music–verbal conjunction much further.

Collier has noted (on *Songs for My Father*) that the jazz composer's problem is 'that of retaining overall control while still allowing musicians their own freedom, and to allow the occasion to dictate some of the content'.

Fig. 10.2 Karl Jenkins on 'Danish Blue'.

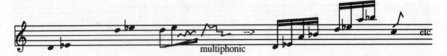

This is a fairly central stance within the spectrum from minimal to maximal composer control, compatible with providing sufficient freedom and stimulus to the improviser, especially when the composer uses the detailed knowledge he has of them. What aspects of that freedom are actually exploited by the performers? We can consider in turn the different musical elements the improviser can use.

Rhythmic freedom was always offered in the cadenza sections, though considerable discipline was required in the metrical pieces. Interestingly, Collier sometimes does not notate precisely the different rhythmic 'feels' needed for a particular piece, leaving them to be generated and decided during rehearsal (for example, on *Midnight Blue*). Improvised transitions from one predetermined pulse to another were also achieved (as on 'Now for Something Completely Different' on *Portraits*). Since *New Conditions*, both pulsed and relatively unpulsed sections have been built in as bases for improvising, so that a complete range of rhythmic freedoms are now included.

As far as harmony is concerned, the early modal pieces do permit a variety of improvising approaches. For example, Karl Jenkins, playing keyboards on the early albums, uses the modes to present harmonies based on thirds, or (as on 'Danish Blue', for example) chordal structures based on fourths. Repeated fourths are also characteristic of some of Beckett's solo trumpet lines, just as are thirds. In 'Darius', Collier uses simple modes, but in the thematic material adds a limited number of foreign notes, to form a harmonic contrast which the soloist can choose to use. Complete harmonic freedom, permitting tonality, polytonality or atonality, was reached by the time of 'Midnight Blue'. For instance in my piano solo there is a loose tonal centre of F, which is submerged at various points and asserted at others. Such complete freedom is precisely expressed within the later works from *New Conditions* by the motives themselves (Fig. 10.1).

Textural variety has also been a permissible improviser's objective since the early records, just as it has always been built into the composition and orchestration. For instance, the remarkable oboe improvising of Jenkins is heard on 'Danish Blue' (Fig. 10.2), where controlled multiphonics are juxtaposed with arpeggiated and scalar playing, and a range of tone production. Similarly, Harry Beckett (trumpet and flugel) uses some controlled microtonal glissandi on theme 6 of *Mosaics*, in high and low registers and over wide pitch ranges. He follows with some 'doodle tonguing' (cf. that used much later on the Berio Sequenza for trumpet) and concludes with a sustained pedal note on E natural concert (below the normal trumpet register produced in a special technique as a pedal tone).

Usually in combination with the percussion playing of Ashley Brown, I have introduced a range of textural and timbral devices on the piano (as discussed in Chapter 7) into performances of his works since *Midnight Blue*. Most recently these have included the digital synthesiser, and real-time timbre modification (for example, *Something British*). Collier himself has also used the synthesiser, providing prerecorded textural and rhythmic elements, as again on *Something British*.

Formal freedom was present in the modular works, although the sleeve of *Mosaics* noted that the composer chose the sequence of elements for the recording. In live concert these freedoms were used. Unlike Braxton's modular approach, these do not permit simultaneous use of previously unconnected material, but rather the formation of new connections successively. On a smaller scale, of course, the cadenza device permits the soloist to move as far away, and sometimes for as long, as chosen, before returning to the next predetermined element.

The soloist can also use elements of the subsequent material in anticipation, thereby creating a new formal link. One of the most obvious examples of this is by Collier himself as bassist, when on *Mosaics* he introduces part of the riff of 'Theme 6' in the preceding cadenza. The composer, as bassist in the early groups, was thus to some degree able to dictate the return from cadenza to composed element, but he jokes about the difficulty of so doing (in other words, the difficulty of distracting the soloist) sometimes.

In his work after *New Conditions*, Collier functions as director/conductor, and subsidiary keyboard player, so that he can concentrate when appropriate on directing the performance. In other words, in some respects he has taken back control of the flexible formal elements, rather than leaving it for the improvising musicians. Collier's partial withdrawal from playing may relate to his wish to direct more, but also to his feeling that *composition* for improvisers would be his most important contribution. He took a decision around the time of *New Conditions* not only to create a new technique for himself, but also to view himself as nothing but a jazz composer. He views his subsequently increased activity in teaching as a simple expression of the organisational abilities required in a jazz composer to influence his improvisers: these, too, are the abilities required to help students of jazz composition and improvisation, in Collier's view.

Collier is interested in 'multilayering' his compositions, just as he sees Malcolm Lowry's writing and abstract expressionist painting as layered. The juxtaposition of words and music provides two layers, but the concept applies within the music, too. Sometimes he differentiates the roles of one section of the group from another so as to have two layers

167

Fig. 10.3 Part of Collier's 'Ryoanji'.

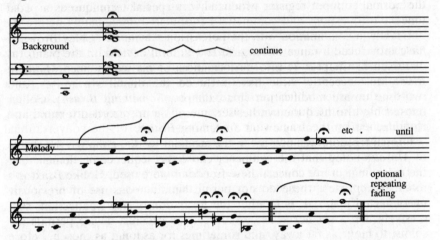

The whole of the 'Background' is shown, but only about half of the 'melody' (after 'etc' and before 'until', the remainder appears in the original score).Each player has the same score.
Collier notes : 'Ryoanji is based on the idea of a particular Japanese Garden where there is a raked sand carpet on which 15 rocks are placed. The observer walks on the sand to see the rocks, which are so placed that various groupings are visible at certain vantage points.
The musical levels representing this are: 1)The burbling background of the bulk of the players softly doodling with the scale. It's important they interact with each other and with 2. 2)The melody: played freely by one or more musicians.... The start of each phrase should be clear. 3)The soloist observer who reacts to what he hears. '

simultaneously expressed; at other times he maintains distinct musical elements intermittently throughout a composition, so that each represents a layer effective continuously whether or not sounded. Conversely, as noted on the sleeve of *Scorpions*, he has sometimes striven to 'obscure the division between melody and background', though this can be seen as a possible corollary of layering, that is, different levels are in a state of equality. An example of this which is interesting from the improviser's point of view is given in Fig. 10.3.

Collier thus made a clear progression in his work from 1969 to 1985, in which harmonic complexity was gradually introduced; textural freedom advanced for the improviser; and an increasingly layered approach to music for/by improvisers became effective. He falls into the conservative subdivision of composers which I outlined in Chapter 9, in that he has preserved strong continuities with some at least of the formulaic elements of jazz (most notably pulse). Within that group, judging by both my improvising experience and my analytical listening to the recordings, he is a composer whose output has been used to influence the improviser's output. And like his hero Ellington, he has made specific compositional responses to the improvising character and abilities of his musicians: for example, the material and placing of the piano solo on 'October Ferry' was clearly designed to exploit my interests of the time.

The fragments of interview which follow are extracted from a two-hour discussion between friends who collaborate. They are based on a sequence of questions and comments I formulated immediately before the interview as a result of analysis of Graham's work. Thus the issues discussed related sequentially to harmony; motive/melody; rhythm; form; words and other non-musical artistic stimuli affecting the composer; signification; and social influences on the compositional activity – in other words, the issues which permeate this book. Not all these issues are represented in the quotations, but some of the responses are necessarily conditioned by the framework of analysis. Some of the conversational expression has been made more grammatical for the purposes of clarity.

The interview contrasts with most published collections (for example, A123) in concerning musical issues rather than biographical ones. Hopefully it is not in the spirit castigated in the following quotation (A123):

> *Rusch*   A lot of the press is made up of glorified fans.
> *Bill Dixon*   They really are. A man collects records for 20 years ...
> when he has a large enough collection, he writes a liner note, he
> becomes a critic.

Graham Collier, interviewed at his home in London by Roger Dean, 23 October 1988

The following are fragments of an edited transcript, prepared in October 1988, approved by both participants and available on request from the author.

Graham Collier (*GC*) [springing from a question on harmony]: There was heavy influence from outside music in 'Tryptych' and 'Scorpions'. I do firmly believe that lots of my musical influences have come from art, and from writers. The conscious one, the obvious one, is Malcolm Lowry. I've learnt a lot from the way he used his language and his different levels of attention. Which is what intrigues me about it. I must also have absorbed a lot subconsciously from writers and film-makers which I've never really articulated properly, although I've paid tribute to Lowry in a conference.

So I think, I want to write a piece of music like *New Conditions*: the idea of that was to put people into new conditions of improvising. Whatever harmonic or musical choices I made in all the different areas were just fuelled because I was trying to write these specific situations. So I've never thought of myself as having a particular method ... And I've always just sat ... and thought about a sound. Quite often, I think especially latterly, the starting process has been harmonic: a chord or a set of chords rather than a kind of bass line or a harmonic line as it used to be. So I think that's been the change ... It's always been part of the stimulus of being a jazz composer to present what I do allied with what the soloist does. And to try to put them into different environments: to complement what I want to say with them, and also to support what they want to say . . .

I've been trying to write music dramatically all my life and that's what I would say I am: a dramatic composer . . . the kind of thing I do is to try to paint a picture . . .

Roger Dean (RD): . . . In the case of *New Conditions*, where there was no programmatic or external artistic object explicit: was there one implicit and not stated? (*GC indicates that there was not.*) . . . Why did you choose harmony to be the primary parameter . . . ?

GC: . . . harmony is what stimulates most jazz musicians anyway. And there are some melodies in there, use of melodic situations. I've always been harmonically based. Even in the old days I based a piece on bass lines which had harmonic structures, or on harmonic implications, . . . as now it may be three chords.

. . . At the opening of *New Conditions* (I've done it in other pieces too) I build up a chord which is very dissonant: maybe you'd call that polytonal but I'd say it was atonal . . . I want to have that kind of sound . . . it doesn't really matter what it is in relation to tonality. I try to find that sound in the same way a painter tries to find a colour . . . More and more . . . I want to get involved in pieces like the Japanese piece ['Ryoanji': see Fig. 10.3] where it's so open and where there are possibilities for somebody to stamp himself (or herself) on it as a player and for me . . . to control the person in some way as a conductor. That . . . is what I'm interested in as a writer.

RD: But in a way that's a tendency which will reduce the overall impact that you the composer have, isn't it?

GC: Yes, but then I see that my role as a jazz composer does involve considering the role of the improviser. To me there's absolutely no point in writing too much for the improviser, like most jazz composers do. So I may veer the other way and make it too free. But it should still be recognisable as me. And the way the piece is structured should still have my stamp no matter what happens within it. And I think it does with 'Ryoanji', 'Hackney Five' and others . . .

RD: Sticking finally with motives: one of the issues, from the performer's point of view, about your use of motives is the degree to which they are varied as the piece goes along . . . One thing you do rarely . . . is transpose the motive. I think there is one place in *New Conditions* where you transpose the first motive in order to make the rhythmic riff on G (*sings riff*) at the end; there you transpose the first four notes. Now is that something you thought about and decided against . . . ?

GC: . . . I go to a lot of trouble to find the space that [motives] inhabit in sound, and so to transpose them changes that space. It's because I have this feeling . . . that there's a certain key that the motive is in . . .

for me there are certain sounds that only work where they are. This is particularly true of chords.

... [after discussion of rhythm] The essence of the constant time/ pulse thing, is that I think it's a very exciting, very important part of jazz ... I'm not really that interested in complicated metres. I did it then in the early 1970s; ... I'm sure I could still do it now, but I'm not terribly interested ...

RD: ... But what you did in the early 1970s was just complicated metre wasn't it? What about ... multiples: sevens, fives, etc.?

GC: I've never been interested in that.

RD: So does complicated rhythm not appeal partly because you want to leave that space for the improviser?

GC: I suppose that is at the root of it ... I've never been very interested in rhythm as such. Rhythm is a pulse-based thing: what improvisers do over it the pulse is what interests me. That may be sevens and fives or whatever ...

RD: Shall we talk about form for a bit? One of the interesting things you did fairly early on after returning from America was to introduce the concept of composition modules which could be shifted around, wasn't it? ... How do you feel about that and how did it arise? Did you have any awareness of a relationship with shifting Earle Brown's pages, etc.?

GC: Not really ... no, I wanted in those particular pieces, *Mosaics* and *Darius* and *Songs*, to reflect in a very broad way the fact that a jazz piece at its best changes from performance to performance ... I wanted to explore ways of achieving that changeability, and I still am, but that was painting with broad strokes, as it were. In ... movable composed modules I thought there were effective ways of writing ... Plus I firmly believe that if the piece is written to allow it, the composer/leader can be very creative with it in live performances; reacting in the same way as the improvisers to the situation ... I sometimes wish I could do it more quickly. You have to cue '1' or '3' and then give four beats and get people in, which all takes time and by then the moment ... inspired ... by the improviser has probably gone. It's still there in the air somewhere but it's not as immediate as if you could press a button on the computer and do it. Maybe that's the next step ...

GC [after extended discussion of motivic relationships in compositions]: ... I'm now able to represent this essentialness of jazz, its ability to be different each time, within a formal framework which I decide before-hand ...

RD: [The opening of *Something British*] ... introduces all the layers, all the materials, musicians, and their links to be retained through the piece, doesn't it?

GC: Yes, and it was written with that in mind. Yes, it's part of the process. I suppose I've learnt how to do this now ...

RD: ... Does your [stance as a composer] relate to the idea that there's only one way the piece, because of the ideas that you've generated at the beginning, could come out? ...

GC: More or less. But ... that what I'm setting up is a 'possible picture': that circumstances (deadlines, influences, even health and state of mind) have shaped the piece ... Then you have the addition of improvisers and composer/leader which again presents a 'possible picture' when it is performed ... I revel in ... the surprise of it, the 'aliveness' of it (the composition) in all its stages from my writing to its performance(s) ...

RD [after extended discussion of words in music]: You're involved in musicals, and you collaborate with several writers, but ... you haven't collaborated with any to produce primarily a jazz work, have you?

GC: There's never been the opportunity ... [but I plan an opera]. I don't yet know who will do the libretto though I want to have a large say in it ... The trouble with jazz and words is that, unless you get a good singer who can improvise with words, then the words are essentially a different stratum of what you're doing. Because the words must be present and whatever improvisation you do is usually around them rather than [with them]. If you do improvise with the words it gets very difficult in terms of what the words mean: if the words are supposed to have a meaning, which for me they usually are. So they need to be said or sung fairly clearly ... I've thought about [other ways of using words] in relation to the planned opera ... In an opera an improvising chorus would be very interesting. Words are important to me and what I've got very consciously from Lowry is this use of different levels of attention. Dividing the jazz picture up in different ways. That's probably been the biggest influence on my life as a jazz composer. The biggest opening, breakthrough, into finding a way of doing things ...

I think there is the very strong connection [with my music] in [Lowry's] use of language: those long spiralling sentences ... And it's that spiralling off 'at a tangent' which I think a good jazz soloist does. I don't think many composers are aware of that and of how to deal with it. Most composers write a tune which with luck inspires improvisation, but they don't really know what the improvisation is doing in or with the tune apart from following it ...

[in relation to outside influences on Collier's music:] I find ... I listen to other composers for enjoyment, Ellington still, but most of the time it has nothing to do with what I'm doing. It's a totally different field. And I get my inspiration from other areas, and the two conscious ones are literature and art. I would say that I think a lot about the overall picture and I may decide that I want a block of colour like a mass improvisation at one particular point in a big piece; or big stab chords as in several. But this idea of using the band by improvising with it is important: like the three saxophones improvising against the stab chords in 'Hoarded Dreams', with the chords being directed freely depending on what the improvisers are doing ... I've always felt these are an inspiration from painting, particularly the splashes of colour ... Like the Clyfford Still paintings where there are tiny splashes of red: that kind of thinking is important to me. That's the thing which really survives from a painting.

Recordings discussed

Collier, Graham (1967) *Deep Dark Blue Centre*, Deram DML 1005.
Collier (1969) *Down Another Road*, Fontana SFJL 922.
Collier (1970) *Songs for My Father*, Fontana 6309 006.
Collier (1971) *Mosaics*, Fontana 6308 051.
Collier (1972) *Portraits*, Saydisc SD1 244.
Collier (1974) *Darius*, Mosaic GCM 741.
Collier (1975) *Midnight Blue*, Mosaic GCM 751.
Collier (1976) *New Conditions*, Mosaic GCM 761.
Collier (1977) *Symphony of Scorpions*, Mosaic GCM 773.
Collier (1978) *Day of The Dead*, Mosaic GCM 783/4.
Collier (1985) *Something British Made in Hong Kong*, Mosaic GCM 871.

SECTION 4

Improvised music and
the artistic context

11 Music-sound-text-image and the futures of improvisation

Written in collaboration with Hazel Smith

> To the extent that we are unpredictable, we improvise ... An additional sense of the word improvisation is that it concerns actions whose effects are indelible
>
> (Pressing in A27).

Could the developments in improvisation which we have discussed have been influences on the development of other arts, such as painting or verbal art? Was there influence in the opposite sense? Since every field needs new technical devices at certain stages in its development, and since around 1960 improvisation was more pronounced in music in the West than in other arts, we might suspect that improvised music influenced some other arts. The analysis of such relationships will be a large project, and subject to many of the difficulties discussed in the Introduction and Appendix 1 relating to music *per se*.

We do not pretend to solve these issues here, but to bring forth pointers towards their investigation, including raising key issues and offering an analytic, if limited, catalogue of instances of improvisation in the other arts. Since such compendia of relevant information are not readily available elsewhere, this will be useful for further analysis in the future. It is also necessary for us to consider inter-artistic forms in order to discuss briefly the future of improvised music, and of improvisation in the arts in general. For it is already apparent that the present art forms will not, or already do not, remain separate in the 1990s and this seems to be true also of the relation of improvised music to the other arts.

We will illustrate how an increased range of improvisatory techniques have been made available within the several western arts. We do not

177

mean to imply that the improvisatory techniques are necessarily more dominant with time, rather that they became established as viable during the period, and have remained so since. We will also point out how the various arts have inevitable continuity with each other, rather than being discrete entities, and how the use of improvisatory techniques has made these continuities the more apparent.

We need first to clarify the concept of improvisation. In its extreme sense we take improvisation as the simultaneous conception and production of an artistic entity. One can contrast 'absolute' and 'referent-based' improvisation (cf. Pressing in A27; and in A134) as at several earlier points in this book. This distinction, in which only referent-based improvisation uses any pre-existing framework (and so is less extreme than absolute improvisation), corresponds to the older confusing distinction of extemporisation (absolute) versus improvisation (referent-based) which still occurs in some literature (for example, Eaton in A84). The extent (cf. A27) of improvised contribution to various activities thus varies from classical ballet (almost none), through rock (a little), jazz (around 50%), some avant-garde theatre (perhaps 80%) to free jazz, Indian alap sections, etc. (nearly 100%).

The frequency and visibility of musical free improvising increased during the period under study. In music there is usually the requirement that if an audience is to experience the improvisation, they have to be present at the time it occurs: thus performance for an audience is often part of musical improvisation. In this sense, conversation is the archetype of improvisation outside the arts. For most improvised arts, the presence of the audience at the time of creation is also necessary: for instance, in the case of performance art, a visual-dramatic entity which is at least partly improvised (see A46; A74a; A103). In some arts other than music, it is not always necessary for the audience to be present at the time a work is made in order to experience it. For example, we could consider the case of an improvised painting, which met an extreme criterion like that proposed in the introductory quotation to this chapter: that there were no erasures or overpaintings (since a painting cannot be 'indelible'). Such a painting, though improvised, would be available to an audience after its completion, and the presence of the audience during the production of the work might not be particularly important. It would be a rare kind of painting.

The concept of improvisation in music normally implies that only a certain length of time should be available for production of the work, and that all the actions by the producer within that time frame should be(come) part of the improvised work. In other words, there is no possibility of removing an element once produced. An element can still be treated as an 'error', and rectified by subsequent actions. Rectification has to be retrospective and cannot be erasive.

The requirement that all actions of the producer should be(come) part of the work can usefully be considered in relation to the other arts, even though the division between the improvised work (operating over minutes and hours), and the composed, preconstructed or premeditated work, being produced over days and weeks, is an arbitrary division. The requirement may be a useful additional criterion for separating improvisation from composition, etc., but the distinction remains inevitably arbitrary: one of gradation rather than discontinuity.

This concept of improvisation does not, of course, preclude the juxtaposition of improvisation with a predetermined framework. Thus in one piece Don Ellis (R53) requested his colleagues to improvise without any defined material but to generate a progression from 'despair to hope'. This could equally be the basis of a theatrical or poetic improvisation, and possibly also of an improvised painting. It is impossible in improvisation to avoid some predetermination in the most literal sense (for example, the performance always takes place within a space, often one whose definitions are accepted beforehand, as when it occurs in a hall or on a mountain, and uses a particular instrument or body, etc.). However, more significantly constructed elements may also be used to provide a framework for improvisation, as elaborated already in relation to music.

Improvised elements in the various arts since 1960

It is remarkable and suggestive that the period under discussion contained a flowering of improvised elements in most arts. We will provide the briefest synopsis. Best known perhaps is action painting, in the work of the abstract expressionists such as Jackson Pollock. There is a film by Hans Namuth and Paul Falkenberg, 'Jackson Pollock', which includes (1950) Pollock painting on glass. He talks as he proceeds, and describes the relationships he holds with a progressing work, which is finished (or rather, stopped) in a matter of a few hours. His 'action painting' normally consisted of dripping paint from a stick or brush onto a horizontal canvas, thereby discarding much precision of control, but gaining much fluidity and freedom of action. The technique again permitted a degree of dislocation between physical movement and artistic output, like some techniques we have discussed in music. Erasure was not involved, but there was retrospective correction of any detected 'errors' by new forms or overpainting, rather than by removal of the errors: again an analogy to the rectification of errors in improvised music which we have mentioned earlier.

That improvising musicians identified with action painting and viewed it as improvisatory is illustrated by the fact that Ornette Coleman's *Free Jazz* (R17) has a reproduction of Pollock on the cover, and that Coleman has stated that his playing had some rapport with Pollock's work (A76, p. 234). A clear analogy also exists between the action painting of the 1960s

179

and the action playing of Cecil Taylor, where, using clusters instead of drips, Taylor for much of the time treats the keyboard of the piano as a one-dimensional pitch map played as a single rapidly moving line. Other musicians were aware of the parallel: for example, the Wolfgang Dauner LP *Free Action*, which we have discussed already, takes its second word advisedly, and has a cover painting not unrelated to action paintings. Daniel Humair, following the improvisations of Alan Davie in painting (particularly in the 1950s, according to Davie in personal conversation), has also been an action artist in both jazz and painting.

The improvisatory technique of action painting can be viewed as largely non-formulaic, non-referent-based. But this need not be the case with improvisatory techniques in painting, as one could improvise in relation to the referent of producing a portrait, or other figurative entity. Such is perhaps the case with some more recent figurative/expressionist painters, such as A.R. Penck (who is also an improvising musician).

Turning to verbal arts, improvised poetry/talk was among the work of the Beats, and of later poets such as David Antin. Many of the Beats of the 1950s and 1960s (see Rolantz in A22), in particular Kerouac and later Ginsberg (in relation to Howl), made a special point of claiming that to be effective their poetry had to be the result of 'blowing'. 'Blowing' was a term borrowed from jazz, and meant producing all in one go a musical statement (as the jazz soloist 'blows' his solo). Similarly, the poets claimed to produce their works often immediately from start to finish. Some of the poetry of Kerouac does have a rhythmic vitality akin to jazz, and it seems quite feasible that an improvisatory process was at work in producing it. Thus Kerouac wrote in the prefatory note to 'Mexico City Blues' (1959):

> I want to be considered a jazz poet
> blowing a long blues in an afternoon jam
> session on Sunday. I take 242 choruses;
> my ideas vary and sometimes roll from
> chorus to chorus or from halfway through
> a chorus to halfway into the next.

Similarly, one of us has argued (A137) that improvisatory elements are important in some of the work around the 1960s of the New York Poets, such as John Ashbery, Kenneth Koch and Frank O'Hara. The influence of the earlier, quite distinct, automatic writing of the Surrealists is readily apparent. Such improvisatory elements also have explicit importance in the subsequent work of Jackson Mac Low (A138).

Among the most extreme cases of improvised poetry/talks may be those of David Antin in the USA and cris cheek in the UK, in the 1970s and 1980s. Antin has been recorded improvising for considerable lengths of time, sometimes using a repetition technique involving permuting patterns of words (see A5), slightly related to some of the processes of repetitive (systemic) music, but more often a kind of narrative structure. Antin used to call himself a 'poet' but later (1984) said that he is a performer of 'talk pieces'. To quote him (A4):

i mean im aiming not to be prepared   so that i can do what i dont expect to do   which is what one means by improvisation ... and what you mean by improvisation is coming and saying something you dont know

A brief example from an equally relevant transcription of Antin's work (A5) is given below:

whos listening out there
this is not really the first time ive done radio piece   the last one was in berkeley on kpfa for a program that peter gordon and cathy acker had put together for the music director   a composer named charles amirkanian   and i guess i was supposed to be some kind of musician or i was supposed to be making some kind of music   by talking   which i suppose i was ... there are a lot of little private audiences ... i think theyre probably worrying because im improvising   because im making up what im saying while im saying it and they may be worrying

In the Sound-Text movement (A74a), a complete integration of verbal and non-verbal sound took place. Sounds were derived from words and phonemes and performed by a speaker-vocalist. Usually there was a text containing such elements, but some referent-based improvising at least was normally involved. Important figures in this movement were Jackson Mac Low, Philip Corner, Dick Higgins (in the USA); and Bob Cobbing (in the UK). The latter has continued to participate in improvisatory activities of many kinds. We will return to Sound-Text later because of its other characteristic of merging two art forms.

It may well be, therefore, that the increasing emphasis on improvisatory elements in music in the 1960s was a factor encouraging similar elements among poets, and we will see additional interactions when we discuss mixed media.

Moving from verbal to moving visual artefacts, we can note that in the 1960s several films and videos were produced by an improvisatory process. For example, *Pull My Daisy*, by R. Frank and Alfred Leslie (R60), depicts an uncontrolled spontaneous gathering of Beat Poets, and has a soundtrack by Kerouac (with music by jazz musician David Amram); and from the 1960s until the present Nam June Paik, the prolific video and multimedia artist, has often produced improvised/environmental work. Here there is some contravention of the idea of no erasure, in that, of course, the filmed segments can (and often have to) be edited and only certain parts used.

In theatre, this process of improvisation followed by editing has often also been applied, in that the performance can be evolved by successive improvisation, and then fairly tightly fixed for repeated performance: this was the case with many works of the Living Theatre (A74b) or Grotowski, and subsequently, for example, in the UK in the procedures of Mike Leigh. An independent line of improvised theatre often without words (as in some of Tadeusz Kantor's work) was operative in Poland in the 1960s, again associated with film (Skolimowski) and jazz musicians such as Kristof Komeda. Similarly, performance works are often a complex amalgam of improvised but then schematised actions, and real-time changes in response to performer sensations.

It is important to realise that most of these improvising techniques in the arts have clear antecedents. Thus in music, the rhythmic developments of the 'rhythm section' were presaged by the work of the improvising soloists in previous generations (as we saw earlier): but they had not achieved the equality between all the members of the group which was subsequently possible. Similarly, several kinds of free abstraction in painting had appeared before Pollock, in the work of the Russians such as Rozanova, of the Frenchman Masson, and elsewhere. Again the physical form of the products had similarities, but the nature of the process, and the attitude of the producer towards the impact of technique upon physical factors (for example, gravity, wind) was quite different, and this is important for the detailed appearance of the work. The work of the Futurists similarly anticipated several aspects of what was later achieved by poetic, theatrical and filmic improvisation (see A46 for example), but again with different intentions and effects, as judged by the writing of the participants. One of the key differences between the attitudes of most of the antecedent artists, and those of the 1960s onwards that we are discussing, is the difference in emphasis on the technical procedure of improvisation. As we are arguing, this became far more important during the recent period.

One common purpose (or at least advantage) of using the improvising techniques in the arts is the dislocation of familiar technique from familiar and predictable effect, just as we have revealed elsewhere in this book in relation to music. An example might be the use in film of an improvised rhythmic technique, not usually found within filming. Because technical innovation is a periodic requirement in every art, the realisation in the 1960s that improvisation could be applied to several arts was an important one which conveyed practical advantages, and contributed to the development of new techniques which did not necessarily remain improvisatory. For example, the aspects of the work of the Surrealists, New York Poets, and David Antin, which dislocate normal verbal expression, could be integrated in that of the Language Poets (Charles Bernstein, Bruce Andrews, Ron Silliman, etc.).

In sum, there has been a variety of distinctive improvised techniques coming to the fore of, and remaining part of, the contemporary arts since

1960. They share the central feature of musical improvisation that has been discussed earlier, that of diversifying the technical language available. They also share a willingness beyond that of composed/predetermined works to permit an interaction with external events, and we will briefly discuss this next.

Environment-space-improvisation

Musical improvisation necessarily involved the possibility of an individual musician facing an event generated by another which was unexpected, even initially undesired. It was not surprising, therefore, that improvisers should develop a preparedness for such events, and even extend the sources of such events outside the activities of the musicians themselves. In this section we will illustrate that such environment-space-improvisation became important in the other spheres besides music.

Oliveros (A102; A103) and others, including Stockhausen, fostered the interest of musical improvisers in utilising every aspect of environmental sound. And in the work of MEV, AMM, among others, one can hear silences, in other words unadulterated environmental sounds, for significant lengths of time. There was a concurrence between the improvisers' interest in environmental contributions to their work, and the composers' interest in it, as influentially illustrated by Cage. His '4'33"' was the most extreme example of this line of thought, consisting only of a pianist sitting down and remaining in front of a piano for the specified length of time (A100). In 1988 Rolf Gehlhaar used a 'sound-space' which is a transducer of bodily movements into instructions to a computer program of musical entities and procedures, so that modifications of the nature of the ongoing music can be effected by the performer's (improvised) movements: a more elegant, larger-scale version of synthesiser control by the two-dimensional movement of a mouse. Other relationships between music and dance are discussed by Silber (A23).

Again this interest developed in music in parallel with similar concerns in the other arts, and may be attributed at least partly to the developments in improvised music. In the visual arts several movements were concerned with juxtaposition of the object with environmental objects: from the conceptual artists, to the work of Richard Long whose natural objects are usually placed in unnatural positions within the environment. In film the most relevant movements were at the origins of Structural film, in that works such as '< >' (La Region Centrale, 1970–1) of Mike Snow involved a camera rotating on its axis from side to side (< to >) and recording whatever happened in the environment (a mixture of improvisation and self-conscious behaviour, with inanimate physical events). Snow was connected more closely with musical improvisers in his direction of the film *New York Eye and Ear Control*, in which Shepp and others appeared; the title is a reference to aspects of the US health system, and particularly that in New York. Some of Warhol's films are, similarly, records of events in uncontrolled domestic and working environments.

But not only could events in the environment be recorded, and then become the work of art, they could also be responded to as they happened (an essence of improvisation) and the resultant sum of the events contributed to the work. Such was more often the procedure of the Fluxus music/artist and of many performance people and theatrical people working with or without words. A pyrogenic example in the UK is the work of the Bow Gamelan, of which improvising percussionist Paul Burwell is a member. Similarly, in Australia Jon Rose gave a performance entitled 'Relative Band Plays Cricket', based on the rules of cricket, and invited the audience to voice loud opinions on anything that happened – 'which is not "fair go", or is getting too close to "art"' (to quote Rose himself). Rose likes 'music to continually attack my preconceptions' (quoted in A62).

The application of improvisation in most arts therefore facilitated the development of an interaction with the environment, whether contributed by inanimate entities or by other people supposedly apart from the work.

Relations between the improvisatory arts

The musical improviser may 'consciously violate syntactic rules' (A148); thus a free jazz performance might be thought the equivalent of the 'creative ungrammaticality' of, for example, the poet e.e. cummings. We have argued that such improvisatory features are shared widely within the arts; and one can also argue that the arts anyway possess many common processes, signs and other entities (A13; A138). The improvisatory elements outlined above thus arose from, reflected and developed anew a variety of pre-existent relationships between the arts in the period under study. We can consider these relations in terms of, first, of simple juxtaposition of different arts into interartistic forms; second, in terms of individuals or collaborators participating in several arts; and third, we can return to the idea of sharing of characteristics by the different arts.

Some examples of juxtaposition have had to be mentioned already in this chapter. Thus we have implied that improvised music was often the companion of poetry performance in the early 1960s. Specifically, Beat poetry was often performed in the 1960s in relation to jazz. Thus Ferlinghetti collaborated with Dorough and a jazz group (on *The Day*; World Pacific WP 1244); and LeRoi Jones with the New York Art Quartet (R82). Tristano's (R133) improvisation on Edgar Allan Poe was an antecedent to these inspirations.

In some cases these juxtapositions had their difficulties. Thus Bryon Gysin (sound poet, painter, film-maker and novelist) has commented (A50, p. 48):

184

But poetry, of course, exists not necessarily on a printed page, nor even in the spoken word – nevertheless, as a so called father of Sound Poetry, I do believe that it's more in the spoken word (and so did the whole movement, it's not my invention that brought it about), in the sense that before we began the Domaine Poetique group ... for example, in 1960–1 ... there had been people trying to do poetry and jazz in America, which was a horrible mess I must say ...

Kuryokhin (A40) has commented similarly on his attempts to persuade poets to improvise in performance (both alone or with musicians):

In our Contemporary Music Club [formed around 1980] we tried to include Leningrad poets in our improvisation performances, but unfortunately these attempts were unsuccessful, as if poets did not understand ... how one can improvise in front of an audience.

Gysin has nevertheless collaborated with the American jazz improviser Steve Lacy to produce an interesting verbal-musical recording (R84). Other interesting text/improvised music collaborations include Archie Shepp's *Fire Music* (R115) (though the improvisation in the text is probably slight); and John Clare and Serge Ermoll's truly improvisatory collaboration in Australia (see Chapter 8). Poempaintings were improvised by Norman Bluhm and Frank O'Hara also: these consisted of verbal elements on a canvas which was painted. The two artists worked successively in the same room on each canvas, and each poempainting was improvised very rapidly (A137).

Improvised music was also often used in conjunction with adventurous films at that time. An interesting example, involving an artist also active in both painting and improvised music, was *New York Eye and Ear Control*, already mentioned, a film by Mike Snow, the Canadian (R117). This used music improvised within the filming, as well as outside it, by musicians in whom Snow was interested. The scenario was based around their activities with apparently little prearrangement. Similarly, the theatrical and musical elements of Fluxus performances (for example, Paik and Beuys); of Sun Ra Arkestra performance (R119); Art Ensemble of Chicago performances; and of instructional pieces by George Brecht ('Jam Box', for example), or the colleagues of Cornelius Cardew in the UK (see A20) cannot be separated because virtually every improvised action had both musical and theatrical effects. Many multimedia works also fit this description.

We can turn now to our second aspect: individual improvisatory artists who were active in several arts rather than one, and who thus tended to combine them in various ways relevant to our thrust here. There are many painters who were proficient in improvised music. Some have been mentioned already in this chapter. Bill Dixon has been mentioned in an earlier chapter: and the ironies of the relationship between the two arts in his case are amusingly revealed (A123). Larry Rivers (see the collection of the Museum of Modern Art, New York) was and is active in fairly conventional jazz improvising, while Mike Snow, as already mentioned, is a dynamic free improviser on keyboard instruments, active in the Canadian Contemporary Musicians' Collective and heard briefly playing trumpet on *Escalator over the Hill* with the Jazz Composers' Orchestra (Chapter 9). The Scotsman Alan Davie, whose work was mistaken at first exposure by Peggy Guggenheim (according to her autobiography) for work of Pollock, is an improvising cellist, pianist and saxophonist, originating within formulaic jazz, but now active in freer improvisation (see, for example, R91).

But perhaps the most interesting of the dual practitioners are those who participate in both improvised music and verbal work. Pauline Oliveros (R106; A102–3) and Robert Ashley were early participants: Ashley's pieces for the Bob James Trio (R75) are interesting, sometimes amusing, interactions of verbal text with improvised music. Some of his sound-texts are in an anthology with Gavin Bryars, Hobbs, Shrapnel and other UK practitioners ('Verbal Anthology' Experimental Music Catalogue, 1972). Sound-text (A74a), whose scores are usually the basis for improvisation, is one area where musical and verbal work are in direct continuity. Thus the scores of Mac Low (A81a and b), often performed by the writers themselves with Lysis, involve whole words and phonemic elements, as discussed earlier (and in A31). Thus performance of his 'Asymmetries' (A81a) can combine musical-sound (where apparently non-verbal sounds derive from phonemes) and text-sound (improvised and verbal). Other performance interactions are included in his 'Representative Works' (A81b). Some of his works also permit a literal translation of the letters used into pitches, which can then be used as an improvising basis, though in fairly strict ways: this generates another source of musical sound (that is, sound which is no longer recognisably verbal or phonemic). As already mentioned, the introduction of such phonemic structures into music has been a most fascinating extension of technical possibilities. Bob Cobbing has said of his ensemble Abana that they try to integrate sound poems with the instruments 'so the voices become instruments, and the instruments speak the poetry' (A77).

We could give many more examples of individuals with talents in several art forms. These examples may simply indicate that the forceful individual can mould the ideas of one art to cohere with those of another. On the other hand, they may indicate some recognition of common features which pre-existed: the third aspect of improvisatory relationships we mentioned at the outset of this section. In either case, they bring to the fore and expand the common ideas which can develop and relate the different arts, largely by the process of enlarging the technical possibilities of each, such that a continuity is formed even if one did not exist previously.

These continuities can also be a consequence of the wish to produce art objects in real time, and to permit interaction with other events, derived from other people and from the physical environment: in other words to improvise them into art processes and objects. We suggest this wish arose partly as a result of the influence of improvised music, its development and power, during the 1960s.

Futures of improvisation

Although one of the values of improvisation is its capacity to develop new techniques, or new, unpredicted outputs from the application of familiar techniques, improvised music has remained viable in cultures of the East (for example, India) even when relatively little change in technique or output has been occurring. On the other hand, several other improvised musics, such as flamenco, are alive and retaining their traditions, but at the same time suffering the depredations of various kinds of amalgamation with commercial music, which may ultimately undermine the tradition. Nevertheless, it is apparent to us that improvised music may remain alive even without any clear sense of change with time. This, of course, is an ethnocentric opinion: perhaps the important scale of change in Indian music is a very small scale compared with that in the West. However, the essential point for our present purposes is that with respect to the kinds of change we have been discussing in this book, Indian music remains relatively static.

Thus western improvisation has reached a stage where a very wide range of techniques are in use in at least some contexts, whether jazz, free improvisation, electronic improvisation or whatever. The same can be said to an equal degree of composition. However, composition has one major technical growing point, influenced by technological developments: digitally synthesised music, and digital control. This technology may also lead to improved techniques of interaction between improvisers, and between composers and improvisers, which will eventually be applicable in real time, and go beyond those presently at work.

Even excluding computer-based development (which has been discussed in A31), the field of improvisation in music has limitless possibilities by means of the techniques already in use; and some specific areas of possible technical expansion within the techniques already opened. Many of these implications for extension of technique have already been described in brief, but here I will summarise them more precisely. I will then outline some of the principles by which computer and digital control may be valuable in the future. As noted already in this volume and in A31, a few remarkable examples of the real-time use of relatively large computers are on record already; and George Lewis has outlined some of the theoretical issues (in A120).

Rhythm and pitch: future extensions of musical usage

The basic principles of rhythmic organisation which seem to offer new possibilities in improvisation can be summarised as rhythmic independence of different parts of a group; and the extension of improvisation of pulse relationships within a piece. Thus the idea of dividing an improvising group into several units which have distinct pulses, or which work on distinct kinds of rhythmic device, has received little attention. Similarly, the possibility of developing the technique of pulse shifts which we have discussed earlier, such that rather more complicated and yet precisely controlled shifts can be achieved, is open. Perhaps even more importantly, the idea of sustaining for significant lengths of time several competing pulses and/or metres in different parts of the group, and improvising the transition to and from this state, is appealing. It leads to a *temporary* subdivision of the group into two or more different rhythmic teams. But this is distinct from permanent rhythmic independence of several parts of a group in that the function of the overlap of rhythmic states is to make the transition, while this is not the function of a continuously established subdivision of the group into different rhythmic functions.

Coming to the realms of pitch, I have suggested the desirability of exploiting microtonal improvisation rather further. There is a clear parallel here with Grainger's aspirations in his 'free-music machine' (cf. A41). This aspiration may be appropriate even for the players of instruments normally treated as suitable for equal tempered playing (for instance, string instruments): they may develop the ability to play without regard for equal temperament. This might involve new fingering systems, playing the instrument in an unorthodox position (for example, playing the double bass while it is lying on the floor), or introducing unusual tunings of the strings of the instrument. Analogous devices can be envisaged for the wind instruments: for instance, using sections of different individual instruments so that the tuning system is not so dictated by the 'unitary' nature of the fingering keys; or permanently closing an individual key so as to be able to use the other keys for microtonal or timbral effects rather than for intonation.

These microtonal (or non-pitch-based) approaches can be extended by harnessing instruments also to digital synthesis through MIDI, as when using wind controllers (like the Yamaha WX7). The WX7 is played as if it were a wind instrument, and has many of the responses, but in fact generates sounds specified by a synthesiser, and thus can be microtonal (or for that matter, percussive and untuned).

Computers and musical improvisation

The previous chapters have indicated that it can be desirable to avoid the intermediacy of notation in the development of improvising abilities (A31; A33; A156), and, similarly, that the speed of improvisation is such that the cognition of the musical elements in other musicians' work often cannot be very detailed, for an improvising response to be initiated. Nevertheless, on occasion a detailed recognition of even a complex element in a continuing improvisation may strike one of the performers, and may be used to some degree.

Computers offer several means by which this recognition in real time (as the piece progresses) could be avoided, or extended and exploited, to produce an additional approach to improvising. Avoidance of the necessity of recognition is possible by live sampling techniques. In these, sounds of other performers are sampled (recorded in brief snippets) by modules whose data can then be played back or modified. Material of other improvisers can thus be acquired and exploited without the need for any recognition or recreation process by the performer (as with Wesley-Smith: see Chapter 8, p. 140 and p. 142).

Other approaches can permit enhancement of recognition rather than avoidance. For example, an improviser on a keyboard synthesiser can readily feed the musical pitches and timings into software which will transmit them onto the screen in various representations, whether spatial or even approximations to conventional rhythms (see, for instance, the automated transcription shown in A113). Thus as one was improvising, one could immediately afterwards view the results, presented in a chosen way, and become aware of aspects of them that might escape one otherwise: these could then become the basis for a further development. Similarly, the material presented to improviser A on a computer screen could originate from another improviser, and could be material not heard by A, or not even sounded at the time of the performance. Thus a silent musical element could be prepared in advance, or during a performance by an improviser whose function is to perturb the ongoing improvisation by silent musical input. All kinds of exchange of information in this way can be envisaged, and might have fascinating effects on the nature of the ongoing improvisation.

While the permutations of this approach are diverse, and easy to envisage, an even more profound development could come when artificial intelligence methods of improvising were added to the mix: for example, an as yet relatively restricted program like 'Jam Factory' (A31) could be fed material from an improviser, and used to generate an output (silent or audible) which is fed back to the performers. Of course, the computer-derived input could also be generated by producers, whether random or systematic, which were programmed independently of the ongoing performance, and not affected by it. But in this case they would merely function like other aspects of environmental input, except that they might be produced as musical sound rather than in any other way. But in the longer term, the use of more sophisticated artificial intelligence programs for controlling musical parameters, working on many of the principles discussed earlier in this book and in A31, might be very provocative for ongoing improvisations, and permit new layers of interaction and control which will be highly productive.

Music improvises poempainting

The relationship and interaction between the different arts, and its accentuation through the involvement of improvisation in each, was discussed earlier. Perhaps the most fascinating perspective on futures of improvisation which one can intuitively glimpse at present is that of a continuous 'translation' of musical input into poetic, filmic or visual output, and reciprocals of all these processes. This could readily be achieved by arbitrary computer programs, just as in a sense it has been achieved in less rigorous ways by some of the interactions already discussed; and is already commencing. The complexity and precision of the translation achieved would be a controllable, expanding facet, and might permit a much fuller appreciation by artists of the common features and functions within their arts. As with the concept of silent musical input into a musical improvisation, so there could be non-visible painterly input, etc. The possibilities are boundless, and likely to be exciting. The increased accessibility and economy of computer hardware encourages the hope that soon most artists will be able to exploit these opportunities.

And equally that the false separation between artist and other beings will finally be undermined if not destroyed by the process. There is no need for reliance on the separation to maintain a belief in the power of art: if art has power it arises by an interaction between mode of production and mode of perception, and it is not necessary that the former involve specialised discriminatory functions; those of most people can probably be employed, just as Cage has employed the functions of most environments. Cheap digital equipment will permit nearly everyone, and nearly every environment, to play a role in improvisatory art.

APPENDICES

Appendix 1 On the analysis
of improvised music

In the body of this text I have largely refrained from sociopolitical interpretation of the musical evolution I have identified. As summarised in the Introduction, the basis for this choice is the view that musical development is largely an autonomous process, riding alongside the sociopolitical streams. The correlations of changing musical choice in the work of individuals, groups and countries which I have documented could be amplified *ad nauseam* to provide an expanding basis for any attempt to distinguish autonomous from sociopolitically motivated development, or to reveal their intermingling, whether internecine or friendly.

In this appendix I argue the issues which have to be handled before a theoretical framework for either kind of causal analysis could proceed. I conclude that the perspective of musical autonomy is tenable, and possibly preferable, and hence my choice throughout the book.

Music as object

There seems to be in most music an excess of information over that which can be fully processed cognitively by listeners or performers (see MacAdams in A27; A52b; A133; A134). For example, psychological studies indicate that only a limited number of musical strands can be recognised (in subject comparison tests) as familiar from within an array of strands presented to the listener previously (A27). Conversely, it is not always clear that all of the repetition of elements of a structure (whether pop song chord, or tonic chord of a tonal work) is necessary in any sense.

One implication of this information overload is that a musical analysis would ideally concentrate on those elements of a musical performance which are cognitively processed, rather than all those simply being received as perceptual stimuli. Even more desirable (and difficult to attain) would be to choose only those elements which are essential to any signification or affective action the music might have. The questions arising from these issues are not fully comprehensible at present: the psychology of musical perception has addressed little beyond simple tonal and timbral systems, while that of cognition has only made opening strides. Similarly, the issues of philosophy and aesthetics of music are in flux and always will be.

191

Since these issues inevitably permeate (explicitly or implicitly) any work of musical analysis, I shall spend a little time on them here, particularly indicating their bearing on improvised music, and the stances I have chosen to adopt in the body of the discourse. It is striking that a very detailed review of analytical procedures in music (A14) makes no reference to improvisation or jazz.

Musical entities

What components of music could one construe as integral wholes separable from each other (as they would need to be for any analysis)? The obvious possibility is the individual sound, taken from commencement to conclusion. But are musical sounds always separable? What of a chord of, say, eight notes, played on the piano? Are the eight notes always attacked at sufficiently different times to be taken as separate? And what of music which is absolutely continuous, in the sense of having no silences for long stretches of time, and no individual instruments or pitches sounding (for instance, passages of circular breathing on wind instruments, or long sustained pitches on string instruments, or much electronic and computer music)? The concept of individual sounds (or instrumental notes) breaks down.

So the individual sound is not necessarily a separable, analysable element in music. Equally, it is very unlikely that when present, an individual sound is a signifier (in the sense of corresponding to another entity, the signified), unless perhaps in the case of the long-sustained and complex sounds just mentioned. Most musical sounds lack the referentiality of, for example, a word. A very few complex sounds might be iconic with another entity, that is, have some predominant physical correlate with that entity: for instance, musical counterparts of some bird sounds or some elements in Javanese music (A13). As a consequence, it is also unlikely that an individual sound would be an affective element. Musical signification must reside in larger structures.

So the musical entities of interest might be either complex sound structures (timbres and textures) which are continuous in time, without necessarily containing separable 'notes' or pitches, or arrays of pitches simultaneous or successive in time. In music based on separable pitches, like classical western music, or much jazz, these arrays of pitches would correspond to harmony and motive. It is, therefore, not surprising that western analysis of music from all sources has tended to emphasise these two parameters of harmony and motive, the latter usually subsuming the parameter of rhythm. This ethnocentricity of musical analysis will no doubt be overcome eventually as awareness of non-western music increases, and as timbral/textural music (a technically developing front of contemporary western music) becomes more widespread and more appreciated. For similar reasons Anthony Braxton has argued that European criticism of black music is usually inappropriate. In its place he advocates a concept of 'affinity dynamics' which seems to be racially based (A79; A118); it remains at an almost mystical level and does not permit precise application.

Thus at present we must still consider the applicability of European concepts of harmony and motive to jazz and freer improvisation. Much jazz is based on repetitive harmonic sequences (the 'chord sequence'), and what has been described as development by intensification rather than extension, the latter being the method of tonal classical music (A90). Thus Fig. A1.1 illustrates some of the repetitive structures of a simple jazz sequence, the blues. Fig. A1.2 contrasts

Fig. A1.1 A Blues with one solo, in C.

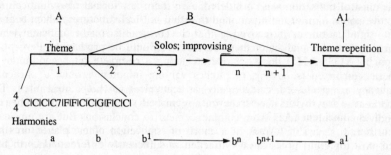

some of the structures of a simple classical exposition. The jazz sequence is tonal, in the crude sense of using diatonic harmonies, and repeatedly emphasising its key centre, in this case C. However the concept of modulation is minimal (there is rudimentary repeated modulation C to F to C); and it is difficult to introduce more distant modulation cohesively into such a pre-existing chord sequence unless the time frame of the sequence (usually a few seconds) is enlarged vastly. Though other new tonal centres can be reached temporarily (for example, G in bar 9) they cannot be sustained for more than a small proportion of the total time taken by one rendering of the sequence. Consistent with this view, a generative grammar for such blues chord sequences has been developed (A144).

In contrast, the classical exposition contains modulations, and these can occupy a large portion of the total time; they can occupy an even greater portion of the development ('extending') section of the classical sonata. The jazz piece is unlikely to emphasise the foreign keys any more in later ('intensifying') choruses than in the first. In summary, in much jazz tonality is present, but used in a very limited way. (Important exceptions have been detailed in Chapter 2.) This deduction points us in our search for possible signifying units towards harmony independent of tonality; and re-emphasises the possible importance of successive pitch arrangements, rhythm, and timbral/textural devices as important entities in jazz, and possibly in improvised music in general.

Fig. A1.2 A simple Classical sonata form.

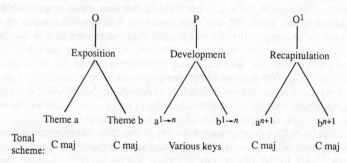

These three topics are the subjects of successive chapters in this book, where their musical utilisation was considered. Are there any formal constraints on the *effective* application of these parameters within musical structures, which bear on their signification or affectiveness? Such constraints might indicate which approaches to the analysis of these parameters would be productive. Perception of pitch (A133; A155) does not operate along a complete pitch continuum in experienced listeners: groups of pitches varying minutely around a particular frequency are perceived 'categorically' as equivalent to that central pitch. The same is true for rhythms, where events separated very briefly in time are perceived as coincident (A113).

Further, the idea of formal constraints on application of pitch structures has been most forcefully propagated by Lerdahl and Jackendoff (A75; and Lerdahl in A134). Briefly, they argue that pitch structures which do not allow octave repetition are unlikely to be musically effective; and that only a limited number of subdivisions of the octave are likely to be useful. Nevertheless, some musics may be able to largely escape octave equivalences (for example, perhaps some aboriginal musics: see A38). For Lerdahl and Jackendoff the main basis in psychoacoustics depends on the concepts of dissonance and consonance.

The elementary acoustics of this issue are outlined in A122, and other textbooks of psychoacoustics; here I will only summarise the crucial background before discussing the important aspects. The necessary information is that pitches on string and wind instruments have associated frequencies: patterns of repetition of waves through the air, reaching the ear. The frequencies of the notes on the piano range from around 20 repetitions (cycles) per second (hertz, Hz) for bass notes, to around 4000 Hz for high treble notes. Octaves (for example middle C and the C below it) have frequencies in the ratio 2:1. However, these instrument-generated notes are all associated with other wave patterns with different frequencies, which are other multiples (of the type $a:b$, where a and b are both integers) of the main pitch frequency. These other patterns are called the 'harmonic overtones'. The proportion of different harmonics varies between different instruments of the orchestra, and contributes their characteristic tone colours. Electronic instruments can control these overtone relationships very precisely, and even largely avoid their occurrence (to produce pure sine waves). In addition, there are on many instruments, such as the piano, inharmonic overtones, which are not frequencies described by integral $a:b$ ratios.

The concept of dissonance (for example, the idea that the interval of a major seventh from C to B nearly an octave above is a highly dissonant interval) has been brought forward as a rationalisation of the structures of western classical music. Partly because of the ethnocentricity of musical analysis, a possible physical (psychoacoustic) basis for the dominance of this interval among dissonant intervals has been sought. It has been argued that the degree of dissonance of an interval is a function of the degree of overlap of the pitches of the interval and of their energised overtones. Without going into the details of the very fascinating studies on this issue (for convenient reviews, see, for example, A122; A29; A32), one can nevertheless see severe difficulties in accepting the idea that dissonance is a necessary psychoacoustic phenomenon. Differences between Indian and western tuning systems (for example) emphasise these difficulties.

One difficulty is that dissonance seems (to moderately experienced listeners) to be retained even when pure sine wave intervals of around a major seventh are constructed; and to be rather similar when major seventh intervals are constructed by instruments of very different overtone characteristics. Relatively inexperienced listeners may possibly identify 'roughness' in intervals in a manner related to the overlap of energised overtones. However, the translation of this into a concept of dissonance seems dependent on experience: in other words it is a culturally conditioned translation, and perhaps dissonance can be recognised without 'roughness'. Indeed, musically trained listeners can recognise tonal melodies more easily than other melodies (see, for example A133; A134; A155), and serial pitch structures are difficult to perceive (A18), or perhaps, as Lerdahl puts it, 'cognitively opaque'.

The theory of the influence of overlapping harmonics, that 'roughness' is a crucial element determining dissonance, has the corollary that suitable manipulation of overtone content could permit other intervals than a major seventh to become just as 'rough' and thus just as dissonant. It follows that microtonal music, in which frequencies closer together than a semitone are used, would be capable of as much control of any intensive action due to this roughness as is tonal music (using only twelve semitones with a key centre), or twelve-tone music (using only twelve semitones, but without a key centre). It seems also that an instrument, and thus a music, could be produced which has no exact octaves within it, elaborating perhaps on the aboriginal elements. For example, the pitch range of the piano could be divided into n equal frequency increments, where n is any of the prime numbers (which are divisible only by themselves and 1).

Many of these ideas undermine the concept of Lerdahl that both octave relationships and the reliance on dissonance are necessarily important elements in music. Some experimental work (for example, Watkins and Dyson in A58) claims to support the 'robustness of tonality', but these particular experiments are almost entirely based on subdivisions of pitch ranges which preserve the octave relationship. In contrast, experimental assessments have been made of the importance of tonal closure (the 'correct' modulation of a piece of music back to the starting central key as in the original classical works taken as experimental material). These experiments indicate that closure has only weak effects on listeners (see, for example, A24). Timbral distortion may be a musical influence which can be used independently of tonality (A35) and this may be a more important application of the 'roughness' mentioned above. These issues are also relevant to the sections of this book on timbre/texture, and on microtonal music.

Lerdahl and Jackendoff (A75) state the 'goal of a theory of music to be a formal description of the musical intuitions of a listener who is experienced in a musical idiom'. They do not define 'idiom', but they state that theirs is intended to be a 'scientific' theory. They spend some time arguing that certain apparently contrary observations do not conflict with their theory, but do not discuss improvisation or microtonality seriously (improvisation is mentioned, but microtonality is not even indexed). A weakness of this impressive and interesting theory is a failure to delineate 'scientific' tests – ones which permit an experimental outcome which would destroy the theory, and thus are dangerous.

Our provisional conclusion should be that there are no necessary constraints on usable pitch relationships. And certainly jazz and free improvisation have been at the forefront of western music which has not totally relied on tonal or serial use of pitches. As we saw, there is as yet nevertheless a surprising lack of use of systematic microtonality in improvisation. It is very interesting that developing children are much more flexible in their pitch and rhythmic usage than adults (A52b).

195

It follows from our provisional conclusion that a variety of approaches to the analysis of pitch relationships in motive and harmony might be applicable to improvised music. And that these pitch relationships might generate signifiers. An application of set theory as developed by Forte for analysis of atonal music (A14; A34) to such analysis of improvised music has already been made (A111). I also use concepts of contour and harmony. Sets and contours are also applicable to the other two main parameters we have identified as targets: rhythm and texture/ timbre. But they abut the problem of identification of a 'motive', and its separation from other adjacent material. This is not simple, especially when outside preconceived contexts with conventional melodic and harmonic frameworks (see the discussion in A136).

We should next consider how the musical entities approached so far are com-

Fig. A1.3 'Bessie's Blues' by John Coltrane, from the album *Crescent*.

bined into larger structures, and whether these structures are important, or rather, too degenerate (in the sense of information overload outlined already). And whether they can be used to reveal changing features of improvised music. The semiotic and structuralist idea of generative grammars (A107; West *et al.* in A58; A144) has been mentioned already. Baker's description (A10) of Rollins's improvising could form the basis of a semiotic approach.

Fig. A1.3 illustrates some structural descriptions of parts of a 'blues' perform-ance (by John Coltrane). A later, stylistically disparate, blues performance, such as '81' played by Miles Davis on *ESP*, has many features in common. Yet it is in 8/8 time rather than 4/4 or 12/8, and has two quite distinct rhythmic feels as it progresses (8/8 and 4/4). In addition, it is more based on quartal harmonies than the Coltrane. Can the common features be taken to be unimportant? Both have twelve-bar sequences: but note that in two successive blues choruses Ornette Coleman recorded playing 'Birdfood' has ten- and eleven-bar sequence lengths, and one bar is 2/4 in the ten-bar version, but 4/4 in the eleven-bar version (A149–151). The twelve-bar nature of blues is thus not inviolate.

Should one instead assume, as does the conventional analysis of sonata form, that the common features *are* rather important? Can one correspondingly assume that the features of difference are important? There seem to be no secure answers to these questions. On the other hand, the differences between the two perform-ances are interesting and are made more apparent by their juxtaposition within structures which are similar. Clearly a practical approach to identifying changes in an intensifying music like jazz is to inspect differences in application of ideas within a relatively constant environment when used at different times or by different musicians.

Because the structures of much freely improvised music do not conform to familiar classical prototypes, they are often construed as simple, and described as if there were nothing more to them than an arc structure (expected to be quiet–loud–quiet or sparse–active–sparse; see, for example, the 'big-bang' des-cription in A142). Thus the following description (A49b) of a performance by AMM (R4):

> The piece makes much use of sustained sounds, and the ritual atmosphere is heightened by regular gong strokes and other periodic rhythms while there is some hint of Indian influence in the steady rise to a climax in the latter part – though this kind of form seems to result all too readily in improvis-ation by a regular ensemble.

As illustrated throughout this book, this attitude to form in improvisations is such a gross simplification, depending on the most elementary appreciation of a very few of the musical parameters in action, as to be useless. The difficulty of identifying appropriate parameters in free improvisation around which to describe structure is hard to overestimate. But the assumption that there is only simplistic structure is itself simplistic.

We arrive from this discussion at primarily practical conclusions, the basis for theoretical ones being insufficient. These conclusions are that in improvised music in particular, the analysis of rhythmic elements, pitch structures, and texture/timbre is appropriate. And that a comparative study of events within common structures may be helpful. Let us turn briefly to the questions of method of transcribing such events.

Fig. A1.4 Transcriptions of the opening bass riff of 'A Love Supreme' by John Coltrane.

(a) By Porter (1985).

(b) By Jost (1974). Modified to same pitch as Porter.

Fig. A1.4(c) and (d) Hancock's repeated pattern in introduction to theme statement of 'Seven Steps to Heaven' (Live Version).

(c) Version consistent with Davies, A29.

(d) Author's version.

Transcription-interpretation-transcription

Just as musical scores are a gross simplification of the content of a resulting musical performance (lacking, for example, any indications of overtone content) so transcriptions of improvised performances necessarily involve comparable or usually greater simplifications. These include assumptions as to the degree of precision with which rhythms and pitches will be analysed; a similiar lack of concern with overtone structure; etc. Perhaps partly because of this there are few published transcriptions (A43).

Indeed automated transcriptions of notated rhythms indicate considerable performance imprecisions; and measurement of the timing of onset of sounds (see, for example, Gabrielson in A134; and Rasch in A134) in performances, improvised or otherwise, reveal major imprecisions (or complexities) of rhythm and tempo. Simple arithmetic errors in transcription, where a constant metre is in effect but manually transcribed note values do not add up to the appropriate number of beats, are also quite common (see, for example A92, p. 216, where bars 25 and 26 lack one beat) as they are also in published compositions.

Thus it is inevitable that the prejudices of the transcriber and the kinds of analysis being attempted will to some degree be reflected in the transcriptions, and so in turn bias the interpretation: a familiar issue in ethnomusicology (cf. A151). The idea of transcription is, of course, itself ethnocentric.

I will briefly illustrate some important disparities. Fig. A1.4 shows two versions of the repeated figure played by the double bass at the opening of John Coltrane's 'A Love Supreme' (R23). Although the rendering of this riff does vary as the piece progresses, and quite significantly, version b (A65) is further from the opening rhythm than is version a. Version b overemphasises the degree of syncopation of the riff (notes 3 and 4) at the outset, and also lengthens the final B♭. The intensity of rhythmic displacement in the riff is increased at later points in the performance. There is a similar disparity between the two versions of a Hancock repeated piano figure in Figs. A1.4c and A1.4d.

Fig. A1.5 is a transcription by Davies (A29) of a piece of drumming by Tony

Fig. A1.5 Tony Williams's drumming on the same performance as the last figure, in different transcriptions. The passage comes shortly after the piano solo, near the end of the piece.

(a) Davies's first version, rewritten to make the beat positions clearer. The repeating pattern, indicated by the brackets, is thus 2+1+3 semiquavers. Note that this whole material is more correctly transcribed with all note values being double those shown, so that the first two notes occupy a whole 4/4 bar. I have retained Davies's system for a, b, and c of this figure for ease of comparison.

(b) Author's version. The repeating pattern occupies two triplet crotchets. Evidence for this is the recurrent triplet crotchet contour on the drums (see c below) matching that of Fig. A1.4c.

(c) Triplet contour on drums at beginning of piano solo.

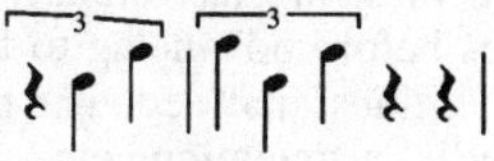

Williams (R43). It is designed to illustrate the complexity of the playing, but does so by emphasising syncopation: the accentuation of notes which occur away from the normally accentuated beats. Davies also presents an alternative version emphasising a different perception of the cross-rhythms involved, but it is not identical in relative rhythmic durations to the first. The length of time between such accentuated notes and the metrically placed beats is undoubtedly a significant variable within jazz performances (see Fig. 2.6b).

However, Fig. A1.5 also shows my own version of the same segment of Williams's drumming: this is conceived in a quite different way. It is based, as are many of the Elvin Jones patterns, on triplet rhythms in which three equal (or at least, as equal as the normal beats are equal) notes are played in the time of two normal notes. Jazz has often spent so much effort in keeping clear the emphasis on and placing of the four beats in its bars, that most other timings have tended to be conceived in relation to those beats (hence Davies's version). However, I have already revealed the tendency in the 1960s towards suspending that pulse or superimposing a new one. Fig. A1.5 in my interpretation is an example of superimposing a faster pulse (six per bar) over the original four. The use of triplet minims over whole bars is an alternative found much in Jones's work (Fig. 2.6) which downplays the second to fourth normal beats of the bars, while retaining the emphasis on the first, but also superimposes a slower pulse (three per bar) over the original four. Kofsky's preliminary analysis (A71–3) of Jones's drumming fails to note this level of triplets, let alone triplets superimposed on this level of triplet minims or on triplet crotchets (see Chapter 2). Such superimpositions add faster pulses than the original basic pulse. While the overall effect of the Williams pattern is complex, the rhythmic elements it contains are rather simpler when viewed in my version than in Davies's, and more concerned with superimposed pulses than with syncopation. Thus can mode of transcription influence interpretation.

This is not to say that these problems of transcription can be simply avoided, nor that they are absent in this book. Manual transcription of such rapidly moving music as much jazz improvisation is very difficult, especially without the use of half-speed tape recorders, etc. I have certainly experienced difficulty in making several of the transcriptions I offer in this book, particularly in deciding the original pitch frame (for example, was the piece recorded in F or F#?). In the absence of any documentary evidence, and finding a disparity between tuning fork A = 440 Hz and the recorded pitches, I have used aural clues with which I am particularly familiar such as the sound of open strings on the double bass, which are clearly distinct from the sound of adjacent semitones. The pitch frame I have chosen must inevitably be an inaccurate reflection of the original in some cases.

Even if readily available, automated timing of complex recorded musical sounds has huge problems: the definition of start time for different kinds of sounds (some of which reach a peak almost immediately, others of which take a significant length of time to peak) will be very difficult to rationalise. The use of a timing such as peak dynamic might seem a simple solution, but this may vary for the different overtones of an instrument and for the several notes played simultaneously on a keyboard or string instrument, etc. It is simply necessary to be aware of these difficulties before advancing to the question of the possibilities of interpreting the musical entities analysed. Far more detailed modes of transcription, representing emphasis, articulation, etc., are needed (A85).

Improvised music as event and process

Documents such as tape recordings of improvisation are essentially empty, as they preserve chiefly the form that something took and give at best an indistinct hint as to the feeling and cannot convey any sense of time and place (A20, p. xvii).

Of course, no music is a fixed object of the kind that this Appendix so far has assumed. It is a process both for the performer and the listener. It also occurs in an environment which inevitably provides some perceptual input to both parties simultaneous with the musical production and reception.

The psychology of musical reception and its development has been the subject of many interesting studies (A133). These reveal how differences in the ability of individuals to identify different kinds of musical element (for example, tonal versus atonal pitch structures) may be related to their musical experience; and how the interest of a given piece of music to professional highly trained musicians from different cultures varies at least as greatly (the Indian musician may find Beethoven very boring). An interesting example of this is given by Cecil Taylor, who said (A143): 'Stockhausen ... doesn't create any music. He never has created any music.'

Available studies on musical reception/production and its development as humans mature indicate relatively little about any culture-independent innate musical preferences which there might be: indeed, they rather tend to undermine belief in such preferences. Thus children usually display greater flexibility in intonation and rhythm, that is, in music production, than adults (A52b). Education influences this (A135) and an amusing example (A52a) involved exposing students to repeated hearings of several kinds of music, and assessing their changing responses: the commonly found 'inverted U' effect for responses to several kinds of music was observed. In such an inverted U effect the liking for a work increases initially as it is repeated (the ascending side of the inverted U), and then declines (the descending side of the inverted U). But it was quite striking in this work (A52a) that the liking for an avant-garde piece of improvising (R131) showed hardly any increase in the experiments. The results were interpreted in terms of stereotyping of attitude, also described as 'musical prejudice'. Another interesting layer of complexity in the analysis of liking for music is that there can be a lack of parallel between stated preferences for music, and purchasing recorded music or listening choice among available music recordings (A45).

One might enquire whether there are sexual differences in the production of music, improvised or otherwise, noting that there are few documented female composers. Oliveros (A103) has argued that female musicians might introduce more 'intuition' into composed music, and probably music in general, than do males. Interestingly, a study (A54) of boys aged 10–15 found positive correlations between compositional abilities and psychological androgyny (using a routine set of associative tests to determine androgyny). It found no such correlation with improvisatory abilities. While one can question the relevance of the parameters measured to the concepts they are named after, it is striking that there were no such correlations in the girls of the same age range. The study also found for the boys a positive correlation between verbalising abilities, general intelligence, and improvisation abilities; but for the girls they showed negative correlations between verbalising ability and all the creative musical parameters measured. It is worthy of note that both referent-based and freer improvisatory abilities were measured. Such studies begin to imply significant differences between the sexes in relation to musical activities, but, of course, they do not suggest a necessary explanation of them.

A biographical survey of a small selection of US jazz women is available (A108) but makes no attempt to evaluate such issues. Wilmer (A154) most often suggests that the female contribution to the production of jazz was in the supporting of the male jazz musician, but she goes on to advocate the necessity and desirability of female participation in improvised music. As one might expect and hope, their preponderance among improvising musicians seems to be increasing. This is especially marked in free improvisation in the UK, where several female musicians are active (for instance, Maggie Nichols, a cofounder of FIG, the Feminist Improvising Group: see A2Ic). It is also possible that some societies, such as Australia, may already have a relatively sizeable input to avant-garde music from women (A61). Perhaps we will only judge adequately whether the female improviser has any characteristics distinct from the male in the future, when both are proportionally represented.

It is appropriate here to discuss the origin of affective responses in listeners to music, with reference to improvised music. Meyer (A89) argued that musical effect is produced by a conflict between expectation and deviation. Thus a particular musical structure leads the experienced listener to have certain expectations, which may be frustrated by deviations (which in turn may be successive or simultaneous). Distortion may also be relevant: while dissonance is within Meyer's framework, distortion is outside it (A35).

Although Meyer's concept is interesting, and impressively presented, in relation to jazz and other pulse-based musics, he has probably overestimated the 'syntactic' parameters, and neglected the 'statistical' parameters, which might result from the intensification by repetition of, for example, pulse (A37). Thus in addition to affect from inhibition of expectation, there may be affect from intensification of an expected and uninhibited activity, such as pulse. Meyer's later work introduced elements of these ideas also, although it did not apply them particularly to jazz. They have not been applied either to the unpulsed yet strongly rhythmic kinds of improvisation such as free jazz which we discuss in this book, but they seem appropriate there, too.

Many other attitudes toward this issue of affect are worthy of consideration, of course, and they cannot be developed here. Let us at least consider a comment by Cornelius Cardew (A20):

> Informal 'sound' has a power over emotional responses that formal 'music' does not, in that it acts subliminally rather than on a cultural level. This is a possible definition of the area in which AMM [the group] is experimental. We are searching for sounds and for the responses that attach to them, rather than thinking them up, preparing them and producing them. The search is conducted in the medium of sound and the musician himself is at the heart of the experiment.

Any of these frameworks in which musical affect might be generated are in turn subject to influence from the changing environments in which music is heard (A35). This is no less true for improvised music than for any other western music, since the distribution by record, tape, compact disc, satellite, etc., has been dramatically changing in the period, and this has had immense effects on the mode of presentation even of public events. Average musical preferences (or frameworks) also vary among social classes, at least in the UK (A101, pp. 242–78).

Perhaps the most interesting studies on musical reception concern musical streaming (A101): they consider the ability of the brain to decide whether successive sounds belong together in a single stream, or separately in several streams. These studies have begun to reveal aspects of musical sonority which are determinants of such fusion or segregation. They have also indicated the limited capacity of the brain for distinguishing multiple streams, which has bearing on the issue of information overload in music mentioned already. One caveat about these studies needs to be kept in mind, however: they are mostly not the results of controlled psychological testing of statistically significant groups of subjects in defined environments, but largely the result of introspective analysis by small groups of musicians and scientists involved closely in the design and interpretation of the work. They may be subject to some bias as a result of this.

The psychology of musical production is rather less studied than that of reception, though there are some very interesting studies on performance inaccuracies (A134). That of musical improvisation is in its infancy. Fig. A1.6, after Johnson-Laird (A63), summarises three possible classes of algorithm (computational pro-

Fig. A1.6 Three Classes of Creativity Algorithm (based on Johnson-Laird).

1. Neo-Darwinian

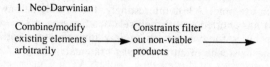

2. Neo-Lamarckian

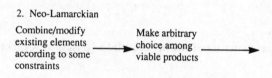

3. Multi-stage

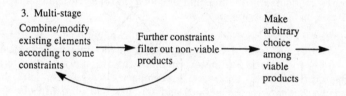

cedure) which might be at work during improvisation. They are based on the idea that computation (in this case, cognitive processing of musical ideas) during improvisation should be minimal (so as to be fast enough): for instance, it should not involve using an intermediate memory after a computation and before generating the note. The computation should lead directly to the note. Computation 'off-line', that is, in deriving frameworks before the note pattern is performed, should be much greater. Off-line in this sense does not necessarily mean prepared a long time ahead, or specifically for the particular improvisation, but these are among the possibilities. Johnson-Laird arrives at a stimulating 'neo-Lamarckian' hypothesis. Because of the general discrediting of Lamarck's ideas in biology, it is also amusing. On the basis of this hypothesis he has developed simple computer programs which generate fairly successful bass lines from jazz chord sequences and melodic lines to go with such sequences, on the basis of regular grammars. Much more computational power is required to generate tonal chord sequences, and this probably requires a more complex, multiple-stage architecture.

The lack of intermediate computations is characteristic of a 'regular' grammar, and thus it is not surprising that generative grammars of related kinds have been investigated by others in relation to musical production. For example, elementary 'jazz' improvised melodic lines have been generated against a predetermined chord sequence, using such a computerised grammar (A152). Rather more computerised attempts have been made in relation to compositional styles than improvisation (see, for example, A36). Interestingly, the acutely self-aware and articulate group AMM has entitled one of their releases *Generative Themes* (R6).

There may well be bases for comparison of jazz improvisation with speech production, such as the existence of an underlying grammar:

> native speakers are seen as having a basic language *competence* that underlies their everyday language *performance*. Performance entails a generative principle – the ability to apply rules to deep syntactic structures to produce a potentially infinite number of surface structure sentences (A148; emphasis added).

Fig. A1.7 Knowledge structures for improvisation (based on Clarke in A134).

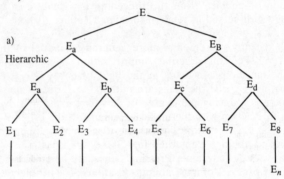

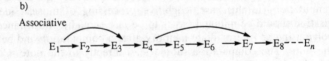

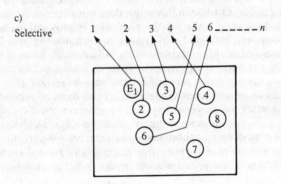

This statement is similar to one by Schuller (A130) concerning improvisation by an African drummer, paraphrased in relation to natural language as follows (A148):

> In a variation by a natural language speaker, what may already be complex expositional material (what linguists call 'kernel sentences') is varied, manipulated, augmented, diminished, fragmented, and regrouped into new variants ... all within, we reiterate, exceedingly strict rules.

It has to be noted, however, that the formulaic element of jazz, which relates to the 'strict rules' has been gradually eroded, and the 'rules' within free improvisation are probably of a more abstracted kind, more distant from musical elements themselves. For example, they may sometimes concern dialogue and problem-solving (A31; A116).

A very simple description of the process of improvising, in the form of some alternative 'knowledge' diagrams, is given in Fig. A1.7. These diagrams make a few of the possibilities for the generation of relationships within improvising quite clear and certainly have real counterparts. For example, selection from a pre-existing group of possibilities characterises the bebop procedure of quotation, while generation of an idea from the preceding is a feature of some motivic improvising, as we discussed in relation to Sonny Rollins, Ornette Coleman and others.

Pressing has recently presented a more generalised model of the process of improvisation (A134). This describes improvisation as a succession of states between which transitions are made in the light of newly decided (or in some cases predetermined) goals; the goals are outlined in terms of musical elements themselves (such as reducing the degree of activity for the improvisers playing, etc.) and their interaction with the musical elements of the other co-improvisers. This seems to bear close relationship with the ideas on development of improvising procedures and abilities elaborated in A31.

However, it is not clear whether Pressing's ideas are immediately applicable to the analysis of the progress of musical improvisations. The problem which arises is similiar to, but greater than, that of transcription discussed above: how should the transition points in an improvisation be defined? How should they be described qualitatively? Or quantitatively? It is probable that, especially for a group improvisation, the choice of parameters for analysis to determine the transition points (if they exist) would be arbitrary, with many giving equally interesting structural descriptions of a given improvisation. It is not obvious how one would be able to distinguish between these different descriptions in terms of their utility or relevance. The theory is intended to be a scientific one, and thus has to meet scientific criteria, the most important of which (as mentioned already) is probably that to be valuable a theory has to lead to experimentally testable predictions. Pressing has since used automated transcription of improvisations done on a Midi-linked synthesiser, to gain fascinating information about the process (A113). However, the interpretations of the transition points he proposes are no more convincing than a range of alternatives, as he admits. Thus the hopefully directive utility of the theory remains to be exploited.

An interesting aspect of the psychology of musical production is that of variability of performance. This has received some attention, beyond the minor inaccuracies mentioned above. Nettl argues that all 'performers improvise to some extent', meaning that their performances, whether of a referent or not, are variable (A97). A referent might be a fully notated composition or a framework, such as a chord sequence, rag, or rhythmic pattern, used for improvising.

He goes on to document this (A98) for repeated recordings of a taqsim (a Middle Eastern improvisatory form) by a single performer, over a considerable span of time. The variations were immense, atlhough the referent remained recognizable:

> those aspects of music which are usually considered by Western musicians to be the most susceptible to improvisatory variation, namely, ornamentation, rhythm, and development of motifs over short stretches of time, are the ones which contribute least to the way in which the concept of taqsim nahawand differs from performance to performance. And on the other hand, it is important to note the rather considerable, though obviously also strictly patterned, diversity in the larger structural aspects of the performances.

In jazz improvisation several studies of variability have been undertaken. One of the first was a description (A150) of changes in rendering of standard bebop tunes by the saxophonist Bunky Green. These indicate systematic repetitions of material in the same passage of the referent chord sequence; they also indicate variations. More interesting perhaps is the comparison (A109) of Coltrane's performance on the commercial version of 'A Love Supreme' (R23) with that on the live concert recording, issued on several small labels (the most complete being R24). As discussed earlier, Coltrane performed a rhythmic translation of the poem printed on the sleeve of the commercial release on that recording. He did no such thing in the live version. This could be taken as a change in the nature of the referent; but besides the difference in scale of the two versions, the concert version being much the longer, there are major differences in the improvisatory devices in use. In the case of freer improvisation marked differences can be heard on the available duplicate recordings of referent pieces such as Coleman's 'Free Jazz' (R17; R18); Amalgam's 'Judy's Smile' (R2); or non-referent works, such as van Hove's 'Solo Suite' (R136) or Guy's 'Statements' (R67).

The studies of performance inaccuracy noted above imply an awareness on the part of the performer of the mistakes created, and an effect of this on the subsequent performance at least for a short time; and concur with the introspective impressions of many performers. Mistakes occur also in improvised music, as is very obvious in some referent-based jazz recordings where the metrical framework is illogically destroyed. This can be illustrated by the illustrious cases of trumpeters Miles Davis and Freddie Hubbard. After the piano solo on 'Circle' (R47) Miles Davis re-enters with the tune one beat late but as if in the normal place. The rhythm section of piano, bass and drums adjust virtually immediately, and shift their down beat by one beat forward. On 'Maiden Voyage' (R69) Hubbard plays an extremely florid scalar run, up and down several times in the high register near the end of his solo, in the last few bars of the middle eight section of this 32-bar structure, and then exits so as to place the down beat ahead of that expected by the rhythm section (and literally early). The rhythm section (the same musicians) make a more complex response to this error than in the former case: they vary the pulse rate slightly, following Carter, and Williams (drums) disguises the beats more, so that he can rejoin Carter's placing (on bass) in the bar within the first bar of Hancock's piano solo which follows Hubbard's error. Unanimity has been achieved again, and it is even very difficult to decide precisely how much time has been omitted to bring everyone back into pulse synchrony; the origin of the error cannot be decided from the recording. Tape editing could conceivably be involved in the first of these two mistakes, though this seems unlikely. Of course, errors also occur in the renderings of the composed part of jazz pieces (for example, the far from unanimous bass Bs at the end of the title track on R32).

Recordings of improvisation which is referent-based may also display errors introduced outside the improvising process itself. A possible example which I in any case find obtrusive, is on Davis's 'SHHH/Peaceful' (R48) which permeates most of the piece, stops temporarily several times, and then restarts. According to Ian Carr (A21b; and personal communication), these stops are all tape-spliced 'pauses', with the implication that, as normally, a pause may be a length of time which is not an integral multiple of the pulse duration. However, nearly all the pauses are integral multiples of pulses and are fitted in with the bass pattern (for example, that at around 1'30"; that at 9'30" in the soprano solo; that at 11'15" (pianos); and that at 12'30" before the rerun of the opening part of the tape and of the trumpet solo. In contrast, the pause at 6' (where the guitar solo begins) is half a beat from an integral number of pulses; and that at 6'30" is two beats too short in relation to the repeated bass pattern. These two pauses come as a real jerk to the listener who remains aware of the pulses throughout the pauses. For me this is a further kind of error, though not for Carr.

It is not so obvious when errors occur within free improvisation (although again introspection indicates that they do, and certainly that misjudgements or faulty anticipations occur). Defining them would be rather difficult, and just as a chance event (as in the work of Cage, for instance) may be a useful element of a work of music, so may a mistake, felt as such by an improviser, be retrospectively incorporated into the improvisation in a productive way. A theory of improvisation would need to incorporate criteria for identifying and analysing such errors, large or small, and their rectification, attempted or achieved. It is not obvious how these criteria would be distinguished quantitatively or qualitatively from those concerning the transition points mentioned above but information could be derived from self-analysis in an automatically transcribed group improvisation.

These areas of musical psychology are fascinating and fertile grounds for research, but until a more solid basis is achieved in them, it seems dangerous to lay too great a store upon them in developing any interpretations of music. Rather, one is again forced towards the practical possibility of the analysis of musical entities envisaged already.

An amusing aspect of the relation between production of improvisation and its reception is the influence that the naming of a piece or of a group can have. While it may be difficult to persuade an audience of a political point through purely musical sound, the context may force the thoughts of the audience in an appropriate direction. For example, as pointed out by Georgina Born (personal communication, 1988) the title, FIG, of the all-female free improvising ensemble of which she was a member, was 'itself a political statement', regardless of whether there was political content intrinsic in the music as object. Music as process, therefore, including the environment in which the music was heard (for instance, a performance by FIG) was undoubtedly of a different significance from an unlabelled tape of the music heard independently. This returns us to the consideration of such social and political signification given in the Introduction.

Appendix 2 References: books and articles

A1.   AIM (1984) *Improvisation – History, Directions, Practice*, Association of Improvising Musicians, London.
A2.   Alperson, P.J. (1984) 'On Musical Improvisation', *Aesthetics and Art Criticism* 43, 17–29.
A3.   Ansell, K. (1978) 'Roger Dean and Lysis', *Impetus* 7, 290–3.
A4.   Antin, D. (1976) *Talking at the Boundaries*, New Directions, New York.
A5.   Antin, D. (1984) *Tuning*, New Directions, New York.
A6.   Attali, J. (1985) *Noise: The Political Economy of Music*, Manchester University Press, Manchester.
A7.   Bailey, D. (1980) *Improvisation: Its Nature and Practice in Music*, Moorland, Ashbourne.
A8.   Baker, D.N. (1968) *Techniques of Improvisation, Vol. 1: The Lydian Chromatic Concept*, Maher, Chicago.
A9.   Baker, D.N. (1973) *Jazz Styles and Analysis: Trombone*, Maher, Chicago.
A10.   Baker, D.N. (1980) *The Jazz Style of Sonny Rollins*, Studio 224, Hialeah, Fla.
A11.   Barnard, G. (1989) 'Az it Was', *New Music Articles* 7, 17–20.
A12.   Bartolozzi, B. (1962) *New Sounds for Woodwind*, Oxford University Press, Oxford.
A13.   Becker, A. (1981) 'A Musical Icon: Power and Meaning in Javanese Gamelan Music' in W. Steiner (ed.), *The Sign in Music and Literature*, University of Texas Press, Austin, pp. 203–15.
A14.   Bent, I. (1987) *Analysis*, Macmillan, London.
A15.   Briggs, N.L. (1986) 'Creative Improvisation: A Musical Dialogue', PhD thesis, University of California, San Diego.
A16.   Brown, B. (ed.) (1988) 'Jazz composition in Australia', *Sounds Australian* 17, 8–28.
A17.   Brown, R.L. (1976) 'Classical Influences on Jazz', *Journal of Jazz Studies* 3, 19–35.
A18.   Bruner, C.L. (1984) 'The Perception of Contemporary Pitch Structures', *Music Perception* 2, 25–39.

A19. Budds, M.J. (1978) *Jazz in the Sixties: The Expansion of Musical Resources and Techniques*, University of Iowa Press, Iowa City.

A20. Cardew, C. (1971) *Treatise Handbook*, Peters, London.

A21a. Carr, I. (1973) *Music Outside: Contemporary Jazz in Britain*, Latimer, London.

A21b. Carr, I. (1982) *Miles Davis: A Critical Biography*, Paladin, London.

A21c. Carr, I. Fairweather, D. and Priestley, B. (1987) *Jazz: The Essential Companion*, Grafton Books, London.

A22. Cerulli, D., Korall, B., Nasatir, M.L. (eds) (1960) *The Jazz World*, Da Capo, New York.

A23. Childs, B. and Hobbs, C. (eds) (1982/3) Forum: Improvisation, *Perspectives of New Music*, pp. 26–111.

A24. Cook, N. (1987) 'The Perception of Large-scale Tonal Closure', *Music Perception 5*, 197–206.

A25. Cope, D.H. (1971) *New Directions in Music*, W.C. Brown, Dubuque, Iowa.

A26. Copland, A. (1952) *Music and Imagination*, Mentor, New York.

A27. Crozier, W.R. and Chapman, A.J. (eds) (1984) *Cognitive Processes in the Perception of Art*, North-Holland, Amsterdam.

A28. Cummings, D.M. and McIntyre, D.K. (eds) (1990) *The International Who's Who in Music*, Melrose Press, Cambridge, UK.

A29. Davies, J.B. (1978) *The Psychology of Music*, Hutchinson, London.

A30. de Lerma D.-R. (1975) 'Black Music: A Bibliographic Essay', *Library Trends 23*, 517–31.

A31. Dean, R.T. (1989) *Creative Improvisation: Jazz, Contemporary Music and Beyond*, Open University Press, Milton Keynes.

A32. Deutsch, D. (ed.) (1982) *The Psychology of Music*, Academic Press, New York.

A33. Dodge, C. and Jerse, T.A. (1985) *Computer Music. Synthesis, Composition and Performance*, Schirmer, New York.

A34. Dunsby, J. and Whittall, A. (1988) *Music Analysis in Theory and Practice*, Faber, London.

A35. Durant, A. (1984) *Conditions of Music*, Macmillan, London.

A36. Ebcioglu, K. (1988) 'An expert system for harmonizing four-part chorales', *Computer Music Journal 12*, 52–7.

A37. Elliott, D.J. (1987) 'Structure and Feeling in Jazz: Rethinking Philosophical Foundations', *Bull Council for Research in Music Education 95*, 13–38.

A38. Ellis, C. (1965) 'Preinstrumental Scales', *Ethnomusicology 9*, 126–43.

A39. Ellis, D. (1972) *The New Rhythm Book*, Ellis Enterprises, North Hollywood, Calif.

A40. Feigin, L. (ed.) (1985) *Russian Jazz: New Identity*, Quartet, London.

A41. Foreman, L. (ed.) (1981) *The Percy Grainger Companion*, Thames Publishing, London.

A42. Gallagher, E. (1989) 'Az Music', *New Music Articles 7*, 9–13.

A43. Garfield, E. (1976) 'More on Jazz Transcription', *Current Contents* (Life Sciences), 26 April, pp. 5–10.

A44. Gaslini, G. (1982) *Tecnica e arte del jazz*, Ricordi, Milan.

A45. Gerringer, J.M. and Madsen, C.K. (1981) 'Verbal and Operant Discrimination–Preference for Tone Qualities and Intonation', *Psychology of Music 9*, 26–30.

A46. Goldberg, R.L. (1988) *Performance Art*, Thames and Hudson, London.
A47. Goldstein, M. (1983) 'The Gesture of Improvisation', *Percussionist* 21, 18–24.
A48. Gottlieb, R. (1985) 'Symbolisms Underlying Improvisation Practices in Indian Music: With Particular Emphasis on Performance Practice Relating to North Indian Tabla Drumming', *Journal of the Indian Musicological Society* 16, 23–36.
A49a. Griffiths, P. (1978) *A Concise History of Modern Music*, Thames and Hudson, London.
A49b. Griffiths, P. (1979) *A Guide to Electronic Music*, Thames and Hudson, London.
A50. Gysin, B. and Wilson, T. (1985) *Here to Go: Planet R-101*, Quartet, London.
A51. Hamm, C., Nettl, B. and Byrnside, R. (1975) *Contemporary Music and Music Cultures*, Prentice Hall, Englewood Cliffs, NJ.
A52a. Hargreaves, D.J. (1984) 'The Effects of Repetition on Liking for Music', *Journal of Research in Music Education* 32, 35–47.
A52b. Hargreaves, D.J. (1986) *The Developmental Psychology of Music*, Cambridge University Press, Cambridge.
A53. Harrison, M., Morgan, A., Atkins, R., James, M. and Cooke, J. (1975) *Modern Jazz 1945–70. The Essential Records*, Aquarius Books, London.
A54. Hassler, M. and Feil, A. (1986) 'A Study of the Relationship of Composition/Improvisation to Selected Personal Variables. Differences in the Relationship to Selected Variables: An Experimental Study', *Bull Council for Research in Music Education* 87, 26–34.
A55. Heiss, J. (1979) 'Some Multiphonic Sonorities for Flute, Oboe, Clarinet and Bassoon, *Perspectives of New Music* 7, 136–42.
A56. Helleu, L. (1988) *The Soldiers – B.A. Zimmerman*, Dernieres Nouvelles d'Alsace, Strasbourg.
A57. Hentoff, N. and McCarthy, A.J. (eds) (1959) *Jazz*, Rinehardt, New York. Reprinted Da Capo, New York (1975).
A58. Howell, P., Cross, I. and West, R. (eds) (1985) *Musical Structure and Cognition*, Academic Press, London.
A59. Ibsen al Faruqi, L. (1978) 'Ornamentation in Arabic Improvisational Music: A Study of Interrelationships in the Arts', *World Music* 20, 17–28.
A60. Jameson, F. (1984) 'Postmodernism or the Cultural logic of late capitalism', *New Left Review*, 146, 53–92.
A61. Jenkins, J. (1988) *22 Contemporary Australian Composers*, NMA Publications, Melbourne.
A62. Johnson, B. (1987) *The Oxford Companion to Australian Jazz*, Oxford University Press, London.
A63. Johnson-Laird, P. (1987) 'Reasoning, Imagining and Creating', *Bull Council for Research in Music Education* 95, 71–87.
A64. Jones, A.M. (1959) *Studies in African Music*, Vols 1 and 2, Oxford University Press, London.
A65. Jost, E. (1974) *Free Jazz* (English edition), Universal, Graz.
A66. Karkoschka, E. (1972) *Notation in New Music*, Universal, London.
A67. Kennedy, M. (1980) *Concise Oxford Dictionary of Music* (3rd edn) Oxford University Press, London.

A68. Kernfeld, B. (1983) 'Two Coltranes', *Annual Review of Jazz Studies* 2, 7–66.

A69. Kernfeld, B. (ed.) (1988) *New Grove Dictionary of Jazz*, Macmillan, New York.

A70. Kofsky, F. (1970) *Black Nationalism and the Revolution in Music*, Pathfinder, New York.

A71. Kofsky, F. (1976) 'Elvin Jones, Part 1: Rhythmic Innovator', *Journal of Jazz Studies* 4 (1), 3–24.

A72. Kofsky, F. (1977) 'Elvin Jones, Part 2: Rhythmic Displacement in the Art of Elvin Jones', *Journal of Jazz Studies* 4 (2), 11–32.

A73. Kofsky, F. (1978) 'Elvin Jones, Part 3', *Journal of Jazz Studies* 5 (1), 81–90.

A74a. Kostelanetz, R. (1980) *Text-Sound-Text*, William Morrow, New York.

A74b. Kostelanetz, R. (1980) *The Theatre of Mixed Neans*, R.K. Editions, New York.

A75. Lerdahl, F. and Jackendoff, R. (1983) *A Generative Theory of Tonal Music*, MIT Press, Cambridge, Mass., USA.

A76. LeRoi Jones (1966) *Blues People: Negro Music in White America*, McGibbon and Kee, London.

A77. Lewis, J. (1972) 'So What Do You Want from Your Music – Security?', *Time Out*, 14 December, pp. 38–40.

A78. Litweiler, J. (1984) *The Freedom Principle: Jazz after 1958*, William Morrow, New York.

A79. Lock, G. (1988) *Forces in Motion*, Quartet, London.

A80. MacAdams, S. and Bergman, A. (1979) 'Hearing Musical Streams', *Computer Music Journal* 3, 26–43.

A81a. Mac Low, J. (1980) *Asymmetries 1–260*, Printed Editions, New York.

A81b. Mac Low, J. (1980) *Representative Works*, Roof Publications, New York.

A82. Manning, P. (1985) *Electronic and Computer Music*, Clarendon, Oxford.

A83. McCarthy, A., Morgan, A., Oliver, P. and Harrison, M. (1968) *Jazz on Record 1917–1967*, Hanover Books, London.

A84. McCue, G. (ed.) (1977) *Music in American Society 1776–1976: From Puritan Hymn to Synthesizer*, Transaction, New Brunswick, NJ.

A85. Meadows, E.S. (1987) 'Ethnomusicology and Jazz Research: A Selective Viewpoint', *Bull Council for Research in Music Education* 95, 61–70.

A86. Mehegan, J. (1962) *Jazz Improvisation Vol. II. Jazz Rhythm and the Improvised Line*, Watson-Guptill, New York.

A87. Mehegan, J. (1965) *Contemporary Piano Styles. Jazz Improvisation IV*, Watson-Guptill, New York.

A88. Mertens, W. (1983) *American Minimal Music*, Broude, New York.

A89. Meyer, L.B. (1956) *Emotion and Meaning in Music*, University of Chicago Press, Chicago.

A90. Middleton, R. (1981) '"Reading" Popular Music', Unit 16 of Open University Course U203 (*Popular Culture, Popular Music and Post-War Youth: Countercultures*), Open University, Milton Keynes.

A91. Miedema, H. (1975) *Jazz Styles and Analysis: Alto Sax*, Maher, Chicago.

A92. Mongan, N. (1983) *The History of the Guitar in Jazz*, Oak Publications, New York.

A93. Murphy, B. (1987) 'Improvisation with Motivic Development Pt II', *Percussionist* 25, 65–7.

A94. Nanry, C. (1979) *The Jazz Text*, Van Nostrand, New York.
A95. Nanry, C. (1982) 'Jazz and Modernism: Twin Born Children of the Age of Invention', *Annual Review of Jazz Studies* 1, 146–54.
A96. National Gallery of Canada (1972) *About 30 Works of Michael Snow*, Ottawa.
A97. Nettl, B. (1974) 'Thoughts on Improvisation: A Comparative Approach', *Musical Quarterly* LX, 1–19.
A98. Nettl, B. and Riddle, R. (1974) 'Taqsim Nahawand: A Study of 16 Performances by Jihad Racy', *Yearbook of the International Folk Music Council* 5, 11–50.
A99. Neubert, D. (1982/3) 'Electronic Bowed String Works – Some Observations on Trends and Developments in the Instrumental/Electronic Medium', *Perspectives on New Music*, Fall and Winter 1982/Spring and Summer 1983, pp. 540–66.
A100. Nyman, M. (1974) *Experimental Music*, Schirmer, New York.
A101. O'Hare, D. (ed.) (1981) *Psychology and the Arts*, Harvester Press, Brighton.
A102. Oliveros, P. (1970) *Sonic Meditations*, Smith Publishing, Baltimore, Md.
A103. Oliveros, P. (1984) *Software for People*, Smith Publications, Baltimore, Md.
A104. Owens, T. (1974) 'Charlie Parker: Technique of Improvisation', PhD thesis, University of California, Los Angeles.
A105. Owens, T. (1976) 'Fugal Pieces of the MJQ', *Journal of Jazz Studies* 4, 25–46.
A106. Partch H. (1974) *Genesis of a Music* (2nd edn), Da Capo, New York.
A107. Perlman, A.H. and Greenblatt, D. (1981) 'Miles meets Noam Chomsky: Some Observations on Jazz Improvisation and Language Structure' in W. Steiner (ed.), *The Sign in Music and Literature*, University of Texas Press, Austin.
A108. Placksin, S. (1982) *American Women in Jazz, 1900 to Present*, Wideview Books, New York.
A109. Porter, L. (1985) 'John Coltrane's A Love Supreme: Jazz Improvisation as Composition', *Journal of the American Musicological Society* 38, 593–621.
A110. Pressing, J. (1977) 'Towards an Understanding of Scales in Jazz', *Jazzforschung* 9, 25–35.
A111. Pressing. J. (1982) 'Pitch Class Set Structures in Contemporary Jazz', *Jazzforschung* 14, 133–72.
A112. Pressing, J. (1983) 'Rhythmic Design in the Support Drums of the Agbedza', *African Music* 6, 4–15.
A113. Pressing, J. (1987) 'The Micro- and Macrostructural Design of Improvised Music', *Music Perception* 5, 133–72.
A114. Pressing, J. (1988) 'Improvisation: Methods and Models', in J. Sloboda (ed.), *Generative Processes in Music*, Oxford University Press, Oxford, pp. 129–78.
A115. Pressing, J. (in press), *Synthesiser Performance and Real Time Techniques*.
A116. Prevost, E. (1985) 'Improvisation: Music for an Occasion', *British Journal of Music Education* 2, 177–86.
A117. Priestley, B. (1982) *Mingus: A Critical Biography*, Quartet, London.
A118. Radano, R.M. (1985) 'Anthony Braxton and his Musical Traditions. The Meeting of Concert Music and Jazz', PhD thesis, University of Michigan.

A119. Roach, M. (1972) 'What "Jazz" Means to Me', *Black Scholar* 3, 2–6.

A120. Roads, C. (ed.) *Composers and the Computer*, Kaufmann, Los Altos, Calif.

A121. Rockwell, J. (1985) *All American Music*, Kahn and Averill, London.

A122. Roederer, J.G. (1973) 'Introduction to the Physics and Psychophysics of Music', Springer-Verlag, New York.

A123. Rusch, R.D. (undated) *Jazz Talk: the Cadence Interviews*, Lyle Stewart, Seacaucus, NJ.

A124. Russell, G. (1959) *The Lydian Chromatic Concept of Tonal Organisation for Improvisation*, Concept, Cambridge, Mass.

A125. Russell, G. (1960) 'Ornette Coleman and Tonality', *Jazz Review*, June, p. 9; also printed in A124.

A126. Schafer, R. Murray (1977) *The Tuning of the World*, Knopf, New York.

A127. Schuller, G. (1959) 'Review: Cecil Taylor', *Jazz Review* 2, 28–31.

A128. Schuller, G. (1961) *Ornette Coleman Transcriptions*, MJQ Music, New York.

A129. Schuller, G. (1962) 'Sonny Rollins and Thematic Improvising' in M. Williams (ed.), *Jazz Panorama*, New York, pp. 239–257 in 1979 reprint.

A130. Schuller, G. (1968) *Early Jazz*, Oxford University Press.

A131. Schuller, G. (1988) 'Third Stream' in A69.

A132. Sidran, B. (1971) *Black Talk*, Holt Rinehart, New York.

A133. Sloboda, J.A. (1985) *The Musical Mind*. Clarendon, Oxford.

A134. Sloboda, J.A. (ed.) (1988) *Generative Processes in Music: The Cognitive Psychology of Music*, Clarendon, Oxford.

A135. Small, C. (1977) *Music. Society. Education*, Calder, London.

A136. Smith, G. (1983) 'Homer, Gregory and Bill Evans? The Theory of Formulaic Composition in the Context of Jazz Piano Improvisation', PhD thesis, Harvard, Boston.

A137. Smith, H.A. (1988) 'The Sense of Neurotic Coherence: Structural Reversals in the Poetry of Frank O'Hara', PhD thesis, University of Nottingham, UK.

A138. Smith, H.A. (1989) 'Image, Text and Performance: Inter-artistic Relationships in Contemporary Poetry' in D. Murray (ed.), *Poetry and Critical Theory*, Batsford, London.

A139. Smith-Brindle, R. (1966) *Serial Composition*, Oxford University Press, London.

A140. Smith-Brindle, R. (1975) *The New Music*, Oxford University Press, London.

A141. Snow, M. (1982–3) 'Sighting Snow', Dedicated Issue of *Afterimage* (Vol. 11).

A142. Solomon, L. (1986) 'Improvisation II, Perspectives', *New Music* 24, 224–35.

A143. Spellman, A.B. (1966) *Four Lives in the Bebop Business*, Pantheon, New York.

A144. Steedman, M.J. (1984) 'A Generative Grammar for Jazz Chord Sequences', *Music Perception* 2, 52–77.

A145. Stewart, M.L. (1974/5) 'Structural Development in the Jazz Improvisation Technique of Clifford Brown', *Jazzforschung* 6/7, 141–273.

A146. Sudnow, D. (1978) *Ways of the Hand: The Origin of Improvised Conduct*, Routledge & Kegan Paul, London.

A147. Sudnow, D. (1979) *Task Body*, Knopf, New York.

A148. Suhor, C. (1986) 'Jazz Improvisation and Language Performance: Parallel Competencies', *Et Cetera* 43, 133–40.

A149. Tirro, F. (1967) 'The Silent Theme Tradition in Jazz', *Musical Quarterly* 53, 313–34.

A150. Tirro, F. (1974) 'Constructive Elements in Jazz Improvisation', *Journal of the American Musicological Society* 27, 294–305.

A151. Tirro, F. (1977) *Jazz – A History*, Norton, New York.

A152. Ulrich, J.W. (1977) 'The Analysis and Synthesis of Jazz by Computer', *Proceedings of the 5th International Conference on Artificial Intelligence*, pp. 865–72.

A153. White, A.L. (ed.) (1987) *Lost in Music*, Routledge & Kegan Paul, London.

A154. Wilmer, V. (1977) *As Serious As Your Life*, Allison & Busby, London.

A155. Winner, E. (1982) *Invented Worlds: Psychology of the Arts*, Harvard University Press, Cambridge, Mass.

A156. Wishart, T. (1985) *On Sonic Art*, Imagineering, York, UK.

A157. Witmer, R. and Robbins, J. (1988) 'A Historical and Critical Survey of Recent Pedagogic Materials for the Teaching and Learning of Jazz', *Bull Council for Research in Music Education* 96, 7–29.

Appendix 3 References: printed musical scores

M1.   Cage, J. (1953) 59½″, Peters, New York.
M2.   Cage. J. (1956) 27′10.554″ for a Percussionist, Peters, New York.
M3.   Cage, J. (1960) Concert for Piano and Orchestra, Peters, New York.
M4.   Cage, J. (1961) Atlas Eclipticalis, Peters, New York.
M5.   Dean, R.T. (1980) Breaking Worlds, Soma Publishing, London and Sydney.
M6.   Hino, T. (c.1985). Miles Davis – Jazz Improvisation, ATN, Tokyo.
M7.   Loevendie, T. (1969) Music for Contrabass and Piano, Donemus, Amsterdam.
M8.   Oliveros, P. (1962) Sonic Meditations, Smith Publishing, Baltimore, Md., USA.
M9.   Penderecki, K. (1971) Actions, Schott, Mainz.
M10. Runswick, D. (1983) Cool↔Warm↔Hot, Faber, London.
M11. Sellars, J. (1986) Music for Double Bass and Drum Machine, Hog River Music, Hartford, Conn.
M12. Sher, C. (1983) The World's Greatest Fake Book, Sher Music, San Francisco.
M13. Stockhausen, K. (1968) From the Seven Days, Universal Edition 1968; English version 1970, Universal Edition, London.
M14. Watanabe, S. (1985) John Coltrane Volume 2: Jazz Improvisation, ATN, Tokyo.
M15. White, A. (1973–8) The Works of John Coltrane (transcriptions), Andrew's Music, Washington, DC.
M16. Xenakis, I. (1976) Theraps, Salabert, Paris.

Appendix 4 References: recordings and films

These are the references given as (R1, R2, etc.) in the text. Note that Chapters 7–10 have their own listings, but some of those recordings may also be discussed elsewhere in the text and so be listed here, too. Some records are listed here because of their great structural interest, but not discussed in detail in the text. Information on how to obtain recordings such as these is given in Appendix 5.

R1. Adderley, C. (1967) *Mercy Mercy Mercy*, Cap5MK 74294.
R2. Amalgam (1969) *Prayer for Peace*, TRA196.
R3. AMM (1966) *Improvisation*, Elektra EVKS7256.
R4. AMM (1967) *Improvisation*, Mainstream MS5002.
R5. AMM (1968) *The Crypt*, Matchless MR5.
R6. AMM (1982) *Generative Themes*, Matchless MR6.
R7. AMM (1987) *The Inexhaustible Document*, Matchless MR13.
R8. Art Ensemble of Chicago (1979) *Les Stances a sophie* Pathé Marconi 20062–11360.
R9a. Brubeck, D. (1956) *Brubeck plays Brubeck*, CL878.
R9b. Brubeck, D. (1959) *Time Out*, CL1397.
R10. Burrell, D. (1969) *Echo*, BYG Actuel 20.
R11. Carter, E. (1975) Double Concerto (composed 1959); Duo (composed 1973), Nonesuch H 71314.
R12. Charles, T. (1953) *Collaboration: West*, Prestige OM2007.
R13. Charles, T. (1954) *Bob Brookmeyer/Revelation*, XTRA 5022.
R14. Charles, T. (1957) *Three for Duke*, LTZ-J 15119.
R15. Coleman, O. (1959) *Change of the Century*, ATL 1327.
R16. Coleman, O. (1959) *Shape of Jazz to Come*, ATL 1317.
R17. Coleman, O. (1960) *Free Jazz*, ATL 1364.
R18. Coleman, O. (1960a) *Twins*, ATL SD 1588.
R19. Coleman, O. (1965) *An Evening with Ornette Coleman*, Polydor 623246/7.
R20. Coltrane, J. (1959) *Giant Steps*, ATL 1311.
R21. Coltrane, J. (1961) *The Other Village Vanguard Tapes*, Impulse AS 9325.
R22. Coltrane, J. (1964) *Crescent*, Impulse A-66.

R23. Coltrane, J. (1964) *A Love Supreme*, Impulse A-77.

R24. Coltrane, J. (1965) *A Love Supreme* (French live recording), FCD 106, INA, France.

R25. Coltrane, J. (1965) *Mastery of John Coltrane Vol. 1: Feelin' Good*, Impulse IZ-9345/2.

R26. Coltrane, J. (1965) *Ascension*, Impulse AS 95 (two different versions).

R27. Coltrane, J. (1965) *First Meditations*, Impulse AS 9332.

R28. Coltrane, J. (1965) *Live at Antibes*, INA FCD 119.

R29. Coltrane, J. (1967) *Interstellar Space*, Impulse ASD 9277.

R30. Coltrane, J. (1967) *Expression*, Impulse S-9120.

R31. Coltrane, J. (1967) *Jupiter*, Impulse S-9369.

R32. Corea, C. (1968) *Now He Sings, Now He Sobs*, CJ325019 (CD rerelease of complete session).

R33. Corea, C. (1968) *Inner Space*, SD 2-305.

R34. Corea, C. (1971) *Piano Improvisations Vol. 1*, ECM 1014.

R35. Coryell, L. (1969) *Spaces*, Vanguard 6554.

R36. Crothers, C. (1974) *Perception*, Steeplechase SC2-1022.

R37. Davis, M. (1949) *Birth of the Cool*, Capitol 60011.

R38. Davis, M. (1958) *At the Plaza Vol. 1*, CBS S 65778.

R39. Davis, M. (1958) *Milestones*, CL1193.

R40. Davis, M. (1959) *Kind of Blue*, CBS 6206.

R41. Davis, M. (1963) *Seven Steps to Heaven*, Columbia PC885L.

R42. Davis, M. (1963) *Live in St Louis*, VGM003.

R43. Davis, M. (1964) *Four and More*, CL2453.

R44. Davis, M. (1964) *My Funny Valentine*, PC9106.

R45. Davis, M. (1965) *ESP*, CL2359.

R46. Davis, M. (1965) *Live at the Plugged Nickel Vol. 2*, CBS Sony 25 Ap291; *Vol. 1*, CBS 460607.

R47. Davis, M. (1966) *Miles Smiles*, CBS 62933.

R48. Davis, M. (1969) *In A Silent Way*, CPC 9875.

R49. Davis, M. (1969) *Jack Johnson*, CBS 30455.

R50. Davis, M. (*c.*1974) *Get Up With It*, CBS 88092.

R51. Davis, M. (*c.*1975) *Agharta*, CBS 88159.

R52. Ellis, D. (1960) *How Time Passes*, Candid 9004.

R53. Ellis, D. (1961) *New Ideas*, Esq 32-183.

R54. Ellis, D. (1967) *Live in (3⅔)/4 Time*, Pacific Jazz 20123.

R55. Ellis, D. (1968) *Electric Bath*, CS-9585.

R56. Evans, B. (1961) *Live at The Village Vanguard*, Milestone 47002.

R57. Evans, B. (1968) *Bill Evans Alone*, Verve 2304005.

R58. Evans, B. (1972) *Live at the Festival*, Enja 2030.

R59. Foss, L. (1961) *Time Cycles*, CMS 6280.

R60. Frank, R. and Leslie, A. (1959) *Pull My Daisy* (B&W film, 27'), USA; sound track on cassette Beat 2.

R61. Ghosh, S. (1966) *Ustad Ali Akhbar Khan Sarod*, EASP 1310.

R62. Ghosh, S. (1967) *Ali Akhbar Khan*, EALP 1319.

R63. Ghosh, S. (1968) *Ustad Ali Akhbar Khan*, EASD 1310.

R64. Ghosh, S. (1980) *Music of the Drums*, Inreco 2407-5138.

R65. Graves, M. and Pullen, D. (1967) *Nommo*, SRP 290.

R66. Gruppo Nuova Consonanza (1969) *Improvisationen*–DGG 643541.

R67. Guy, B. (1976) *Statements V–XI*, Incus 22.
R68. Hancock, H. (1963) *Takin' Off*, BST 84109.
R69. Hancock, H. (1965) *Maiden Voyage*, BLP 84195.
R70. Hancock, H. (1971) *Mwandishi*, Warner K46077.
R71. Handy, J. (1965) *Live at Monterey Jazz Festival*, CBS 62678.
R72. Harriott, J. (1960) *Free Form*, Jazzland JLP 949.
R73. Harriott, J. (1961) *Abstract*, Columbia SX 1477.
R74. Henderson, J. (1969) *Power to the People*, CBS 64068.
R75. James, B. (1965) *Explosions*, ESP 1009.
R76. Jarrett, K. (1968) *Life Between the Exit Signs*, Vortex 2006.
R77. Jarrett, K. (1969) *Somewhere Before*, Vortex 2022.
R78. Jarrett, K. (1971) *Facing You*, ECM 1017.
R79. Jazz Warriors (1987) *Out of Many One People*, Antilles AN 871Z.
R80. Johnson, L. (1970) *Synthesis*, Columbia SCX 6412.
R81. Jones, E. (1963) *Illumination*, Impulse A-49.
R82. Jones, LeRoi (1965) *LeRoi Jones and the New York Art Quartet*, ESP Disc, Fontana STL5521.
R83. Kagel, M. (1988) *Oral Treason*, BBC TV film.
R84. Lacy, S. and Gysin, R. (1987) *Songs*, Hat Art 1985/86.
R85. Loose Tubes (1968) *Delightful Precipice*, LTLP003.
R86. Lysis (1976) *Lysis Live*, Mosaic GCM 761.
R87. Lysis (1977) *Cycles*, Mosaic GCM 774.
R88. Lysis (1978) *The Solo Trumpet*, Soma 781.
R89. Lysis (1978) *Dualyses*, Soma 782.
R90. Lysis (1979) *Lysis Plus*, Mosaic GCM 791.
R91. Lysis (1980) *Superimpositions*, Soma 783.
R92. Lysis (1987) *Wings of the Whale*, Soma 784.
R93. Mac Low, J. (1976) *First Milarepa Gatha*, Pari & Dispari, Cavriago.
R94. Mack, D. (1964) *New Directions*, Columbia 33SX-1670.
R95. Mahavishnu Orchestra (1972) *Birds of Fire*, CBS 32280.
R96. McLaughlin, J. (1969) *Extrapolation*, Polydor 2310 018.
R97. Musica Elettronica Viva (1967) *Spacecraft*, Mainstream MS 5002.
R98. Musica Elettronica Viva (1969) *Soundpool*, BYG 529326.
R99. Milhaud, D. (1952) *String Quintet and other Chamber Music*, played by Sonant, KNEW LP 305, CD 305/306.
R100. Mingus, C. (1963) *Black Saint and the Sinner Lady*, Impulse AS-35.
R101a. Mitchell, R. (1966) *Free Sound*, Delmark DL 408.
R101b. Mitchell, R. (1968) *Congliptious*, Nessa 2.
R102. Mulligan, G. (1953) *Midnight Session*, Pacific Jazz 688 105ZL.
R103. Music Improvisation Company (1970) ECM1005.
R104. Naughton, B. (1976) *The Haunt*, OTIC 1005.
R105a. New Phonic Art (1971) *New Phonic Art*, Wergo 60060.
R105b. New Phonic Art (1973) *Free Improvisation*, DGG 2740105.
R106. Oliveros, P. (1982) *Accordion and Voice*, Lovely Music VR 1901.
R107. Parker, E. (1978) *Abracadabra*, Beak Doctor 2.
R108. Parker, E. (1978) *Monoceros*, Incus 27.
R109. Parker, E. (1979) *Around 6* (with K. Wheeler), ECM 1156.
R110. Parker, E., Bailey, D. and Bennink, H. (1970) *The Topography of the Lungs*, Incus 1.

R111. Richards, E. (*c.*1966) *Emil Richards and the Microtonal Blues Band: Journey to Bliss*, Impulse ST As 9166.

R112. Risset, J.C. (1987) *Sud-dialogues*, INA C1003.

R113. Russell, G. (1983) *African Game*, Blue Note BST 85103.

R114. Schuller, G. (1960) *Jazz Abstractions*, Atlantic 587043.

R115. Shepp, A. (1965) *Further Fire Music*, Impulse IA 9357/2.

R116. Sheppard, A. (1987) *A* Antilles AN 8720.

R117. Snow, M. (1964) *New York Eye and Ear Control* (film), National Gallery of Canada, Ottawa.

R118. Stockhausen, K. (1969) *Set Sail for the Sun*, Harmonia Mundi 34.795.

R119. Sun Ra (1983) *A Joyful Noise* (film by R. Mugge), available from Rhapsody Films, New York.

R120. Taylor, C. (1955) *In Transition*, BNLA 458HZ 0798.

R121. Taylor, C. (1962) *Live at Cafe Montmartre*, SFJL 928.

R122. Taylor, C. (1962) *Early Unit 1962*, Ingo 16.

R123. Taylor, C. (1966) *Unit Structures*, BST 84237.

R124. Taylor, C. (1966) *Cecil Taylor*, BYG YX 4003-4.

R125. Taylor, C. (1969) *Second Act of A*, 3 vols, Shandar SR 10.011.

R126. Taylor, C. (1976) *Dark to Themselves*, Enja 2084.

R127. Taylor, C. (1981) *Garden*, Hat Art 1993/4 (double).

R128. Taylor, C. (1984) *Segments II*, Soul Note SN 1084.

R129. Taylor, C. (1987) *Live in Bologna*, Leo CD LR 100.

R130. Terroade, K. (1969) *Love Rejoice*, BYG Actuel 22.

R131. Touch of the Sun (*c.*1977) *Milk Teeth*, Bead 1.

R132. Tristano, L. (1949) *Sextet: Crosscurrents*, Capitol EASP 1-491.

R133. Tristano, L. (1953) *Descent into Maelstrom*, Inner City IC 6002.

R134. Tyner, M. (1963) *Reaching Fourth*, Impulse A-33.

R135. Tyner, M. (1968) *Tender Moments*, BST 84275.

R136. Van Hove, F. (1972) *Fred van Hove*, Vogel 001-S.

R137. Weather Report (1971) *I Sing the Body Electric*, CBS 32062.

R138. Wired (1970) *Free Improvisation*, DGG 2740105.

R139. Wishart, T. (1978) *Red Bird*, Yes 7.

Appendix 5 An illustrative core collection of improvised music and how to obtain it

This very select list is intended to indicate the key recordings which illustrate the musical developments discussed in the book; where possible a relatively available recording is chosen among alternatives. The list is not intended to replace the function of the discographies given elsewhere in this book. In addition, more comprehensive discographies, and catalogues of recordings such as those published by *The Gramophone* (London) or W. Schwann, Inc. (Boston), may be useful in providing alternative local issue numbers and CD equivalents of LPs.

There is real difficulty in obtaining even some of these records in certain countries; and the more so in the case of some of the older recordings in Appendix 4 and in the discussion of Chapters 7–9. A general strategy for this quest can be offered, and a few specific contact points. For records which are still in press, independent small distributors often exist, and can be helpful: for example, New Music Distribution Services in New York. A second line of enquiry, and this can be fruitful even with deleted recordings, are the key national libraries. Thus the British Institute of Recorded Sound, a branch of the British Library, holds an extremely interesting collection of music within the purview of this book; and comparable sources exist in some other countries. In the USA, the Institute of Jazz Studies at Rutgers University, New Brunswick, NJ, also holds a large relevant collection, which is available to the public. Finally, addresses for a few of the labels which are most difficult to obtain are given below: these companies will sometimes supply recordings on other 'difficult' labels from their own country, and very often offer a contact address.

AMM (1968) *The Crypt*, Matchless MR5.
AMM (1982) *Generative Themes*, Matchless MR6.
AMM (1987) *The Inexhaustible Document*, Matchless MR13.
Bailey, D. (1969) and Han Bennink, *Instant Composers' Pool*, ICP 004.
Bailey, D. (1970) *Solo Guitar*, Incus 2.
Bailey, D. (1971) *Improvisations for Cello and Guitar*, ECM 1013.
Bailey, D. (1979) *Time*, Incus 34.
Bailey, D. (1982) *Han*, CD Incus CD02.
Bley, P. (1961) *Jimmy Giuffre Trio Live in Europe, Vol. 1*, Raretone 5018–FC.

Bley, P. (1961) *Jimmy Giuffre Trio Live in Europe, Vol. 2*, Raretone 5019–FC.

Bley, P. (1964) *Turning Point*, Improvising Artists IAI 373841.

Bley, P. (1967) *Ballads*, ECM 1010.

Bley, P. (1986) *Fragments*, ECM 1320.

Braxton, A. (1968) *Three Compositions of New Jazz*, Delmark DS 415.

Braxton, A. (1968) *For Alto*, Delmark DS 420/1.

Braxton, A. (1974) *Duo Live at Wigmore Hall*, Emanem 3313/4 (UK, Australia) or Inner City IC 1041 (USA).

Braxton, A. (1976) *Creative Music Orchestra 1976*, CD RCA ND86579.

Breuker, W. (1967) *New Acoustic Swing Duo*, Instant Composers' Pool ICP 001.

Brubeck, D. (1959) *Time Out*, CL1397.

Charles, T. (1953) *Collaboration: West*, Prestige OM2007.

Coleman, O. (1959) *Shape of Jazz to Come*, ATL 1317.

Coleman, O. (1960) *Free Jazz*, ATL 1364.

Coleman, O. (1965) *An Evening with Ornette Coleman*, Polydor 623246/7.

Collier, G. (1976) *New Conditions*, Mosaic GCM 773.

Collier, G. (1985) *Something British Made in Hong Kong*, Mosaic GCM 871.

Coltrane, J. (1959) *Giant Steps*, ATL 1311.

Coltrane, J. (1961) *The Other Village Vanguard Tapes*, Impulse AS 9325.

Coltrane, J. (1964) *A Love Supreme*, Impulse A-77.

Coltrane, J. (1965) *A Love Supreme* (French live recording), FCD 106, INA, France.

Coltrane, J. (1965) *Ascension*, Impulse AS95.

Coltrane, J. (1967) *Interstellar Space*, Impulse ASD 9277.

Coltrane, J. (1967) *Expression*, Impulse S-9120.

Corea, C. (1968) *Now He Sings, Now He Sobs*, CJ325019 (CD rerelease of complete session).

Dauner, W. (1964) *Dream Talk*, CBS S 62478.

Dauner, W. (1967) *Free Action*, MPS 161017.

Davis, A. (1981) *Episteme*, Gramavision Gr 8101.

Davis, M. (1949) *Birth of the Cool*, Capitol 60011.

Davis, M. (1958) *Milestones*, CL1193.

Davis, M. (1959) *Kind of Blue*, CBS 6206.

Davis, M. (1964) *Four and More*, CL2453.

Davis, M. (1964) *My Funny Valentine*, PC9106.

Davis, M. (1965) *ESP*, CL2359.

Davis, M. (1969) *In A Silent Way*, CPC 9875.

Dolphy, E. (1964) *Out to Lunch*, Blue Note BST 84163.

Dolphy, E. (1964) *Last Date*, original issue Limelight LS 86013.

Ellis, D. (1960) *How Time Passes*, Candid 9004.

Ellis, D. (1961) *New Ideas*, Esq 32-183.

Evans, B. (1961) *Live at The Village Vanguard*, Milestone 47002.

Ganelin Trio (1982) *New Wine*, Leo LR 112.

Gruppo Nuova Consonanza (1969) *Improvisationen*, DGG 643541.

Guy, B. (1972) *Ode*, Incus 6, 7.

Guy, B. (1976) *Statements V–XI*, Incus 22.

Guy, B. (1980) *Stringer*, FMP SAJ-41.

Guy, B. (1988) London Jazz Composers' Orch, *Zurich Concerts*, Intackt 004/005.

Hancock, H. (1965) *Maiden Voyage*, BLP 84195.

Hancock, H. (1971) *Mwandishi*, Warner K46077.
Harriott, J. (1960) *Free Form*, Jazzland JLP 949.
Harriott, J. (1961) *Abstract*, Columbia SX 1477.
Hill, A. (1963) *Smokestack*, Blue Note BVLP 4160.
Hill, A. (1964) *Point of Departure*, Blue Note CD reissue CDP 7 84167 2.
Hill, A. (1965) *Compulsion*, Blue Note BLP 421.
Hill, A. (1965/70) *One for One*, Blue Note BN-LA-459-H2-0798.
Iskra 1903, New Phonic Art and Wired (1973) *Free Improvisation*, DGG 2740 105.
Jarrett, K. (1968) *Life Between the Exit Signs*, Vortex 2006.
Jazz Composers' Orchestra (1968) JCOA J 1001/2.
Kuhn, J. (1967) *Transfiguration*, Saba SB 15118.
Kuhn, J. (1967) *Impressions of New York*, Impulse A-9158.
Kuhn, J. (1971) *Piano*, MPS 2121330-7.
McLaughlin, J. (1969) *Extrapolation*, Polydor 2310 018.
Mengelberg, M. (1970) *Instant Composers' Pool* ICP 005.
Musica Elettronica Viva (1967) *Spacecraft*, Mainstream MS 5002.
Musica Elettronica Viva (1969) *Soundpool*, BYG 529326.
Mingus, C. (1963) *Black Saint and the Sinner Lady*, Impulse AS-35.
Mitchell, R. (1966) *Free Sound*, Delmark DL 408.
Music Improvisation Company (1970) ECM1005.
New Phonic Art (1971) *New Phonic Art*, Wergo 60060.
New Phonic Art, Iskra 1903 and Wired (1973) *Free Improvisation*, DGG 2740 105.
Oliveros, P. (1982) *Accordion and Voice*, Lovely Music VR 1901.
Oxley, T. (1969) *Baptised Traveller*, CBS 52664.
Oxley, T. (1970) *Four Compositions for Sextet*, CBS 64071.
Oxley, T. (1971) *Ichnos*, RCA Victor SF 8215.
Parker, E. (1970) *Topography of the Lung*, Incus 1.
Parker, E. (1978) *Abracadabra*, Beak Doctor 2.
Parker, E. (1978) *Monoceros*, Incus 27.
Parker, E., Bailey, D. and Bennink, H. (1970) *The Topography of the Lungs*, Incus 1.
Rose, J. (1983) *Tango*, Hot 1009.
Russell, G. (1965) *Sextet at Beethoven Hall*, MSP BAP 5079.
Russell, G. (1983) *The Living Game*, CBS S 65010.
Schlippenbach, A. (1966) *Globe Unity*, Saba 15 109 ST.
Schoof, M. (1969) *European Echoes*, Free Music Production FMP 0010.
Schuller, G. (1960) *Jazz Abstractions*, Atlantic 587043.
Schweizer, I. (1973) *Ramifications*, Ogun OG500.
Stevens, J. (1976) *Longest Night*, Ogun OG120.
Stockhausen, K. (1969) *Set Sail for the Sun*, Harmonia Mundi 34.795.
Sun Ra (1983) *A Joyful Noise* (film by R. Mugge), available from Rhapsody Films, New York. (1970/1) *The Solar Myth Approach*, BYG 529340/1.
Taylor, C. (1955) *In Transition*, BNLA 458HZ 0798.
Taylor, C. (1962) *Live at Cafe Montmartre*, SFJL 928.
Taylor, C. (1966) *Unit Structures*, BST 84237.
Taylor, C. (1981) *Garden*, Hat Art 1993/4 (double).
Taylor, C. (1984) *Segments II*, Soul Note SN 1084.

Taylor, C. (1987) *Live in Bologna*, Leo CD LR 100.
Tristano, L. (1949) *Sextet: Crosscurrents*, Capitol EASP 1-491.
Tristano, L. (1953) *Descent into Maelstrom*, Inner City IC 6002.
Wired, Iskra 1903 and New Phonic Art (1973) Free Improvisation, DGG 2740 105.

Some contact addresses:
Anthony Braxton, Music Dept, Mills College, 9000 MacArthur Boulevard, Oakland, California 94613, USA (for writings and scores)
Free Music Production, Mierendorfstrasse 19, D-1000 Berlin 10, Germany
Hat Hut Records, Box 127, West Park, NY 12493, USA
Improvising Artists, 26 Jane Street, New York, NY 10014, USA
Incus Recordings, 112 Hounslow Rd, Twickenham, Middx, UK
Intakt, c/o Rec-Rec-distribution, Magnusstrasse 5, CH-8004 Zurich, Switzerland
Leo Records, 35 Cascade Ave, London N10 3PT, UK
Matchless Recordings, 2 Shetlocks Cottages, Matching Tye, Harlow, Essex CM17 0QS, UK
Mosaic Records (UK) 38 Shell Road, Lewisham, London SE13, UK
Soma Records, 135 Nicholson Parade, Cronulla, Sydney, NSW 2230, Australia
Spiral Scratch Records, PO Box 282, Rose Bay 2029, Australia
Sun Ra, 5626 Morton St, Philadelphia, PA 19144, USA (in this case, obtaining a reply can be difficult, and direct contact at concerts is more effective!)

Index

224

Blakey, Art, xxiii, 7
Blanchard, Terence, xxiii, xxv, 7
Bley, Carla, 111, 112, 148, 156
Bley, Paul, 8, 52, 66, 92, 95, 98, 103,
104–12, 128, 132
blocks, 17, 19
blowing, 180
blues, 6, 193, 195, 197
Bluhm, Norman, 185
Born, Georgina, 207
Boulez, Pierre, xxii, 3
Bow Gamelan, xiv, 184
Brant, Henry, 104, 105
brass instruments, 89, 137
Braxton, Anthony, 68, 98, 101, 133, 136, 137,
138, 139, 157, 161, 192
Brecht, George, 7, 185
Breuker, Willem, xvi, xviii, 7, 59, 68, 135, 136,
151, 153, 154, 155, 156, 159
Brotzmann, Peter, xvii, xviii, 136
Brown, Ashley, ix, 86, 126, 167
Brown, Clifford, 20
Brown, Earle, 4, 171
Brubeck, Dave, 20, 27, 57, 58, 69, 147
Bryars, Gavin, 186
Buck, Tony, ix, 86, 139
Budd, Harold, 131, 132
Burchell, Chas, 52
Burrell, Dave, 68, 136
Burton, Gary, 91
Burwell, Paul, xiv, 184

Cage, John, xxii, xxiii, 4, 7, 77, 83, 92, 121,
124, 134, 157, 183, 190, 207
Canada, 103
canons, 145
Cardew, Cornelius, 7, 132, 140, 143, 144, 185,
202
Carr, Ian, 134, 139, 207
Carter, Elliot, 39, 41, 42, 157
Carter, Ron, 22, 28, 36, 37, 116, 206
categorical perception, 194
cello, 119, 137, 149
Chadbourne, Eugene, 93
chain improvising (c.f. metonymy), 49, 52
Chambers, Joe, 116
chant, 148
Charles, Teddy, xxii, 7, 8, 54, 58, 60, 105
cheek, cris, 180
Chekasov, Vladimir, 162
Cherry, Don, 83, 106, 123, 152, 156
children, 195, 201
Childs, Barney, 161
chromatic playing, 59
chromaticism, 62
Circle, 39, 41, 106, 161
circular breathing, 46, 86, 137, 192
Clare, John, 139, 185
clarinet, 87, 94, 119, 122, 147, 148
classical exposition, 192
clusters, 64, 110, 119, 124, 180
Cobb, Jimmy, 17, 35
Cobbing, Bob, 181, 186
Coe, Tony, 95, 148

cognition, 89, 191–207
cognitive processing, 203
Coleman, Ornette, xviii, xxii, xxiv, 7, 8, 10, 22,
23, 25, 26, 42, 43, 44, 49, 52, 53, 54, 60,
74, 83, 105, 106, 132, 134, 143, 147, 151,
155, 179, 197, 205, 206
collaboration, 184
collage, 124, 147
collective improvisation, 133
Collette, Buddy, xxii
Collier Graham, xxvi, 7, 26, 71, 73, 98, 127,
162, 164–73
Coltrane, John, xviii, xxiii, xxiv, 7, 10, 14, 15,
20, 30, 43, 44, 46, 48, 49, 50, 55, 56, 57,
58, 61, 62, 64, 65, 67, 70, 72, 73, 83, 87,
88, 108, 113, 123, 132, 135, 145, 155, 196,
197, 198, 206
Company, 95
complexity, xi, 5, 12
composition, xxiii, 3, 9, 69–78, 143–73
computer composition, 66
computerised grammar, 204
computers, 4, 46, 51, 66, 82, 98, 140, 171, 183,
187, 188, 190, 202, 203
conducting, 121
consonance, 194
constructed instruments, 46
contour, 199
control, 3
Cooper, Lindsay, 95
Copland, Aaron, 52, 95
Corea, Chick, 13, 14, 39, 55, 56, 57
Corner, Philip, 181
Coryell, Larry, 132, 155
Courbois, Pierre, 155
Cowell, Henry, 64, 91
creativity, 203
Cresswell, Lyell, 4, 76
Crothers, Connie, 52
Crumb, George, 91
Crusaders, xxiv
cultural conditioning, 195
cymbals, 91
Cyrille, Andrew, 45

damping, 92
dance, 183
Dankworth, Johnny, 148
Dauner, Wolfgang, xvii, 10, 83, 103,
119–22, 135, 152, 180
Davie, Alan, 180, 186
Davies, Hugh, 46, 96
Davies, John B., 198, 199, 200
Davies, Peter Maxwell, 157
Davis, Anthony, 143, 144, 149
Davis, Miles, xviii, xxiv, 7, 16, 20, 22, 28,
34–9, 41, 50, 51, 55, 56, 57, 68, 70, 106,
108, 112, 114, 115, 197, 206, 207
Davis, Richard, 113, 116
Dean, Roger, 31, 42, 92, 103, 126–8, 166, 167
degeneracy, 197
Dempster, Stuart, 137
Desmond, Paul, 19, 20
development, 193

225